Dear Reader:

The book you are about to read is the latest bestseller from the St. Martin's True Crime Library, the imprint *The New York Times* calls "the leader in true crime!" Each month, we offer you a fascinating account of the latest, most sensational crime that has captured the national attention. St. Martin's is the publisher of bestselling true crime author and crime journalist Kieran Crowley, who explores the dark, deadly links between a prominent Manhattan surgeon and the disappearance of his wife fifteen years earlier in THE SURGEON'S WIFE. Suzy Spencer's BREAKING POINT guides readers through the tortuous twists and turns in the case of Andrea Yates, the Houston mother who drowned her five young children in the family's bathtub. In Edgar Award-nominated DARK DREAMS, legendary FBI profiler Roy Hazelwood and bestselling crime author Stephen G. Michaud shine light on the inner workings of America's most violent and depraved murderers. In the book you now hold, CRUEL GAMES, acclaimed author Rose Ciotta looks into the case of a brilliant professor and a mysterious death.

St. Martin's True Crime Library gives you the stories behind the headlines. Our authors take you right to the scene of the crime and into the minds of the most notorious murderers to show you what really makes them tick. St. Martin's True Crime Library paperbacks are better than the most terrifying thriller, because it's all true! The next time you want a crackling good read, make sure it's got the St. Martin's True Crime Library logo on the spine—you'll be up all night!

CRUEL GAMES

A Brilliant Professor, a Loving Mother,
a Brutal Killing

ROSE CIOTTA

St. Martin's Paperbacks

This is a work of fiction. All of the characters, organizations, and events portrayed in this novel are either products of the author's imagination or are used fictitiously.

CRUEL GAMES

Copyright © 2009 by Rose Ciotta.

Cover photo of house © Michael S. Wirtz/*The Philadelphia Inquirer.* Cover photo of Rafael Robb © Ron Tarver/*The Philadelphia Inquirer.* Cover photo of Ellen Robb courtesy Gary Gregory.

For information address St. Martin's Press, 175 Fifth Avenue, New York, NY 10010.

ISBN: 0-312-94703-8
EAN: 978-0-312-94703-3

Printed in the United States of America

St. Martin's Paperbacks edition / February 2009

St. Martin's Paperbacks are published by St. Martin's Press, 175 Fifth Avenue, New York, NY 10010.

10 9 8 7 6 5 4 3 2 1

For my mother, Carmela Ciotta, my first mentor.

ACKNOWLEDGMENTS

This book is based on scores of interviews and hundreds of pages of documents, including police reports, court records and transcripts. During the approximately two years I spent reporting and writing this story, I relied on the generosity of many members of law enforcement and others in the community who knew Ellen and Rafael Robb. Their contributions helped me re-create the Robbs' years together and Ellen's final days.

I thank my editors at St. Martin's Press, notably Charles E. Spicer, Jr., whose vision launched this book, and his assistant, Allison Caplin, who, as a South Jersey native, read with a critical eye for local details. My gratitude also goes to Jane Dystel, my literary agent, who made it possible for me to do this book and helped guide me along.

A special thanks to my editor at *The Philadelphia Inquirer*, William K. Marimow, for his support; to Deputy Managing Editor Vernon Loeb for his critical reading and support; and to Susan DiIanni of Philadelphia Media Holdings, who assembled the works of photographers for *The Philadelphia Inquirer* and *The Philadelphia Daily News* and arranged for their publication in this book.

This book would not have been possible without the cooperation of the professionals in the Montgomery County District Attorney's office and Detective Bureau and Upper

Merion Police Department, notably former District Attorney Bruce L. Castor, Jr., who made time for interviews despite his busy schedule and campaign for County Commissioner. He also made it possible for me to work with detectives and prosecutors in his office. Likewise, my thanks to District Attorney Risa Vetri Ferman, who gave her time and insight and patiently answered my questions (even if they landed on her Blackberry on a Saturday afternoon), and Deputy Chief of Detectives Samuel J. Gallen, who shared his experiences and made it possible for the detectives to walk me through the investigation.

I am indebted to the lead investigators, Montgomery County Homicide Detective Drew Marino and Upper Merion Police Detective David Gershanick, who helped me re-create their painstaking investigation.

I reserve special thanks for Ellen's friends, who believed her story needed to be told to help other women find the courage to leave. These women courageously agreed to share their memories of Ellen and what they knew about her marriage. I especially commend Mary Beth Pedlow, Ellen's best friend. I can only hope that I earned the trust you all placed in me.

Many others also gave their time to help me report on the case. Judge Paul W. Tressler helped me with legal issues; Assistant District Attorney Robert J. Sander assisted me in tracking the unfolding court proceedings; and Upper Merion Lieutenant James Early connected me with the officers who worked the case.

I interviewed nearly all of the thirty officers from Montgomery County Detective Bureau and Upper Merion Police Department who played roles in this investigation. I thank you all for your help.

To veteran undercover narcotics detectives Tony Spagnoletti (now retired) and Stephen Forzato, thank you for allowing me to get a glimpse of the fascinating world in which you work.

I thank attorneys Frank DeSimone, Jules Epstein and Francis J. Genovese for their assistance.

For help of a different kind, I am indebted to Dr. David K. Levine, a game theorist and scholar who teaches at Washington University in St. Louis, for answering my questions about game theory and allowing me to use material from his website.

Beth Sturman, executive director of Laurel House, which operates a shelter for victims of domestic violence in Montgomery County, helped guide my research on the issue.

This book builds on the reporting, photography and videography of my colleagues in the Philadelphia area media, especially at *The Philadelphia Inquirer*. An important part of the story is how the investigation unfolded, and I thank you all for giving me a place to start. I am especially indebted to the talented photographers whose photos are included in this book.

To my first critical readers—my husband, Joseph J. Cultrara, my brother, Peter J. Ciotta, and my dear friend, Kate Nelson—who provided keen feedback at a crucial time. And to my niece, Melina Rose Ciotta, who graciously understood why her godmother couldn't make it to Buffalo for her thirteenth birthday. And, lastly but certainly not least, to my husband, who kept the rest of our lives going while I retreated on evenings and weekends to my office to work on the book. I hope to make it up to all of you.

CHAPTER 1

December 20, 2006
Morning

The screeching telephone stopped Mary Beth Pedlow before she reached her front door. She was already late for her appointment. Maybe she should just let the answering machine pick it up. But, as the mother of four, ages 9 to 16, MacBeth, as her friends liked to call her, knew better than to ignore any calls.

"Hi, MB. You're home! I thought I'd get your machine," exclaimed Ellen.

"I was on my way out. I've got this appointment. What's up?"

"Do you have anything in Avon? I need a couple more gifts to take with me up to Boston."

"I have a couple of Avon gift boxes I know you will like. It's a great deal. They are cloth-covered jewelry boxes trimmed with beads. There's one in blue and the other in green. And they're on sale marked down from fifteen dollars to four ninety-nine," said Mary Beth, recalling the latest items in her Avon inventory. "I'll drop them off on Thursday or Friday before you leave."

"OK, great," said Ellen, satisfied that she'd not only found the gifts she needed, but had gotten them at a good price. Mary Beth knew that her friend loved a bargain. They'd started their working careers together as management trainees at Bamberger's department store, then a division of Macy's, for which it was renamed in 1986. And, after they each married, it was Ellen who'd told MacBeth to check out the house for sale down the street. What could be better than having a best friend living nearby?

There was so much joy in her friend's voice that day that Mary Beth found herself sitting down just to listen. She gladly missed her appointment to hear her friend's good news.

For the next hour, Ellen talked excitedly, recounting the latest developments. It was time to put an end to her loveless marriage to University of Pennsylvania Professor Rafael Robb. She especially wanted their 12-year-old daughter, Olivia, to know that there was another way to live. For the last ten years, Ellen and Rafael had lived separately in the same house, sleeping in separate bedrooms, keeping separate bank accounts and arguing—often over money. Rafi, as his friends called him, kept his bedroom door locked. Ellen feared he was hiding his money in foreign banks, but she needed to get to his financial records to prove it. She had plans to hire a locksmith to force open the door.

"I'm turning fifty, my life is changing," Ellen said. "I want a better life for me, and I want a better life for my daughter."

As a stay-at-home mom, Ellen was devoted to her daughter, and had spent a lot of time—especially when Olivia was in grade school—volunteering at her school, fundraising for special activities and running the Brownie troop. What disturbed her greatly in recent years was that Olivia was starting to turn on her—starting to mimic her father's demeaning ways.

Ellen was determined now to get out. Her brother, Gary Gregory, was coming down the next day from his home outside Boston. Their plan was to leave Friday with Ellen's mother, Mary Janette Gregory, so they could join the rest of the family for a big party to celebrate Christmas and Ellen's 50th birthday on December 26. They would know that she had a lot more to celebrate than Christmas and her birthday.

But one of the issues still up in the air was when Rafi would see Olivia. Ellen told Mary Beth that she was worried about how it would all work out. Their plan was to meet in New York on December 27 so Rafi could take Olivia and spend a few days with her. He really wanted her to join him on December 26, but Ellen had convinced him to let her keep her daughter on her birthday, and promised him he and Olivia would still get to spend a lot of time together. At the very least they would have a couple of days in New York to go to a museum or see a play—the kinds of things that he used to do with his wife, but had increasingly enjoyed doing with his daughter. Olivia was a pro at all of it, having learned from an early age how to get what she wanted from both of her doting parents. As she got older, she especially liked going to fancy places with her daddy. Their plan was to stay in New York at the Plaza Hotel and see the musical *Wicked*.

Ellen said Rafi was also talking about taking Olivia to Israel for one last visit with his dying mother. She didn't mind Olivia going on the trip. In fact, it would give Ellen a chance to get packed up and ready to move right after they returned. But she was worried that Olivia would not return in time to start school on January 3.

Robb didn't need to be back in Philadelphia until January 8 for the start of the spring semester at the University of Pennsylvania where he was an economics professor and well-known expert in game theory—a discipline that blends economics, psychology and mathematics in order to make decisions by calculating what others might do.

Ellen couldn't hide her nagging worry, one she had told Mary Beth and other friends about many times over the years. Ellen had long been afraid that Rafi, 56, would make good on his threats to take Olivia away from her, take her to live with his family in Israel, and Ellen would never see her again.

"We'll work it out," Ellen declared to Mary Beth.

Ellen excitedly told her friend that she had met with a lawyer who'd told her she could expect to get about $4,000 per month from Robb, more than enough to lease a townhouse she had found on Susan Drive, in a complex nearby. Robb had toured it recently with a realtor and had agreed that Ellen and Olivia should take it. The plan was for them to move in around January 1, or as soon as they could. She wasn't going to take very much from the Forest Road house, a three-bedroom split-level in a wooded area of Philadelphia's Main Line suburbs. There wasn't too much there that she really cared about anyway. Rafi could trash it all for all she cared.

"How about if he moves in there?" asked Mary Beth. "Wouldn't that be easier?" Mary Beth, a former accountant who had worked at a brokerage firm, couldn't help thinking that, while she wanted her friend to get away, she also wanted her to be financially secure. Getting the house in a highly desirable leafy suburb was worth a lot more than getting money for rent.

"He won't," Ellen replied. "He's already gone to check out the townhouse and he told me he'd never move into it. He doesn't want to move out of *his* house. Besides, this will be better. It's easier for me to go out and start fresh."

Fearing there was more, Mary Beth pressed Ellen to know whether he had ever hurt her. "Is there anything he's done that we can get the police involved to get him out and change the locks?"

"No, I'd rather do it this way . . . I still love him."

"Is there any problem with Olivia?"

"No, Olivia is actually looking forward to moving in with me."

Ellen had arranged it so Olivia would still be near her father and school friends. She could even stay in the same school.

Mary Beth was elated. It was like the sun had finally come into Ellen's life to replace the darkness that had enveloped her for so long.

Ellen's voice was strong and broke out easily in laughter. She was obviously excited by the new life that awaited her.

"Are you definitely doing this?" asked Mary Beth, reminding her friend that they had talked about this scenario many times before.

"Yes, for sure," said Ellen.

"OK then, when you come back, we'll have our birthday lunch and we'll get you packed up and moved into the new place," said Mary Beth, referring to the celebration they would have in honor of her own birthday on December 23 and Ellen's on December 26.

As she hung up the phone, Mary Beth couldn't help talking

to herself: "Thank God I took that phone call. The old Ellen is back."

And talking to her had actually been enjoyable. So different from the many depressing phone calls she had taken over the last couple of years from her friend. Mary Beth knew it: 2007 was going to be a great year for Ellen.

CHAPTER 2

Rafael Robb walked through the garage to his car, parked in the driveway. He reached in and retrieved his cell phone from the floor before punching in the ten-digit non-emergency number to summon the Upper Merion police to his home in the quiet, exclusive suburb of Wayne. "I just came home and found my wife murdered on the kitchen floor," he told Dispatcher Matt Markland in his heavily accented English.

Just hearing him say "murdered" sent a shiver through the young dispatcher as he recorded the details of Incident #06-27106. In his five years on the job, this was his first homicide and he wanted to get it right. His training automatically kicked in. He needed to keep the caller safe and find out what the officers would encounter when they got there.

After getting his location, the dispatcher continued, "And what's the matter with your wife?"

"She is killed," Robb said.

"How can you tell?"

"I know, her head is cracked. . . . She's on the kitchen floor."

". . . Is there anyone in the house?"

"There is a broken window in the back."

"Sir, can you step outside for me?"

Robb did as Markland asked and walked out of the garage to stand in front of his brick and tan split-level home with attached garage. As is typical of mid-Atlantic weather in late December, there was a light icy rain that, as darkness fell, turned into a downpour.

"OK, just calm down," Markland told Robb after getting him to spell his name and repeat his address. "Step outside and wait for me, OK?"

"OK."

Just calm down so you can talk to me, all right?

"OK."

"Do you see anyone else around the house?"

"No, I don't see anything."

"OK. Was there blood coming from her or what?"

Before Robb could answer, Robb hung up and Markland called him back.

"It's the police. Are you standing out front? You need to stay on the phone with me."

"Yes, I'm out front, yes."

"OK, stay out front. There are police and an ambulance coming."

Within minutes, four Upper Merion police cars converged on Forest Road. Officers Patrick Krouse, Jerry Davis, Mike Ballman and Andy Fidler met Robb in the driveway. They were responding to the alert tone that Markland had sent out over the department radio—the kind of loud lingering alarm that told them this call was a priority emergency.

"Mike, you talk to him," shouted Krouse as he and Davis ducked into the garage toward the house. They immediately noticed a trail of bloody footprints that continued into the den. Turning toward Robb, Krouse asked, "Is there anybody in there?"

"No," Robb answered. With their guns drawn, Davis, an eight-year patrol veteran, and Krouse, an officer for twelve years, walked through the garage and den and up the two steps into the kitchen, where they immediately saw Ellen Robb's body sprawled on the bloody floor, her feet pointing toward them. The officers' immediate concern was whether anyone was hiding in the house. To get beyond the kitchen, they braced their arms and feet toward each other so they could step over the body without disturbing anything. They were very cognizant about not adding or taking anything away from the scene.

Officer Keith Christian headed inside toward the back of the house where Robb had reported finding the glass shattered on the outside door of the laundry room. 'How could anyone have gotten through here?' Christian asked himself as he checked out the area. There were too many boxes near the door to let anyone enter through it.

Outside, Ballman took out his notebook and looked at Robb. "What's going on?" he asked, giving Robb an opening so he could start telling the officer when he'd found his wife and what else he'd done that day. Robb calmly recounted how he'd last seen his wife in the morning before leaving for the University of Pennsylvania where he was a professor of economics. There were no tears, not even any noticeable emotion, when he described finding her bloody body on the kitchen floor.

Upper Merion Officer Joseph Bennett started stringing the yellow plastic police tape around the perimeter of the home and the front yard—a first signal to neighbors that there was a lot more than a medical emergency at the Robb house.

The neighbors could see Robb standing outside in front of the garage as he spoke with Ballman while other officers searched outside. Police were checking for anyone in or around the home, including the woods behind the house. After that, they were looking for any possible evidence, including a weapon or bloody discarded clothes. Because Ellen Robb was lying in heavy pools of blood, they didn't know if perhaps she had killed herself and was situated on top of the weapon. Or, as sometimes happens, she could have killed herself, but Robb had come home and removed the gun before police arrived. At this point, anything was possible.

At first glance, all they knew was that it certainly looked like Ellen Robb's head had been blown off.

Upstairs, Krouse and Davis cleared each bedroom, one at a time. As Krouse pushed on the door to Olivia's room, Copper, the tiny shih tzu family dog, came charging out and scurried down the stairs, startling Davis, who quickly followed and grabbed him just as he was about to step in the thick black-red blood pooling around Ellen Robb's head. After putting the dog back in the bedroom, the officers retreated to the living room and shut down the house. No one else would be allowed to go inside.

Talking to Davis and Krouse from behind the front screen door, Patrol Lieutenant Thomas Nolan decided to alert the Montgomery County detectives. This could still be a suicide, but there was too much that the officers told him "just didn't look right." If this was a burglary, as Robb had said, why wasn't there any ransacking inside? And why had the burglar broken the glass on a back door when the front door was unlocked? Even more puzzling, why would a burglar pick the Robb house, where Ellen Robb's Subaru wagon was parked in the driveway, when the house next door was unoccupied and a UPS package on the front steps advertised that fact to anyone driving by?

Nolan directed Officer Fidler to position himself by the front door and start keeping a log of everyone who entered the crime scene.

As Detective David Gershanick stood by the door, he queried the officers inside on what they were finding.

"What do you have?" he yelled out to Krouse and Davis.

"It looks like she's been shot, but we don't know, there could be a gun underneath her."

From his vantage point, Gershanick could see even from afar the severe trauma to her head and face.

As he turned away, Detective Sergeant Jeff McCabe came up to him. "Dave, you're going to take this one," he told him, giving Gershanick his first job as the lead investigator in a homicide investigation.

"Are you sure?"

"Of course, you can handle it."

Before Gershanick got too involved, he reminded himself that the job could evaporate, like that, if they found out this was a suicide. It surely had some indications of a self-inflicted gunshot wound, but they wouldn't know at least until the body was moved.

For now, Gershanick needed to call his fiancé, Karen Faix, to let her know that he wouldn't be going Christmas shopping at the mall with her that evening. He walked down the driveway for a private moment: "Look, there's been a murder or a suicide," he told her, adding that he would be late getting home. Their only break would be if this turned out to be a suicide. That would mean some paperwork, but not much more.

If it turned out to be a homicide, Gershanick knew he'd be missing a lot more than a shopping trip. "I don't know when I'm going to be home or when I'm going to be done," Gershanick told her. A substitute teacher at Roberts Elementary, the same school that Olivia had attended the year before, Karen would get her first dose of what it would be like to be married to a police detective. They had planned to spend a lot of time together while she was on Christmas break, but now that was all in jeopardy. They had met at school—Gershanick had been visiting there for several years as part of a "Cops 'N Kids" program that sent Upper Merion officers on field trips to teach safety tips. It was on one of those trips that Gershanick had first met Robb.

None of that mattered now as Gershanick told his fiancé that it was Olivia's mother who had been found dead. The news stunned Karen, who remembered Olivia and even her father. He had often escorted her to school and had to sign her in at the office because she was late.

CHAPTER 3

December 22, 2006
Afternoon

The only cars that traveled down Forest Road were driven by people who lived there. A police car rarely made the trip. Today, there were at least six parked every which way on the street. And the brass had yet to arrive from Upper Merion, the Montgomery County Office of the District Attorney or the county detective bureau.

Just seeing the police at the Robb house drew the Forest Road neighbors out of their well-kept homes, many of which were decorated with lights, outside wreaths and ornaments for Christmas. It was the kind of place where every year, on Christmas Eve, children would come out of their houses to greet Santa, who rode through town on a fire truck, tossing out candy canes.

On this day, the mood on Forest Road was somber. In a cold driving rain, a steady stream of neighbors came up to the officers demanding answers.

"Can you tell me what's going on?" one woman probed as Gershanick returned to the police car.

"No, but you are safe. Everything is fine."

"Do we need to lock our doors?" the woman insisted.

"No, everything is safe. We just can't tell you anything right now."

She left, agitated and, like many others, perplexed: "Why couldn't the police tell us what is going on?" What the police couldn't tell them is that—at that moment—they didn't really know what they had on their hands. All the officers knew at that point was what Robb had told them—that he had come home and found his wife dead on their kitchen floor, and a back door window had been broken. Gershanick knew the rules in a situation like this: "We didn't want to say someone was murdered and find out later that it was a suicide.

"It didn't make sense to panic anybody until we were sure about what we had."

As he spoke to Officer Ballman, Rafael Robb nervously looked at his watch. Olivia was due to return home any minute from school, which was letting out early at 2 p.m. for the start of an eleven-day Christmas holiday. And, he didn't want her to walk in on all of this.

Rather than take any chances, Ballman got on his radio and told dispatch that the couple's daughter was en route home. Markland contacted the school bus dispatch to track the bus's location. After learning that it had already left Upper Merion Area Middle School and was nearing Forest Road, a supervisor directed Upper Merion police evidence technician Kim O'Keefe to get there to meet Olivia as she climbed down the steps.

At the first break in the action, Krouse, who lived down the hill from the Robbs in the Bob White Farms section, an enclave of upscale homes, called his wife. Everybody in the neighborhood knew he was the local resident cop, and her phone was going to be ringing off the wall. Other than to say he'd be late and couldn't make it to set up for Christmas Mass at their church, Krouse couldn't tell her much. "We don't know what we have," he told her.

Robb began pacing nervously, his hand rubbing his upper right arm. "I'm feeling shoulder pain," he told Ballman as they stood in the driveway outside the garage. Looking over at him, Ballman couldn't tell whether this was a totally understandable anxiety attack or a heart attack in progress, but he wasn't going to take any chances. He walked Robb to his squad car to sit down and get out of the steady drizzle, and called for an ambulance. Shortly—just nineteen minutes after Robb had first summoned police—he was inside an ambulance where paramedics were checking his vital signs and giving him oxygen.

As the school bus made the turn toward her normal stop at the corner of Forest and Brookwood Roads, Olivia could see the cluster of police cars and feared that something was wrong at home. She borrowed a cell phone from her friend, Brooke Dubin, and nervously pressed the ten digits for her home number and her father's cell phone. No one answered. Inside, the officers could hear her as she left a frantic message on the answering machine: "Mom, why are all the cops there? Is everything OK? Mom, why are the cops out front?" They knew they had only minutes to stop the little girl from walking in on the horrific scene. That job fell to O'Keefe, who walked up just as Olivia was getting off the bus. Olivia's friend Brooke stayed on the bus to the next stop, so she could go home and get her father, Jeff, who quickly got in the car and drove them both the short distance from Bob White Road to the Robbs' house. En route, Jeff called his wife, LuAnn, one of Ellen's closest friends, who had been out shopping, telling her to get there quickly.

Brooke and Jeff stood with Olivia near the bus stop as if to shield her from the commotion. "What's going on?" Olivia repeatedly asked O'Keefe. "What's happened to my mom? Where's my dad?" No one would answer her questions.

When LuAnn arrived, she could see the police stripping the yellow plastic "Police Line—Do Not Cross" tape across the front of the house, and Olivia standing with her family and O'Keefe. As she walked toward them, LuAnn was able to look in the back of the ambulance and spotted Robb sitting inside.

Her mind was racing. "I knew it was Ellen and I knew it wasn't Olivia and I knew it wasn't him. I happened to look inside the ambulance and he was sitting inside."

To the first officer she saw, LuAnn blurted out: "I know this isn't good. I know it's my friend Ellen and I know he did it." The officer immediately took out his pad and started writing down what LuAnn was saying. He also took down her name and phone number, and promised to send someone over later to find out more of what she knew.

LuAnn was one of the first to accuse Robb of having

something to do with Ellen's death. As she talked to the officer, all she could think of was Olivia and how much Ellen loved her, and how LuAnn had to be there for her. "Where is Olivia going?" she asked the officers, who explained that they needed to get a statement from the little girl. "Please don't take her to the police station right now." LuAnn offered her home if Olivia wanted to go there. The girls were friends. "I wanted her in a safe spot," LuAnn would say later. The officers agreed and walked over to Olivia, who told them she wanted to go around the block to her friend's house.

As they walked away, Olivia caught a glimpse of the back of the ambulance where her father was resting inside. As the little girl climbed inside, Robb tearfully told her everything would be OK. It was the first time that day that any of the officers had seen him show any emotion.

He didn't say any more. That was left to O'Keefe and veteran investigator and father of four, Lieutenant Rich Peffall, a Montgomery County detective, later that afternoon. When they arrived at Olivia's friend's home on Crestwood, directly behind the Robbs' house, Olivia was with her friend in the family room. Peffall asked if there was a room where they could have some privacy, and Laura's mother took them to a bedroom upstairs.

The adults felt the tension, knowing that the officers were about to deliver traumatic news to a 12-year-old girl. Peffall began telling Olivia that "something bad had happened" to her mother, and she was dead. Although the little girl, her long brown softly curled hair falling over her shoulders, said nothing and asked no questions, Peffall reached out his arms to comfort her. She appeared to stiffen instead, pushing back quickly. He couldn't help thinking that perhaps she didn't quite grasp all that was happening. She appeared stone-faced, showing no emotion and shedding no tears. The officers were encouraging her, telling her it was OK to cry. She never did.

She asked for one thing—her dog. O'Keefe went to First Assistant District Attorney Risa Vetri Ferman, who gave a quick approval and even dug into her own car and pulled out a purple rope for a leash.

* * *

Olivia wouldn't be the only person shocked that afternoon.

Detective Les Glauner was supposed to be off that day, but had volunteered to work overtime to help direct holiday traffic at the King of Prussia Mall, which promotes itself as the largest retail complex in the country, with 13,000 parking spaces. As soon as he heard the all-car alarm, he redirected his car to the Robb house, where Detective Sergeant McCabe told him to stand guard at the southern end of Forest Road, three houses away.

Robb had told the officers that his brother-in-law, Gary Gregory, was expected to come by to pick up Ellen and Olivia. It was supposed to be Gary's first stop in a journey back to his home in Sherborn, Massachusetts, outside Boston, with Ellen, Olivia and his mother, Mary Janette Gregory, who lived in Honey Brook, another Philadelphia area suburban town. Gary, the CEO of a medical device company in Waltham, Massachusetts, had elected to spend the night at a nearby hotel so he could spend the morning working. He knew of his older sister's plans to get a divorce. He had given her the $5,000 retainer she had needed to hire an attorney in October. But, instead of Ellen's beaming smile and warm hug, Gary was intercepted as he maneuvered his Ford Explorer SUV down Forest Road. As he approached the barricade, he pulled over to one side, got out and walked apprehensively toward Glauner.

"Mr. Gregory?

"I'm Detective Glauner from the Upper Merion Police Department. There's been an incident at your sister's house. I need you to come with me."

Gary asked the officer what was going on and looked puzzled at the scene in front of him—police cars blocking the street, yellow police tape encircling his sister's house, an ambulance parked out in front.

"I can't tell you right now, but if you come to the station, I will be able to tell you there."

With that, Gary climbed into the police car as Glauner took the wheel. What was supposed to be a ten-minute ride seemed to go on for a half hour as they fought the late afternoon holiday traffic. The rhythmic flapping of the windshield wipers to clear off the steady rain filled in the silent moments.

Mostly, Gary was doing the talking. As they made their way, he peppered the officer with questions about Ellen and what had happened to her that the officer couldn't answer. Glauner tried to answer without telling him that Ellen was dead. As an eleven-year police veteran, Glauner had learned that one of the worst jobs in policing was to deliver to family members the news that their loved one had died. It was excruciating for both of them. Glauner purposely didn't want to tell him while they were driving. He feared that Gary would become so enraged and emotional inside the car that Glauner would lose control of the situation.

With every question, Glauner repeated that there had been an incident and he would tell him more at the station. Finally, as they pulled into the station parking lot, Gary looked at Glauner and asked him directly whether Ellen was alive.

Seeing the look on Glauner's face, Gary knew the answer and began sobbing. Inside, Glauner told him everything they knew—that Ellen had been found dead on her kitchen floor by her husband, who had called police at 1:45 p.m., saying he had come home to find her dead and the back door window broken. They were investigating all of the possibilities.

Before he began a formal interview, Glauner had to ask Gary two questions:

"Do you know anyone who would want to burglarize her house?"

"No."

"Who do you think would do something like this?"

Gary didn't hesitate.

"Rafael."

With that, he told Glauner about Ellen's plans to get a divorce, and how much she hated and feared her husband, "but I could never get to the bottom of it. When he blows his top, she didn't feel very secure." He described Robb as having a cool nature, but a short fuse when he got mad, at times about little things. Asked if Ellen had talked to him about Robb, Gary said, "I know all about their relationship and their plans for divorce." Their relationship had been bad for the past thirteen years, "and the past ten years have been really bad," he told Glauner. Asked if Ellen had ever said anything about any abuse, Gary described how Ellen had endured "heavy verbal abuse and she denied any physical abuse but I am not so sure about that." Asked about Ellen's medical conditions, Gary told Glauner, "She has colitis from her nerves and [sic] been depressed from the verbal abuse."

Gary also told police that Robb may have owned a handgun. Ellen had told her brother that the gun was kept in Robb's bedroom, which was locked when he wasn't there.

Glauner had to cover another possibility. "Did your sister ever mention anything about suicide?"

"Never."

Glauner couldn't tell Gary much about what had happened to Ellen except to say that the crime-scene specialists were still working on it. Once the body was moved, they would know more about whether she could have killed herself.

Gary was adamant. He knew his sister, and she would never kill herself.

Obviously emotionally distraught as he answered Glauner, Gary would alternately weep and ask questions. He took a break to call family, starting with his brother, Art, who lived about 30 miles away across the Delaware River in Haddonfield, New Jersey. When he first picked up a message from Gary to call him right away, Art feared that something had happened to their 81-year-old mother. When he reached Gary, he immediately asked what was wrong with her. When Gary said it wasn't their mother, Art knew it had to be Ellen and told police he thought, 'What did Rafi do?' When he asked Gary what happened is when he learned that Ellen had been killed.

"Did Rafi do it?"

It was too early to tell, Gary told him.

Back at the Robb house, the detectives had to simultaneously process what they were seeing and what Robb had told them. His story was that someone had broken into his home and killed his wife. Hearing that stirred the neighbors, who feared that there was a killer burglar on the loose. Many called into Upper Merion police with tips that went nowhere. Neighbors locked their doors and traded phone calls: If there was a killer and he had a gun, he could kill again. And, if he had tried to burglarize the Robb home and was surprised by Ellen Robb, then maybe he would be looking to break into other houses.

Before television or radio would spread the news, cell phones and instant messaging alerted neighbors and many of Ellen's friends.

Patty Volpi was driving her daughter Kelly home from her job as a gymnastics coach when she got a call from her younger daughter Jenna, a classmate of Olivia's. The kids were trading text messages that Olivia's mother was dead from an asthma seizure and her father had suffered an attack and been taken to the hospital. Olivia was staying with friends.

"Do you want to drive up and see?" Patty asked her daughter.

"Yes, let's go."

Patty turned the wheel on her silver Toyota SUV onto Brookwood and down Forest Road, where she was forced to stop three doors away from the Robb house by a police barricade. Thankfully she recognized Krouse, who was standing guard behind a barricade in the icy rain now that the forensic team had taken over at the house.

Patty told him what the kids had told her.

"Is any of that true?"

"It's an open investigation," he said. "I can't tell you anything. But, one thing I can say, it is Ellen."

"Is she dead?"

"Yes."

Patty's first thought was that there was a crazy person running around the neighborhood. She immediately started peppering the officer with questions.

"Have you checked the area? Have you caught anybody? Is the area safe?"

"We're checking the area," said Krouse, who was trying to reassure her. Finally, just as the television news truck pulled up nearby, he told her that she could tell her daughters not to worry about going to sleep that night.

"Should my children be scared?"

"I don't think so."

Patty took that to mean that the police had the area covered. Nobody was going anywhere that night. Her first thoughts were that if there was a killer in the area, everyone needed to lock their doors and get their children inside. Her first instinct was to get her daughter home.

She returned to her car, climbed in and sat, motionless. She was overwhelmed with the shocking news. She couldn't believe her friend Ellen was gone.

"Mom, what's wrong?" her daughter Kelly implored. "What's wrong? Mom . . ."

The reality of the moment was starting to sink in—Ellen wasn't alive anymore. As if in slow motion, she somehow directed her car to take her home.

When she arrived, her first thought was to tell her husband, Paul. The Volpis had formed a warm and close relationship with Ellen Robb in recent years while their daughters were classmates at Roberts Elementary on nearby Croton Road. That's where Ellen had earned her "Volunteer of the Year" honors in 2004 for doing it all, from bringing treats for the children after reading to them to running complicated fundraising projects. She'd often worked with the Volpis.

It must have been the pale look on Patty's face that stopped Paul, a friendly guy with a solid grip who runs his own business. "What's wrong?" Paul asked as they stepped out of the kitchen and onto the porch.

"Ellen, she's dead," Patty answered, trying hurriedly to fill her husband in on the details as she knew them. "We just sat there. It hit us. It was like a building had floated and fell down on us. It was like the weight of the world was on us. My first thought was, 'Was Olivia taken care of?' "

At about the same time, Lieutenant Bruce Saville and Detective John Finor were in Norristown, driving in their Montgomery County Detective Bureau cars toward the Robb house—Finor in front of Saville—when Saville radioed Finor to pull over.

"Do you have a gunshot residue kit in the car?"

"Yes," said Finor. "I always carry it."

With that, Saville redirected Finor to get to Montgomery Hospital Medical Center and test Robb's hands.

When he arrived at the hospital, Finor found Robb in the emergency room, sitting up on a gurney in a side examining room. Ballman attached paper bags to each of Robb's hands while Robb sat in the ambulance. With so many questions unanswered, it was standard procedure that they preserve any evidence by anyone who could have been there.

As he applied the testing chemical to Robb's hands, Finor couldn't help noticing that he had blood there too—a small amount of blood on the web of his right hand between the thumb and forefinger. Finor carefully preserved it all. With so much blood at the scene and Robb's movements around the house in question, Finor had no idea how important that speck of blood could become.

CHAPTER 4

December 22, 2006
Afternoon

News of a murder in Upper Merion sent town officers and county detectives scurrying to the scene. On the Friday before Christmas, the Upper Merion Township Police Department's attention was at the King of Prussia Mall, where patrol officers and even some of the department's eleven detectives had been pressed into service just to keep traffic moving and to handle the fender benders and car burglaries that are routine when your territory includes a super-sized mall.

During the same hours that they were called to the Robb house, police also picked up three guys for smoking dope inside a 2006 Jeep parked outside a movie theater, and a GPS was stolen out of a 2005 Toyota Camry parked at the mall.

Murder rarely happens in the town and the Robbs' neighborhood was especially quiet. As the most populous suburban county in Pennsylvania, Montgomery handled about twenty a year—twenty-two in 2005 and seventeen in 2006. But, when they do happen, it's intense, and detectives work around the clock to solve them. That's why the Montgomery County Detective Bureau's Deputy Chief, Sam Gallen, was happy when he could give his crew some time off. On the day Ellen Robb was killed, the county detectives had just finished a holiday luncheon in the detective bureau conference room. The table was still littered with the leftovers of lasagna, roast pork, baked ziti and trays of cookies and other holiday goodies. The luncheon, an annual gathering, brings together not only the detectives and office staff, but also the district attorney and assistants.

Gallen, a former local police chief, who'd worked as a detective on over 100 homicide investigations, had figured he would use the rest of the day to catch up on paperwork. It was rare that he got a quiet day in the office. Gallen oversaw the six detectives in the elite homicide unit and indirectly supervised the other units with some thirty-four detectives.

Risa Ferman had also told the staff to go home. In charge that day while DA Bruce L. Castor, Jr., was out for a long weekend holiday, she was also counting on a free afternoon to prepare for the upcoming trial of Patrick "Lex" McCarthy, who was charged with killing Anna Nicole Fowler, 19, in Room 252 at the Motel 6 on October 5, 2004.

Montgomery has a well-oiled machine for handling homicides. The protocol of joint local and county investigations was long-standing, but as first assistant DA, Castor had perfected it by having the prosecutor run the investigation from the field in the belief that cases were won or lost on the fruits of the field work and not on what happened in the courtroom. The idea was to be able to get key evidence promptly that the prosecutor could foresee would be needed at trial and to close off defense options as soon as possible.

In his fourteen years as either the first or second in command, Castor pushed the team approach with the resources and manpower to get the job done. The first few hours in a homicide case were critical and he wanted enough people to be able to jump in immediately. Once local officers determine that a death was criminal, protocol calls for the local department to notify the county's deputy chief of detectives, who would coordinate the investigation with the first assistant district attorney. They would work together like the hub on a wheel, sending assignments out to local officers and county detectives. On a parallel track, depending on the case, officers would team up to do the forensic work. On each part of the investigation, the two agencies would assign detectives to work together when needed or they would parcel out the interviews to cover the broadest area in the shortest amount of time. The idea was to match the local knowledge with the resources of a countywide bureau. The assistant DA would be sure to keep the DA informed of the status of the case.

When Upper Merion's Lieutenant Nolan called Gallen to tell him of the Robb murder, everyone knew what to expect. Gallen's first call went to Ferman and then to the detectives, many of whom were spreading out for the holiday weekend. Gallen was getting them all back—the generalists, the specialists and the seasoned veterans.

Drew Marino, a homicide detective for a third of his twelve years in policing, was just about to step into Brother Paul's, his favorite watering hole, fifteen minutes from the office, for a holiday drink with friends, when his cell phone went off and he heard Gallen's voice telling him to get over to Forest Road. Marino had just stepped in the front door, and literally turned on his heels, waving a quick hello to those waiting for him. Before hanging up, Marino heard Gallen say, "This one is going to be yours."

That meant that Marino would take the lead for the county detectives working jointly with Gershanick from Upper Merion. While he had worked on other homicides, this was only the second case in which Marino would take lead position. In a high-profile case like this one, taking lead carried with it a lot of responsibility to coordinate the investigation, collect all of the evidence and statements as they came in and make sure everyone knew what the other officers were finding out.

Gershanick, who had just stopped in at his house to grab a quick lunch when he got the high alert call, was already at the scene when Marino arrived.

"Hey, I guess it's you and me," said Gershanick, offering his hand in welcome. The young detectives knew each other from when they'd jointly investigated a fire death, but they had never worked a case together. What they didn't know then was just how much time they would be spending with each other over the next several weeks. On that Friday night, they stayed at it until about 3 a.m. and started back in the next morning at 7:30.

Included in Gallen's roundup were Bruce Saville and J. Michael Santarelli, seasoned veterans of both homicides and crime scenes. Gallen wanted them to get there as soon as possible to start examining and collecting evidence, key tasks in the critical first forty-eight hours following a homicide. He could almost hear Castor's directives from other investigations: "If it can't be perfect, it better be as close to perfect as you can make it. Don't leave any stone unturned and don't cut any corners." Everyone in the office knew the bottom line so well, they could have put it on bumper stickers: 'We don't want to lose a homicide case.'

As she grabbed her coat, Ferman couldn't help thinking, 'My husband is going to love this.' She reached into her purse for her cell phone and pushed the speed dial on Michael's number. "I've got a job," she told him. "I'll let you know later how long I will be." Michael Ferman, an executive in the family's paper mill business, knew all too well to keep things flexible.

Michael knew Risa would call later when she learned more, but for now he and their three children would be having Chinese dinner without her. Ferman usually prepared a Shabbat dinner for her family on Fridays, but on this day, she'd planned an outing to their favorite Chinese restaurant to give her more time to prepare for next week's so-called Motel 6 murder trial. At risk were their plans for the weekend, which included birthday parties for both grandmothers and Risa's parents' anniversary.

She couldn't think of any of that now. As a veteran of thirteen years in the district attorney's office, Ferman and her family had learned that the job comes first. In the five years since Castor had tapped her to become first assistant district attorney, Ferman had become a veteran at running homicide investigations. That's the way the office was organized. As DA, Castor could take over any case he wanted to, but the job routinely fell to the first assistant. That's how Castor made his name in the Philly area, first as the wunderkind 32-year-old first assistant to Drew's father, Michael Marino, and then as district attorney. Castor joined the office in 1985 as a legal intern while attending Washington and Lee University School of Law where he won the graduation prize in criminal law. He returned after graduation and spent five years as an assistant district attorney in the major crimes and sex crimes units, making his way to captain. His fast track led him to deputy district attorney in 1991 and Marino's first assistant in 1993. When Marino left the office, Castor took the top job, elected in 1999 and re-elected in 2003 by wide margins.

In the last four years, his office had racked up a nearly perfect conviction record—90 out of 91 homicides. The one they lost was an unusual case in which a gun had been left unattended and a child found it and killed his playmate.

A petite, no-nonsense prosecutor, Ferman clicked into her investigator mode—she knew they had to get as many officers as possible to work on the case while memories were fresh and evidence was undisturbed.

CHAPTER 5

December 22, 2006
Late Afternoon

When Finor finally got to the Robb house, a blur of blood greeted him as he pushed open the kitchen door. What he saw next took him back to the streets of Philadelphia, where he had put in thirty-two years as a street officer and firearms expert. The city racked up so many killings—377 in 2005 and 406 in 2006, alarmingly high even for Philadelphia—that Finor got special training as a ballistics expert. Thin, tanned and tall, Finor was well-known in law enforcement circles as an ace investigator who knew his stuff and kept his cool under pressure. He had done ballistics work for some of Philly's most notorious shootings. He'd been there on December 28, 2000, to examine the array of bullet holes left in the city's worst mass murder in recent history when four men perpetrated a shootout inside a West Philadelphia crack house that killed seven and injured three others. The gun blitz was to get revenge on a drug dealer who'd ruined a clutch on one killer's car. When Finor worked the night shift in Philly, he spent his nights checking out dead bodies and his days testifying in court about the guns that had killed them.

When he retired in early 2006, Finor had lots of options, but the one he jumped at was the detective job offered by Montgomery County. He was happy to move into Montgomery County to get away from the daily grind of gun killings in the city.

And he wanted to use his skills to the fullest in a department with a reputation for throwing in everything they had and everything they needed to solve a homicide.

That day had arrived.

Finor's first task was to take photos of the crime scene so that the other detectives could have them in hand when they went out to question potential witnesses. There was no reason to allow everyone to go walking into the kitchen to get a look. And his colleagues who were already forming their own opinions about how Ellen Robb had been killed wanted to know what John had to say.

The smiling photos of Ellen around the house bore no resemblance to the bloody corpse sprawled on the kitchen floor. As he looked closely at Ellen Robb's body, Finor figured she had been shot in the face. Looking at the horrific wounds, he concluded that the killer had pulled the trigger on a high-powered shotgun at close range. That's the only thing that could explain the pool of blood, cracked skull and horribly disfigured face.

He instinctively scanned the bloody walls and ceiling for bullet holes. Looking around the room, the veteran officer was struck by what he saw: Christmas wrapping paper unfurled on the kitchen table, a partially wrapped box, scissors and eyeglasses lying nearby, a television on low in the background. And blood everywhere—on the floor, on the walls, up to the ceiling and down to the baseboards.

Ellen had been wrapping presents at the kitchen table—a common scene just three days before Christmas. The "to" and "from" tags had been filled in with a pink pen, the same one the officers found clutched in her hand in a pool of blood. The tip of the pen was sticking to the blood on Ellen's body.

The pen was apparently all Ellen Robb had had to fight off her attacker.

"What are we looking at?" asked Saville as Finor emerged from the house joining Marino and Gershanick, the lead homicide detectives on the case.

"It looks like either a shotgun or a high-powered rifle to the head," said Finor, who had won the respect of everyone since he joined the Montgomery County detectives. It was hard not to defer to him as the gun expert. In his career, he had testified 700 times in various courts on ballistics evidence. On top of that, Finor had military and advanced police training, which included stints at the FBI Academy in Quantico, Virginia, making him one of the country's foremost experts in firearms and the damage the bullets leave on the human body.

As he joined the others, Finor went on to explain what he saw. It definitely looked like a shotgun blast to the face. The more they talked, the more they realized that what they were seeing on Ellen looked a lot like that kid at Springfield High School last month—the one who'd shot himself with a an AK-47 blast up through his chin.

A crime-scene specialist who put in twenty-seven-and-a-half years with Upper Merion before joining the county detectives, Saville knew exactly what Finor was talking about. Detective Santarelli, a homicide detective who is also a crime-scene specialist, nodded in agreement. That image of what they'd seen inside Springfield High was something they would never forget. Was it possible that this death had occurred the same way?

Mary Beth Pedlow had meant to stop in to see her friend Ellen that Friday morning, but, as usual, she was running late for work. She figured she'd catch up with her later. But by then, she was rushing to get to her 9-year-old daughter Lily's holiday party at Roberts Elementary School. She missed the party, but she got there in time to meet Lily. She whisked her into their Toyota Sienna minivan to take her home. Ellen lived at 670 and Mary Beth at 573 Forest Road. Her route from school took her home up Croton Road to Brookwood and down Forest Road from the opposite direction, so she didn't pass in front of Ellen's house. It was an unusual route and one that kept Mary Beth from seeing for herself all of the commotion going on in the neighborhood at Ellen's end of the street.

Mary Beth's split-level sits down a steep incline. If she knew she'd have to go out again, she would leave the car parked up on the street. She pulled up and walked down the steps to her front door. As she walked in, Mary Beth got a phone call from another neighbor. Something was happening at Ellen's house. There were police cars everywhere and an ambulance was there too. Someone was hurt.

"Oh, my God. What's going on?"

She closed her eyes. "Dear God, please let her be OK."

Before she could compose herself, Upper Merion Detective Jim Godby was knocking at her front door. Ellen's husband had told police that Mary Beth was Ellen's best friend.

"I have really bad news for you," he told her.

"Please tell me she'll be OK," Mary Beth pleaded as she tried to move past him. "I've got to help her."

"No, you can't do anything to help her. She's dead."

"It can't be. It can't be. It can't be," she sobbed, as tears rolled down her face. She was in shock.

"When was the last day you spoke with her?"

"Just two days ago."

The words came tumbling out as she told him about her last talk with Ellen—her plans for the divorce and the move. She tried to remember whether Ellen had told her the name of her lawyer, but could only recall that Ellen had chosen him because of another friend's recommendation.

There was a lot more for them to talk about, but they'd have to do it at the police station. Mary Beth promised to pick up her son from the high school and meet the officer later at the Upper Merion station a few miles away on West Valley Forge Road.

When she arrived, there was one subject Detective Godby was anxious to ask about.

"I need to ask you a question," the officer said. "Do you know whether there were any guns in the house?"

"No. They don't have guns."

"Do you think she would ever shoot herself?"

"No."

As Pennsylvania's most populous suburban county, Montgomery gets its share of headline-grabbing homicides. But not so in Upper Merion, a well-heeled suburb where the cops are more likely to be chasing robbers at the nearby King of Prussia Mall. If it weren't for the mall, there would hardly be any crime in this affluent town, where houses in some sections sell for over a million dollars. Most of what the police deal with in Upper Merion are property crimes. Between 2000 and 2006, police responded to 5,991 thefts, 419 burglaries and 60 robberies. There were 163 assaults.

Along Forest Road, split-level, ranch and two-story homes were tucked amid rolling hills and tall, majestic trees, a leafy enclave with a prestigious Wayne zip code in the Philadelphia suburbs.

The Robb home itself was fairly modest in size—2,077 square feet—and style, but its approximately $400,000 value was largely dictated by its location on the famed Main Line, which derives its name from the Main Line of the Pennsylvania Railroad. Originally built by wealthy industrialists to ease their commute from the city to their country homes, the Main Line parallels Lancaster Avenue or Route 30.

The moniker comes from the law that authorized the construction of the first eighty-two miles of rail, from Philadelphia through Lancaster with its terminus on the Susquehanna River, which were described as part of the Main Line of Public Works of the State of Pennsylvania. Eventually, the label applied to the rail line from 30th Street in Philadelphia to Paoli.

The "Main Line" conjures up the kind of privileged lifestyle of socialite Helen Hope Montgomery Scott in the Broadway hit and classic movie, *The Philadelphia Story* (1940) starring Katharine Hepburn. More than sixty years later, the Main Line label still has lots of cachet among Philadelphians of wealth and status. And the easiest way to be included is to buy into the townships west of the city along Route 30.

It's no wonder then that a murder on Forest Road would draw everyone's attention in a way that a similar killing in the crime-infested streets of North Philadelphia would not. Over that holiday weekend, news reports drew millions to the tragedy of the Penn professor's wife found bludgeoned in the kitchen of her Main Line home.

That tragedy, in a place that typically reported no murders. There'd been four in 2005, an unusually high number, compared to only one in 2004. But even when there are killings, they don't occur like this—in a home in a quiet residential area. Robb's report that the back door had been broken into suggested that Ellen Robb had been selected at random. That just didn't happen in this town. Of the four murders in 2005, three had been carried out by John C. Eichinger, 33, a supermarket clerk who killed a woman who had spurned his romantic advances, and two witnesses, one of whom was a child. He was also charged with another killing that had occurred in 1999, of a 20-year-old woman who had rejected him. The old killing was solved only because detectives investigating the 2005 killings noticed that the distinctive wound marks from the large knife used looked similar to those in the 1999 killing.

Two other murders in Upper Merion had occurred in local motels, one in 2004 and the other in 2005.

The murder in 2005 was of a 33-year-old man with a long criminal record in Montgomery County who'd been found shot to death on January 31 in a Best Western near the King of Prussia Mall. Police had been led to the motel room by a receipt found on another body, that of a dead pregnant woman with a bullet in her head, who'd been discovered by a passerby in a Philadelphia park. The deaths, which were later ruled drug-related, led to the arrest of three men who were expected to be tried again, following a mistrial. The defense appealed a ruling that the trial judge was wrong to grant the mistrial.

The town's only murder in 2004 had occurred next door in a Motel 6 on West DeKalb Pike where Anna Nicole Fowler, 19, was raped, stabbed and strangled to death by Patrick "Lex" Mc-Carthy, 22, who had lured her there. She had been blindfolded, bound and gagged, before McCarthy slashed her throat, police said. McCarthy's trial was set to open on January 8. That was the case Ferman was working on when Gallen called to alert her of the brutal death of Ellen Robb.

As she drove up the exclusive Forest Road enclave, Ferman was pleased to see that the town police had secured the site by stripping yellow plastic tape around the perimeter of the house and its property. The street was closed to all traffic, and onlookers were being kept away. Word of the incident was trickling out in the neighborhood, but it hadn't yet hit the airwaves. Soon the scene would be swarming with television trucks all staging their live shots.

"All right, guys, what do we got?" Ferman asked as she walked up the driveway to a circle of detectives standing in the garage. As the crime-scene commander, Saville was the first to brief Ferman and then take her on a tour of the murder scene and the inside of the house.

As she stepped around the body, careful not to disturb anything, Saville told her that the consensus among them was that Ellen Robb had been shot with a high-powered shotgun—much like the teenage boy who'd taken his father's AK-47 to nearby Springfield High School ten days earlier and blown his head off. Ferman nodded as Saville reminded her of that scene. The contingent at Springfield that day had included Castor, Ferman, Gallen and Finor. The scene of the 16-year-old with his head caved in had been a first for Ferman, and it was clearly something she wouldn't forget. Looking down at Ellen Robb, Ferman agreed that it looked like Ellen had been shot in the face. She noticed how the trauma to the bones in her skull had caused her face to collapse inward—much like a basketball looks when it has lost its pressurized air. The rest of the room looked like someone had exploded a balloon filled with blood and brain matter.

They kept going, making their way through a pathway in the house, which was cluttered floor-to-ceiling with boxes, many of them online shopping deliveries. While standing in Robb's master bedroom, Ferman took out her Nextel, which gave her a direct link to Castor.

"Hey, boss, we've got a job," she said, catching Castor as he was having lunch with friends on a dreary rainy Friday before Christmas. They were all supposed to have ended up at a holiday party later that day, but it was obvious Ferman wouldn't get there. "A woman, inside her home in Upper Merion, residential neighborhood, found dead in her kitchen, looks like a shotgun blast—just like that kid in Springfield," said Ferman in the staccato shorthand of a crime investigator.

"Her kid was about to come home from school. The husband called it in. I'm standing in the master bedroom—his room. She had a different room."

The details were beginning to sound interesting to Castor. There was nothing routine about this death.

"Do you need me to come out?"

"I've got it covered. I will call you if I need anything else. Keep you posted."

After five years as Castor's first assistant, Ferman knew how he wanted things done.

A perfectionist, Castor has described himself as "a policeman who wears a suit." He loved the hunt, and as first assistant, he always went to the scene just so he could see the evidence for himself.

He also knew talent when he saw it, and had promoted Ferman from deputy to be his second in command in 2002, fully confident that she could handle anything that came their way.

Although he was off for a few days for the holiday, Ferman knew he'd want to know how the case was progressing. If the media called, he also wanted to be able to answer their questions. He would need to know whatever the police knew about how Ellen Robb was killed. Details mattered. There was no telling the boss that a gun had killed her if anyone had any doubts. The handsome, hard-driving Castor enjoyed making news and giving the sound bites. After twenty years as a prosecutor—seven as district attorney—he was comfortable in front of the television cameras. Looking dapper in tailored pinstriped suits, he knew what the media needed and what would get airtime and headlines.

Facing re-election in November 2007, Castor would surely take every chance he could to show the public that he was firmly in command and doing what he loved best—fighting the bad guys. The Robb case would give him lots of opportunities.

But, at the scene, it was Ferman who was in charge, working closely with Gallen to insure that all of the questions were being asked as quickly as possible and that the crime-scene evidence was being preserved. Just like Castor trusted Ferman, she knew she could trust the department's ace forensic team, led by Saville.

Castor knew that too, so he had no reason to question Ferman when she told him that the detectives, including ballistics expert Finor, had concluded that Ellen Robb had been shot to death. With those details in hand, he was ready to tell the public what they knew and to reassure them that they were doing everything they could to find the killer. Castor doubted there was a murdering burglar on the loose, but he didn't know for sure.

Still surveying the scene, Ferman couldn't help noticing what a mess the Robb household was. "How could anyone live like this?" she asked herself as she stepped around the clutter. There were boxes everywhere. Every surface in the kitchen was covered with something. Even before she got a look at any evidence, Ferman knew there was something dysfunctional about this house and this family. The parents slept in separate bedrooms. There was so much everywhere that the house was claustrophobic. Something may have come to a head, she thought.

Anyone who walked into the house was taken aback by all of the stuff inside. There were boxes stacked on boxes, many new purchases that remained unopened. Dishes were piled in the sink. A small house—remarkably modest in size for the home of a Penn professor on a $200,000 salary—that looked even smaller. It was split-level and had three bedrooms, one bath, a first-floor powder room and a den/family room.

As the detectives started to work the case, access to the house was very limited, but those who had to go in wore gauze-like paper booties to protect the scene from stray matter that could come in on a person's shoes. As the lead detectives, Marino and Gershanick needed to take a look at the scene before Ellen's body was moved. With that, Saville took them inside and pointed out to them the blood trail and how it could end up telling the story of how Ellen Robb had died. Pointing to the blood spatter on the blond wood kitchen cabinets and marble pattern linoleum floor, Saville told them there were lots of scenarios—including a beating death—although the scene was more consistent with the damage caused by a gunshot.

"This is what you have. I don't know what it is, but this is it," he told them, waving his arms around the kitchen.

The officers worked out of the county's command center—a trailer positioned in front of the Robb house. By the end of the night, Ferman and Gallen relocated the working group to the county detectives' offices in Norristown. It was there, over the next forty-eight hours, that they would collect evidence that would point them to Ellen's killer. While mapping out the next steps, Ferman was guided by one question: "Who would want to do this to her?"

As the last person to see Ellen, Robb became the first witness and potentially the first suspect. If he didn't murder her, he would have valuable information that could lead the detectives to the killer. They all knew the drill. Their focus was to try to eliminate him as a suspect. "We're looking to disprove someone's involvement," Ferman said. "We're going to find out if he's telling the truth or not. . . . That's the goal—to eliminate all of the people that you can, so you can find the person responsible."

Talking to Robb was their first priority.

CHAPTER 6

December 22, 2006
Evening

The police investigation into who killed Ellen Robb started with her husband, Rafael, the first person to see her dead and, except for the killer, the last person to see her alive. All that police had to go on was what he had said when he'd called police minutes earlier. Taken to the Montgomery County hospital for treatment of anxiety, Rafael had had his hands swabbed for gun residue. The officers weren't taking any chances. If a gun had been used, and if Robb was involved, any gun residue could easily be wiped or washed off. Robb also signed forms allowing the officers to search his car and his home, and later, he would even trade his clothing for blue hospital scrubs. Robb's demeanor was one of calm, unemotional cooperation. Whatever the police asked for, he went along with. He asked no questions and never protested. There was no antagonism or push back. The officers gave him a glass of water and began what would be a twelve-hour marathon of questioning, with breaks for medical tests, including x-rays and blood pressure readings. Although he was in the hospital to check out what appeared to have been an anxiety attack at the house, Robb was free to leave at any point. He was submitting to the police inquiries voluntarily.

Upper Merion Detective Elbert Lee rode in the ambulance with Robb to the hospital and met Montgomery County Detective Christopher Kuklentz. On the way, Lee was there to listen and try to pick up any clues Robb was willing to give. For a man who had just lost his wife, Lee was struck by what Robb didn't say. He had no questions about what could have happened to her and certainly was not distraught. As a domestic violence specialist, Lee was used to dealing with people in emotional situations, and this one was significant for the husband's lack of emotion, despite the fact that his partner was dead.

Regardless of how Robb appeared, Lee and Kuklentz knew what Gallen wanted: interview Robb immediately. Making the assignments, Gallen, a veteran of numerous investigations during his years as a county homicide detective, wanted to collect as much information as quickly as possible. It was classic investigating—start at the inner circle, those closest to the victim and, depending on their answers, work your way to those in the outer rings.

Their first mission was to verify Robb's claim that someone had broken in. So far, the officers at the scene were not finding any evidence to back him up.

Even the patrol officers who were first on the scene were shaking their heads. "Something just doesn't look right," they told their superiors. They'd all been on enough burglary calls to know that the way the glass was shattered and lying undisturbed on a floor mat just didn't look like the work of a burglar. The crime-scene team would move in quickly to do their analysis.

For now, they all wanted to find out: What did Robb know?

The hospital staff gave them a private room in the ER wing.

"Mr. Robb, I am Detective Kuklentz and this is Detective Lee. We are investigating the shooting death of your wife, Ellen. Do you mind answering a few questions?"

"No," replied Robb, who looked every bit like the spectacled nerdy-looking professor known for his quiet ways.

After asking whether he was making the statement voluntarily and having him sign forms to allow the police to test his hands and search his cars and home, the officers got right into the day's timeline.

"When did you last see Ellen alive?"

"This morning around eight-thirty or nine a.m." Later Robb would change the outside time to 9:20 a.m.

Before they could get too far, the officers halted the questioning when Robb began asking the whereabouts of his daughter. The officers spent a few minutes calling to check on Olivia, who was at her friend's house on Crestwood, which is directly behind the Robbs' house. Within a short while, she would be with her Uncle Gary and the rest of the family. In addition to Gary, there was a second uncle, Art, his ex-wife, Mary Ann Jones, their son, Andrew, and daughter, Lauren, and Ellen's mother. Gary's wife Kim and their three sons were home near Boston. Robb approved of Olivia staying with her friend until Gary could get there.

Once that was settled, the officers resumed their questioning of Robb:

"Where did you last see your wife alive?"

"At home, it was just my wife and I."

"Do you know what your wife had planned for today?"

"She was going to do some last-minute Christmas shopping on the Internet. She was going to send gifts. This was likely for the family and her brothers, nephew, niece."

"Was your wife having any problems?"

"We both suffer from depression. We are both on medication."

"How long has your wife suffered from depression?"

"Years, maybe six or seven."

Because they didn't yet know how Ellen had died, even whether she'd been shot, or if there was any possibility of suicide, the officers questioned Robb on the medications she'd taken. ("Many," he said.) They also asked whether she had ever tried to harm herself, or even talked about it. Did they have any guns in the home?

"No," Robb said to it all.

While at home, Robb said, he and his wife had talked about her upcoming trip to Boston. "I asked if she was packed and when she was planning to drive. She said tomorrow. I said I would be back a little early today to help them pack for the trip."

When he last saw Ellen, Robb said she was "standing in the kitchen. She was getting a drink from the refrigerator. I'm not sure what she was getting to drink. She stopped what she was doing to talk to me about the trip."

The studious professor appeared calm and eager to please. He answered all of the officers' questions and described his every step on December 22, 2006:

Robb said he'd left the house at about 9:30 a.m. and driven his car, a 1999 blue BMW, to his office at the University of Pennsylvania in West Philadelphia. First, he stopped at King's Market on North 10th Street in Chinatown for about forty minutes, where he paid $6.00 in cash for some fruit that was still in his car.

"The bag might tell you the name of the store. I bought the fruit for my wife and daughter. They were driving to outside of Boston, Massachusetts, tomorrow." Police found a bag of fruit in the front seat of his car from King's Market, but there was no receipt inside.

He'd continued to the Penn campus and parked in the ramp near his Locust Walk office where he spent about a half hour. He took his grades to Lynn Costello, the undergraduate grade coordinator. He also called and left a message for Bruce Carlin, a University of North Carolina professor with whom Robb was collaborating on a research paper. A recognized expert in game theory, a discipline applied in many fields to assess how a person's goals match or clash with others, Robb was in demand from other professors and other universities to teach, lecture and collaborate on research.

He'd headed for the parking ramp to get his BMW and driven it to Chestnut and 36th Street, where he parked his car so he could go into Wawa, a convenience store at 3604 Chestnut Street, and paid cash for a 20-ounce bottle of Coke that he drank and discarded before reaching his car. When he got there, he found a parking ticket for an expired meter at 11:52 a.m. Security tape later showed that Robb had bought the soda at 11:56 a.m. He was wearing the same clothes that he had on later in the day when he was interviewed by police.

Robb said he had driven himself home from his office at

the University of Pennsylvania, arriving at 1:45 p.m. Because his car's garage remote control was broken, Robb said he'd parked his car in the driveway and manually opened the door. He'd walked through the garage to the family room and climbed the few steps to the kitchen. It was from there that he'd first spotted his wife's body on the kitchen floor—her feet visible through the door.

Robb told police he'd entered the room and put down his laptop and briefcase before walking over to her and touching her face with his right hand. He'd then picked up his laptop and computer and took them upstairs to his bedroom and put them on his bed. Hearing the family dog Copper barking, he'd gone to his daughter's bedroom to see if she was there. Seeing that she wasn't, he'd closed the door and gone to the kitchen to look for a cordless telephone to call police. When he didn't find one, he'd headed to the laundry room, intending to use the bathroom there, but noticed instead that the glass was shattered on the door leading to the outside. Spotting the big chunks of glass strewn all over the carpet, Robb abandoned his plans to use the bathroom and instead retraced his steps through the garage back to his car to get his cell phone, and called police.

With the investigation moving so quickly, the detectives regularly gathered with Gallen and Ferman in the conference room in their offices at One Montgomery Plaza, the office building across from the courthouse, to update everyone on what was coming in and to reassign officers to check out new leads. It didn't take long for the officers to focus on what they called Robb's odd behavior and the holes in his statement—starting with the phone call. Why did he go out to his car to use a cell phone and dial a non-emergency number rather than use a house phone to call 911? Could it be that Robb had mistakenly thought that only 911 calls are taped? His session with police, which was still ongoing, was generating a lot of unanswered questions.

In fact, at one point during the session, Kuklentz and Lee

advised Robb that some of his responses were actually suspicious, although they were quick to add, "You're not in trouble." If he wanted to clear himself, he could always take a polygraph.

Robb refused.

Robb raised even more suspicion by changing some of his answers when officers intermittently gave him the chance to review his statement and sign it. Most of the changes gave him more time in his alibi. As police wrote later, his corrections were "significant to us in that these corrections reveal Dr. Robb's caution concerning his alibi, his relationship with his wife and the physical evidence found at the scene."

Initially, Robb said he had seen Ellen alive around 8:30 or 9 a.m. He extended the time to 9:20 a.m. On his visit to the Chinatown store, Robb initially said he'd been there at about 10:15 or 10:30 a.m. for about a half hour. He extended the time, saying he was there twenty to forty minutes. When asked if he'd shared the bedroom with his wife, Robb answered, "No. We sleep in different bedrooms. We have slept in different rooms for many years. We don't get along. We have fights. We don't see eye to eye." He crossed out "We have fights." When asked if he was thinking clearly during the interview, Robb had answered, "More or less." He corrected that to add, "I am still agitated."

Asked how he'd approached his dead wife when he'd first seen her, Robb said, "I approached her from the direction of the feet. I leaned down and touched her face with my right hand." On correction, he added, "I think."

It was Detective James McGowan's job to monitor the questioning and inform the detectives about other developments in the investigation—other facts uncovered by other officers that might allow them to probe deeper into what Robb knew about Ellen's killing. By then, information was starting to come in from others about Ellen Robb's plans to leave her husband.

"Do you know if your wife saw a lawyer about the divorce?"

"She told me she did. She told me a year or two years ago. She has told me many times since then."

Later, the officers returned to the subject:

"Did you get upset when your wife spoke of getting a divorce?"

"Yes, it was upsetting. I don't know what would happen to my daughter. It is a traumatic event."

"Did you want a divorce?"

"Sometimes I did."

Robb said he'd contacted a lawyer years ago, and, when asked if his wife had told him that she'd recently gone to a lawyer, Robb responded, "She has said it many times. It was always the same thing."

As Robb gave up details to police interrogators about his whereabouts on December 22, Gallen was dispatching detectives to check out his story, and—if he was the killer—showing that he had no alibi. If any part of Robb's statement was made up, then why not all of it?

The assignment of checking out Robb's trip to the fruit stand went to County Detectives Mark Minzola and Jeff Koch. Driving the 20 miles from Norristown to Center City looks easy on the map, but at rush hour on the Friday before Christmas, it was an exercise in patience. With Minzola behind the wheel of his sea foam Ford 500, they opted to stay off the car-clogged Schuylkill Expressway and take the back roads toward the city, dumping off on Kelly Drive, which also paralleled the Schuylkill River. En route, Koch worked the phone.

With King's Market as their destination, they made their way down Vine Street and turned right onto North 10th, a busy narrow street of shops, apartments and storefront offices that serves as the main street of Philadelphia's Chinatown with its ornate, red-and-gold carved archway. Known as the Friendship Gate, a 25-year-old landmark, a gift from Philadelphia's Chinese sister city of Tianjin. The market is actually a small fruit stand, on the east side of the street, just north of the neighborhood's city fire station. Robb told police he had spent about forty minutes there that morning picking out fruit to give to his wife and daughter for their trip to Boston.

On their own, the officers first tried speaking with the elderly man standing outside sweeping the sidewalk. His real job was to watch so no one stole fruit or vegetables from the cardboard boxes on the store's stoop. He either didn't understand or he wanted nothing to do with them. His "No" was emphatic and accompanied by a sharp shaking of his head. In any language, they knew he wouldn't be helpful.

Looking around, they spotted a fish market across the street. Inside, the young woman cashier said she spoke English and would be glad to help them. She followed them back into the tiny fruit stand where their translator helped them locate the cashier, Liu E. Sai.

Their translator, Yanmei Zhu, did a pre-interview, asking Liu whether she recognized the man in the license photo. Liu said she knew him, but he had not been in the store that day.

With that, the translator told the officers that she needed to return to her store to get another woman who also spoke the Fukienese dialect to best understand what Liu was telling her, and shortly after, returned with Le Hong. The officers relayed to Philadelphia police that they needed translating help from the Fukienese dialect. There was no one who could help. They were on their own.

They were taking up too much space in the store, attracting stern looks from the owner. While he had the women cooperating, Minzola suggested that they find someplace else—a restaurant perhaps—where they could talk. Together, they walked down the street to the Zhong Gang Bakery, a small store with a few tables where the police conducted a three-way interview with Liu, a petite woman of 39 who lived across from the market.

While they would have to get police translators later so she could make an official statement, they needed to move quickly right now. Robb's claim that he had stopped at the fruit stand was a major part of his alibi. If the clerk had seen him earlier that day, it could very well mean that he was telling the truth that he hadn't had anything to do with Ellen's murder.

With the help of Le Hong and Yanmei Zhu, the officers asked Liu to tell them everything she knew. They learned that Liu had been working as a cashier all day, since 8 a.m. She was then shown a photo from Robb's driver's license and asked if she recognized him.

"Regularly, he comes to shop at the market."

"Did you see this man today, shopping at the market?"

"No."

"This man may have been shopping in King Market this morning between ten a.m. and ten-thirty a.m. Are you certain you didn't see this man shopping in the store during this approximate time frame?"

"Yes, I am certain. The only bathroom break I took was about 11 a.m. I wasn't in there long, because there were two customers in the store, and when I came back out they were still shopping. I was only in the bathroom for about a minute."

Liu said Robb, who paid in cash like everyone who came there, had been in the store previously—about two weeks ago. "He's not a regular like some other customers, but he comes in around two times a month. I started this job about three months ago and he's been coming in since then."

Although they couldn't understand what she said, Minzola and Koch knew from her body language that she was adamant that she knew who Robb was, and he had not been there that day.

As they left the women, Minzola, who had done a three-year stint in undercover narcotics during his nearly fourteen years in policing, grabbed his Nextel and called in to Gallen, who was eager to pass the latest information back to the officers interviewing Robb.

It was nearly 6:30 p.m. and they had already covered a lot of ground with him. That Robb had already lied was important for the officers to know.

Gallen, who also passed Minzola's critical information on to Ferman, stepped up the pace by assigning officers to remaining interviews. It was important to finish checking out Robb's alibi before the officers finished interrogating him.

CHAPTER 7

December 22–23, 2006

After a battery of tests, including an EKG, x-ray, blood pressure and a request for Tylenol, Robb got a medical clearance to leave the hospital. He hadn't had a heart attack or even an anxiety attack. He was treated for hyperventilation.

In fact, when McGowan arrived late that night, he had found Robb looking "just fine."

Robb said he'd be willing to answer more questions, so he was transferred to the offices of the county detectives.

After a three-hour break, during which Robb was given some food and beverage, the officers started in again, trying to pin him down to exactly what he had done earlier that morning.

At 8:15 p.m., it was McGowan's turn to push Robb to take a polygraph. Robb had given them information that was at odds with other things they were hearing from Ellen's friends and family. A polygraph could help clear him.

McGowan, a streetwise veteran homicide detective, found Robb very quiet and very willing to change the subject at any mention of taking a polygraph.

"No," Robb repeatedly told McGowan. He wouldn't take the test.

McGowan explained that the polygraph couldn't be used in court as evidence, but could be used to exclude someone as a suspect in an investigation. Robb responded that he got nervous, and feared failing the test. To calm him, McGowan went on to explain that the examiner would use control questions to identify what made him nervous and he would know the questions before submitting to the test.

Robb told him he wanted to think about it and said he "may feel more comfortable" if they spoke for a while.

Robb went on to tell McGowan about himself: that as a native of Israel, he'd been required to serve a tour of military duty. He had earned his first degree in 1976 in economics and mathematics from Hebrew University in Jerusalem and then gone to California, where in 1977 he'd earned first a masters and then a doctorate in economics from the University of California at Los Angeles.

McGowan wasn't changing his mind. He went right back to pushing Robb to take the polygraph, impressing upon him that that would be the best way for him to remove any suspicion about whether he'd played any role in Ellen's death.

Robb said nothing. There were long stretches of time when Robb and McGowan faced each other—in silence. At one point, after explaining about his military experience, Robb told McGowan, "Again, we arrive at the question of the polygraph."

"Yes," McGowan told him, exchanging hard looks.

In refusing to answer questions while hooked up to a monitor, Robb repeatedly asked, "What if I fail? Then I will be in more trouble." McGowan sat back. He had all the time in the world. Robb, who sounded lucent and coherent, appeared calm and cool. As if he were playing a game. By then, McGowan and the other officers had been briefed on Robb's academic expertise as a game theorist. They were ready to deal with a brilliant mind, someone who was likely analyzing their every move so he could maximize what he could control. "He thought he was smarter than we were, is the bottom line," McGowan recalled.

Finally, Robb told McGowan he wanted to see the questions. McGowan read them aloud:

"Did you cause the death of your wife, Ellen?

"Did you dispose of the object used to cause the death of your wife, Ellen?

"Did you have someone else cause the death of your wife, Ellen?"

Robb asked McGowan, "What if I fail the test?" to which McGowan told him they could decide if and when that happened. Robb's response was to stare at McGowan for seven minutes. He ended it by saying, "I do not think I would take the test, and I may fail because I get agitated and nervous."

But he was willing to continue cooperating with the police and their investigation.

The offer didn't impress McGowan. He knew what Robb was trying to do. McGowan figured that by cooperating with the police, Robb would also be able to monitor what they knew so he could stay one step ahead of them.

It was 9:03 p.m. Robb would continue in police custody answering questions until 2:31 a.m.

Gallen, who was monitoring the questioning from the adjoining room, was pleased that the detectives had gotten as much as they could out of Robb. They couldn't get him to take the polygraph, but they had gotten him to detail critical information about what he'd done and seen that day. All of it was helping them put together the puzzle of who had killed Ellen Robb.

While Detectives Kuklentz, Lee and McGowan questioned Robb, the other detectives were looking closely at the evidence in the house—and there was a lot about the scene that made them suspicious about Robb's story.

They were curious about the bloody footprints close to the body that led out to the garage.

At 2:31 a.m. Kuklentz told Robb they had a few more questions. "Is that OK?"

"Yes."

Kuklentz asked him about the Timberland boots he had told them earlier that he owned. "How many pairs do you have?"

"Two or three. They are like work boots. They should be upstairs in my bedroom closet. I haven't worn them in years." He then changed his statement to include, "Maybe I don't have them anymore."

And the black-and-gray warmup suit that he'd worn in the morning?

"When did you wear this suit?"

"I wore this when I drove Olivia to school this morning. When I came home, I took a shower and changed into the clothes you took from me tonight."

"Where is the black-and-gray suit?"

"It should be in my room. Maybe on the bed or chair."

Investigators found the suit where he said it would be, but not the boots.

Finding them would allow police to see if they matched the partial bloody footprints they had found on the kitchen floor. If only they could find Robb's boots, they would have a significant piece of evidence.

CHAPTER 8

December 22, 2006
Late Evening

When they started talking to Rafael Robb, the officers told him they were investigating the "shooting" death of his wife. It took an autopsy later that night to tell police that Ellen had been beaten to death—the victim of a blitz attack with a cylindrical object that experts would say was aimed at wiping her off the face of the earth.

Police theorized that Ellen had been struck as she wrapped presents. They couldn't tell if she'd been sitting at the table or standing up. Her killer had stunned her by swinging a crowbarlike object that landed on her head, knocking her to the floor on her back. As she lay there helpless, her killer kept swinging at her head, crushing her face and cracking open her skull in multiple places, her brain exposed in a bloody mass of purple and white. Ellen Gregory Robb existed no more. The pretty, smiling mother had become a ghoulish remnant of a once human form.

Whoever did it, didn't stop. The killer kept swinging and swinging, landing blow after blow even after she died.

With blood spurting from her head, Ellen fought mightily, using her hands and arms to fend off the repeated blows to her head and face. Two of her fingers were crushed and her hands were bruised, evidence of her fierce struggle to survive.

Montgomery County Coroner Jeanne Ottinger pronounced Ellen Robb dead shortly after 4 p.m. in the kitchen of her home. In her examination of Ellen's body, Ottinger found her very cold to the touch, with rigor mortis setting into her arms and legs. That told her that Ellen Robb had been dead since well before noon. She had died sometime between 8:15 and 10:30 a.m.

But what the officers really needed was an official word on the cause of death. Dr. Ian Hood, widely considered one of the best forensic pathologists in the area, usually spends his time working in Philadelphia, where he's the deputy medical examiner. He came into Montgomery County when needed, especially after the death of Dr. Hal Fillinger, the county coroner and forensic pathologist.

After a long day working cases in Philadelphia, Hood drove up to the Montgomery County Morgue in Norristown that evening to perform the autopsy on Ellen Robb.

A New Zealand–born pathologist, Dr. Hood had presided over autopsies for some of the area's most notorious killings.

Detective Albert Dinnell, a forensic specialist and veteran cop, got the call from Gallen at 6 p.m. to cover the autopsy. He was joined by Upper Merion Police Detective Glauner.

As Hood prepared to begin on case MCC06-1769, Dinnell pushed open the door of autopsy room #1. As he glanced at the body lying on the gurney, Dinnell checked to confirm that ELLEN ROBB was written on the tag attached to the toe. Not having gone to the scene himself, he wanted to be sure.

"This is the body sent to us from Upper Merion," Deputy Coroner Gary Schmoltze told him.

Ellen wore blue-and-white pajama bottoms with pink underwear and a pink shirt covered by a blue short-sleeved sweater, much of which had turned black as it soaked up the blood flowing from her face and head. Her thick, short brown hair had been freshly coiffed with highlight streaks.

Dinnell's job was not only to get Hood's opinion, but also to photograph the victim and her wounds, and to handle the evidence. Through his camera lens, Dinnell captured what remained of Ellen Robb after the blood had been cleaned away—a gruesome, teeth-clenched image of a woman in her final desperate moments.

The photos, shot with a Nikon D100 digital, recorded the

devastation of the attack on Ellen Robb. Crushed skull bones to the back, left and center; massive injuries to the left ear. He captured the concaved face with its multiple broken bones and the large hole inside her mouth above the top row of teeth, some of which were missing. And, not surprising to anyone, there was blood everywhere on her face, arms and abdomen.

Hood pointed out to the officers what he was seeing, like the horrific damage to Ellen's fingers, one nearly severed on her left hand and another crushed on her right, and a long cylindrical mark on the outer side of her left arm. Those were defensive wounds that could never have been caused by a gun.

Before entering the autopsy room, Dinnell had been told by Gallen that, looking at the scene and the injuries, the detectives figured she had been shot in the face. But looking at the injuries up close through the lens of his Nikon, Dinnell watched as Hood measured the wounds and examined them closely. None looked like they had been caused by bullets entering or exiting the body. There was nothing related to a gun here.

Hood, assisted by Schmoltze, morgue technician Tony Guzman and intern Rachael Rymann took three hours to work his way through the autopsy, stopping after every segment to describe his observations into a tape recorder.

In the end, there was no doubt to him that Ellen Robb had been beaten to death or, in official language, had died of multiple blunt force traumas to the head. As he wrote later:

> The entire skull is deformed by multiple, intersecting fractures that fragment the vault and base as a result of these several massive blunt impacts to the left frontal, left posterior parietal and occipital regions. None of the multiple lacerations exhibit significant abrasion of their edges suggesting that a relatively thin but very hard object was used to produce them.

The Upper Merion Township Police Department had its one and only homicide of 2006.

Word quickly filtered out to the detectives who were still

actively working the case, including those who continued to interrogate Robb at the office of the county detectives.

For Saville and Santarelli, Hood's autopsy fit right in with what they had observed in the Robb kitchen. Not only was the body lying in thick pools of blood, but also there was blood and brain matter spattered on the walls and the door leading out to the laundry room.

Knowing that Ellen had been beaten to death with a crowbar-like object fit with the so-called cast-off evidence that the crime-scene veterans found in the room. Castoff occurs when an object that is saturated in blood is swung in such a way that it leaves a trail of blood.

Hood also gave Dinnell blood samples that would be tested and matched to any other blood found at the scene. If the killer had left any blood or tissue behind, the detectives wanted to be able to distinguish it from the victim's. Glauner, a former volunteer fireman who had witnessed his share of gory accident scenes, was conducting his first autopsy as a homicide detective. He helped Dinnell collect specimens, and bagged and recorded everything they found.

Before the officers left, they recovered one last item—a tiny pink plastic pen that had fallen off of Ellen's body as they removed her clothing. She had been using the pen as she sat barefoot at her kitchen table writing out a gift card, "To: Mrs. Becker, From: Olivia." When her attacker had come for her, all Ellen had in her hand to fight back was the plastic pen. She'd clutched it and held on to it even as she tried to shield her body from the constant blows of a heavy metal object.

Glauner held open the plastic bag as Dinnell dropped in the pen.

The autopsy results were center stage when the officers and prosecutors gathered late that evening at the Upper Merion Township Police Department. Ferman and Gallen got the meeting going, though it didn't require much supervision, as the officers took turns sharing what they had come up with during an intense ten hours. Much of it was contradictory to the version of events that Robb had given them earlier.

By midnight, Ferman and Lieutenant James Early of the

Upper Merion Township Police Department were ready to issue their first carefully worded joint press release to the media
the next morning.

> *The victim is identified as Ellen Robb (49 year-old, DOB*
> *12/26/1956). Robb's husband, Professor Rafael Robb*
> *called the Upper Merion Police at 1:45 p.m. on Friday,*
> *December 22, 2006 and reported finding his wife de-*
> *ceased in their home. Dr. Robb reported last seeing his*
> *wife in the morning when he drove away from the cou-*
> *ple's home in his blue 1999 BMW 328i sedan (PA reg-*
> *istration EBR817) to go to his office in the McNeil*
> *Building at the University of Pennsylvania . . . He said*
> *that when he returned home in the afternoon he found*
> *his wife's body in the kitchen . . .*

They needed the public's help to solve Ellen Robb's murder,
hoping someone would call in if they'd seen anything unusual:
anyone attempting to discard the murder weapon—a long
cylindrical object—or trying to get rid of bloodied clothing and
footwear. In addition to identifying Ellen, the press release
also identified Robb as being the last person known to have
seen Ellen alive when he'd driven away to go to his office at
the University of Pennsylvania.

Since the interrogation of Robb was continuing, the autopsy results also gave McGowan and Kuklentz fresh ammunition to challenge Robb on details of his story. In the twelve
hours since he'd first called police, the investigators had found
evidence that Robb had been misleading during their two earlier go-rounds. Following through on his pledge to cooperate,
Robb signed a consent form to give up his cell phone and his
clothes so they could be taken to the lab for testing. He pulled
on police-issued hospital-blue scrubs.

McGowan was ready to make him squirm.

"Do you celebrate Christmas or Hanukkah?" McGowan
asked knowing that Robb was Jewish.

"A little bit of both."

"You have forever ruined your daughter's memory of all

future Christmases, because three days before Christmas she will always recall that her father killed her mother, and you haven't offered an explanation to why it happened."

McGowan was verbally pushing at him, and all Robb could do was sit there silently.

Finally, McGowan decided to go for it. "You've never once said you didn't do this," he said firmly.

Robb turned toward him and blurted out, "I didn't do this. I didn't kill my wife."

"Good answer!" McGowan shouted.

No matter what the detectives asked, Robb said nothing or very little. There would be no admission that night and no sign that he was cracking.

But, he had left an impression. By the time the session ended at 2:21 a.m., McGowan was convinced that Robb had either killed his wife or had hired someone else to do it. Proving it would be another matter.

With Robb still in his hospital scrubs, the officers drove him to the Crowne Plaza Hotel in King of Prussia, where he would stay until Christmas Eve morning.

Just twenty miles from Philadelphia's Center City, Upper Merion is typical of the area's economically strong suburban towns with its mix of residential and commercial properties to help pay for services and schools. Along with 27,000 people, Upper Merion is home to some 50,000 jobs and 9.5 million square feet of office space. Its biggest employers are the pharmaceutical giant GlaxoSmithKline and the aeronautical company Lockheed Martin, each with more than 2,000 employees. The town's claim to fame is the King of Prussia Mall which hails as one of the nation's largest retail shopping complexes, with seven major department stores like Neiman Marcus and Nordstrom and Bloomingdale's, and 400 stores, boutiques and restaurants. It boasts more "pure retail shopping space than any other attraction in America," with stores not found elsewhere in the Philadelphia region. The town is also home to the Valley Forge National Historical Park with its 1,300 acres of mostly open land.

In a lot of ways, Upper Merion is typical of the sprawling suburbs surrounding Philadelphia. Its population grew slightly in the 2000 census (up 4.4 percent); its face is largely white (84.8 percent) and getting older (its biggest population change was the increase of 3.3 percent of those 65 years and older) but it is also more highly educated (49.8 percent with bachelor's degrees or higher) and slightly more affluent than the rest of the county, with a median household income of $65,636.

The Robbs' home is located in the hilly and wooded Croton Woods area in the southwestern portion of the town, which borders the Schuylkill Expressway. It's an enclave of the educated and affluent. The homes are worth more there than in the rest of the town—a median value of $241,400 compared to $165,700.

CHAPTER 9

December 23, 2006
Morning

Marino had given Robb his cell phone number and told him to call if he needed anything.

When the phone rang that morning, a subdued Robb asked if he could leave the hotel and if Marino could bring him a change of clothes. He had spent the night in the hospital scrubs and needed street clothes.

Although he had previously turned over his passport, Robb remained free to do anything and go anywhere—except home. But he acted like he was in police custody. Before promising Robb anything, Marino said he would check it out. He called Detective Rich Nilsen, asking if there were any of Robb's clothes that were safe to take offsite. Nilsen was among the officers gathering evidence and searching through all of the boxes and clutter, and recording the scene with photos and video. They weren't going to let Robb select or even ask for specific items, for fear that he would be trying to destroy them.

En route to a meeting at the Upper Merion Township Police Department, Marino stopped at the Robb house and picked up a plastic bag with a full set of clothes and a pair of shoes—jeans, a shirt and fleece top.

At the hotel room, Marino held out the plastic bag to Robb, who immediately started pulling the shirt and pants on right over the scrubs.

"Rafi you can take them off," Marino told him, referring to the scrubs.

"No that's OK," he answered as he quickly put on the fresh clothes.

The room was dark, with drawn curtains and an undisturbed bed. A food tray sat on the table. Robb had apparently spent the last eight hours sitting there in the dark.

Ellen's friends and family were quick to offer to help—anything they could do to help police find her killer. For Ellen's brother, Gary Gregory, the offer would take him into the world of undercover police work.

After meeting with Ferman, Gary agreed to wear a wire and try to get his brother-in-law to incriminate himself in Ellen's death.

He called Robb, who agreed to meet him in the hotel parking lot. On his way, he stopped at the Upper Merion police station, where Kuklentz, who was certified in wiretapping, taped to Gary's chest a small microphone that was connected to a battery pack. Gary was ready to record everything that he and Robb said to one another while the officers watched from nearby—Marino and Kuklentz from an upper parking deck at King of Prussia Mall, and Gershanick and Minzola from an adjoining parking lot. While they could see the encounter, they could not hear the conversations, which were being recorded.

After alerting Robb by phone that he was in the parking lot, Gary stepped out of his car to greet his brother-in-law. They stepped toward each other and embraced.

Once the men were in Gary's Ford Explorer, they talked about Olivia and the arrangements for Ellen's funeral. Telling Robb he didn't want Olivia to grow up without a father, Gary offered to synchronize his story with Robb's. Robb refused to take the bait.

Robb didn't crack, even as his brother-in-law told him he'd like to help him stay out of jail—for the sake of his 12-year-old daughter. The police were listening for Robb to give Gary a version of what had happened different from the one he had already given them. Robb said that he knew Gary thought he'd killed Ellen, but denied doing it.

Back in Waltham, Massachusetts, Gary was the chief operating officer of a publicly traded medical device company, NeuroMetrix, Inc., which sells products that allow physicians to pinpoint the source of back and spinal pain. A personable executive, Gary spoke well in public and greeted even strangers with a strong handshake. Talking about Ellen, even in the presence of the man Gary blamed for her murder, brought him to tears. Robb sounded to police like he too was crying, but Gary would later tell them that Robb shed no tears and the emotion he displayed was false.

As Gary told police: ". . . He had no true emotions of the loss [or] any concern. He had no discussion of finding the intruder and he didn't push back on the concept of me helping him getting away with it."

The only thing Robb gave up was admitting to Gary that he didn't tell police that he and Ellen had been planning to divorce.

During Gary's debriefing with police that evening, he described getting a phone call from Robb at 3:49 p.m. that day.

Robb told Gary he was waiting for the police to return his clothes and that he had spoken to Gary's mom, who told him Gary was meeting with the police.

"Yeah, they wanted to talk to Olivia for a couple of minutes," Gary told him.

Gary didn't tell Robb about the other questions the officers had for him.

Robb spent another night at the Crowne Plaza.

CHAPTER 10

December 23–24, 2006

Gallen easily had thirty detectives working the case from both the county detectives and the Upper Merion force. For something like this, where time mattered, Gallen was pulling officers from narcotics, major crimes. Anyone available got a job to do. While one group attempted to verify Robb's statement, the others focused on the crime scene, where they were in a race against time.

Ferman's initial description of the inside of the Robb house was only the beginning. When the detectives got inside, they were astounded at how cluttered and messy everything was. There were so many boxes and bags and just plain stuff that they had a difficult time searching for a weapon or even determining whether anything could have been taken. They were looking for anything that could help them—bloody clothes, footprints, a weapon, an empty purse discarded by a would-be burglar.

In directing the officers to begin their search, Saville had them clear one corner of the family room so they could start looking through the boxes and work their way out. The painstaking process took six officers working for hours—long into the first night and then into the second.

After getting his first look at the interior of the house, DA Castor said it looked like the inside of a Salvation Army depot. As they dug deeper, the officers found lots of new items—most of them recent online purchases. In the living room, beneath the clothes and boxes, there was even a sofa and chair, wrapped in heavy plastic, that had been delivered two years earlier.

Beneath the boxes there was a nice mahogany dining room table, a reminder of another time when Ellen Robb had kept a meticulous showplace house with vases filled with fresh yellow roses, her favorite flower.

There were other remnants of that bygone life—a vase of flowers in the dining room, wreaths on the front and back doors and Olivia's artwork on the refrigerator door.

To get around the house, the officers followed a pathway that led from one room to the other and upstairs to the bedrooms.

There, the officers found Robb's room jammed with clothes and books—including several on economics: *Nonlinear Pricing*, *The Structure of Economics*, *Mathematics for Economists*. They also found pain and sleep medicine. Unlike the rest of the house, Robb's room was organized. His clothes hung in an orderly way.

As they looked around the house, there was a lot about Robb's statement and behavior that made police suspicious: after he'd arrived home and found his dead wife, he'd taken his time calling police, and then called the non-emergency number, instead of 911. He and his wife had recently made plans for her to move out, yet he hadn't told the police about the pending divorce.

But what really got police thinking was when they saw that the glass had not been stepped on or tracked through the house, an impossibility for a burglar who had smashed a windowpane to gain entrance.

In the first call from Upper Merion's Lieutenant Nolan to Chief Gallen, the officer alerted him that "things didn't look right." Robb had called in a burglary and led them to the busted-out glass, but they weren't quite sure what they had.

Once crime-scene experts Saville and Santarelli got a look, they too agreed that Robb's version of events "didn't make sense."

"This had to be staged," said Saville as they looked down at the chunks of glass sitting undisturbed on the floor.

"Yep," said Santarelli, a veteran of scores of burglary investigations from his twenty-six years on the police force in

Cheltenham, a small town of about 9 square miles that borders Philadelphia. "We've all worked burglaries before, and this doesn't fit anything we know."

As a first-ring suburb—a so-called bedroom community to Philadelphia—Cheltenham's 15,000 homes are on smaller lots than the McMansions in the outlying newer developments. Home burglaries are a major focus for police.

In his dozen years as a detective there, Santarelli figured he had investigated some 200 to 250 home burglaries.

As he stood in the driveway of the Robb home, Santarelli was intrigued by something else. A white Subaru station wagon that turned out to belong to Ellen Robb was parked in the driveway, to the side of the garage entrance. In his experience, burglars usually skip houses where there is a car parked outside. To get into the Robb home from the rear laundry room door, a burglar would have had to step down into it. The most direct route into the kitchen was to step in from the laundry room, turn right at the doorway that led to the family room and take a left to the stairs that go directly to the kitchen.

"If anyone broke that glass and entered that door, you would walk through the glass and it would pulverize under your feet," said Saville. "The glass from the door was shattered, but it wasn't pulverized like someone stepped on it."

And there was something else.

The footprints of blood led from the kitchen down through the family room and into the garage, where they came to an end.

For Saville, there was a lot that didn't make sense: A burglar wouldn't enter through a door secluded from the front of the house and hidden from the sides of the home, and then leave by opening a double garage door. "If it were true that it was a burglar, he already knew his way out, because he knew his way in rather than search another method to get out of the house."

The third flag for the investigators was the blood on the kitchen walls and behind the door.

"The blood we found along the wall in the kitchen is actually behind the door. That would indicate to us that someone had to have entered the home, break the glass, entered the home, come up the steps into the kitchen, close the door behind him before he begins his assault on her, without her possibly knowing that he's there," said Saville.

Once the detectives did the trajectory analysis—drawing string to show the path of the blood spatter—it became clear that the door would be a significant piece of evidence.

For Ferman, the fact that the door had to be closed during the murder convinced her that Ellen Robb had been targeted for murder. There's no way she had come into the path of a random burglar.

Perhaps the footprints, especially the ones on the floor linoleum could reveal something, the officers agreed. The shoe size, the boot brand. Perhaps there would be clues there. They cut out the flooring so it could be sent to the FBI crime lab for sizing and testing.

But there was another set of prints conspicuous for their absence. Olivia had told police that Copper, the family's dog, usually had the run of the house, although he typically slept underneath her bed.

But what the investigators saw in the kitchen was puzzling. When she'd hit the floor, Ellen's body had lain near the dog's food and water bowls. The dog's bones, blanket and towel were nearly touching her.

Yet there were no dog prints anywhere in the house. When he'd arrived home, Robb said, he'd heard the dog barking and found him closed up in Olivia's bedroom. He said he'd gone there to check on whether Olivia was home.

As Gallen, Ferman and the rest of the team analyzed what they knew so far, their suspicion deepened. Had Robb left the house at all that morning? Had anyone seen him at the University of Pennsylvania, where he said he had gone to turn in his course grades?

For those answers, Montgomery County Detective Michael Reynolds and Upper Merion Detective Michael Milke drove onto the Ivy League university's West Philadelphia campus and headed straight for the McNeil Building, a six-story nondescript 1970-era structure that housed the Economics Department.

Robb said he'd spent about thirty to forty minutes in his office, Room 512.

The McNeil Building, on Locust Walk, was located in the heart of the 280-acre Penn campus, where historic buildings share the terrain with some of the world's most modern and sophisticated education complexes. Envisioned by Benjamin Franklin as an institution that would prepare its students for lives of business and public service, Penn has evolved as one of the world's premier universities, attracting the top students and faculty, and more than $780 million per year in annual research money.

Penn also employs some 20,000, making it Philadelphia's largest private employer. That doesn't even count the University of Pennsylvania Health System, which includes the Hospital of the University of Pennsylvania, which employs another 14,000. Because of its size, Penn also has its own police force, and while the Robb killing did not occur on campus, campus security were very helpful to the Montgomery County detectives who needed to trace Robb's steps on December 22, 2006.

The detectives went up to the office area. They couldn't help but notice that there were working vending machines in the building, and all sold twenty-ounce bottles of soda. And, outside, along the very path that Robb would have had to walk to go to his car, there were cafes and vending carts that also sold soda. The officers also retraced Robb's steps. The store where he'd bought the soda was a short walk from his office. Clearly, they thought, there was no reason for Robb to get in his car and drive to the nearby Wawa convenience store except to be photographed by the security camera and to get a parking ticket. Expired meters or parking in no parking zones were the easiest ways to get a ticket anywhere on campus. The city's Parking Authority did a brisk business giving out tickets on the streets of the Penn campus, especially on heavily traveled thoroughfares like Walnut and Chestnut Streets.

At this point, the officers had not yet been able to confirm that Robb had gone to Penn that morning. Their questioning of people they saw around McNeil and the Economics Department didn't help. All they knew is they were having trouble finding anyone who'd seen Robb that day at Penn. They had yet to check out his e-mail or his phone records.

Around midnight, Gallen dispatched Minzola and Koch to go back to the city. They needed to verify that Robb had gone to Penn and turned in his grades, as he had claimed. Getting that nailed down was critical. Eventually, investigators would get the electronic records and security camera films with time stamps on Robb's moves. That night they needed to find someone who could verify that Robb had been on campus. Their last shot was Lynn Costello, the coordinator of undergraduate records for the Economics Department. Robb had told police that he had turned in his grades to her that morning.

Arriving at her home in Philadelphia's Roxborough neighborhood at around 1 a.m., the detectives told her about the death of Robb's wife. Sitting on the couch, Costello expressed shock, saying she couldn't believe that Robb would have anything to do with his wife's death. She knew he was married and had a daughter, but knew little else. While he was friendly, they didn't spend much time together. "He came in and dropped off his grades sheet," Costello said. "He asked if I had a good holiday." Their contact was all of about three minutes, she told them.

To learn more about Robb, the detectives returned to campus over the next few days, looking for anyone who knew him well. Although he had been teaching at Penn since 1984, when he'd begun as an assistant professor in economics, the detectives were hard-pressed to find anyone who really knew him. One problem was timing. It was the end of the semester, and no one stayed around any longer than they needed to. Those who knew Robb never came forward to volunteer information about him. The professors the police spoke to said they knew him to say hello but never went to lunch with him. The police had already learned from Olivia that her father "wasn't very social" and spent a lot of time on the phone with colleagues who lived elsewhere.

After getting a tip that Robb had taken books on murder out of the Penn library, Detectives Marino and Gershanick returned to campus to find out what Robb had checked out. When the university librarian balked at turning over the records as a violation of Robb's privacy, Marino secured a warrant from the grand jury. They could show them the records, or someone would be subpoenaed to testify about the information. What the officers learned from Robb's library book records was predictable. He'd taken out various books on economics. There was nothing even remotely connected to murder.

Those closest to Ellen, while shocked by her killing, told police—often unsolicited—that they knew her husband had killed her.

Ellen's friend Mary Beth was the first person to tell police that Ellen had recently seen a lawyer about divorcing Robb. She could only remember a portion of the lawyer's name, but it was enough for prosecutors to track him down, the first clue toward unlocking the details of the couple's stormy marriage.

With just a portion of the name, Ferman got working on the Internet and narrowed the possibilities down to Albert Shemtob, who conveniently used to work in the district attorney's office. Now, if only she could locate him on a holiday weekend. With no answer at his home or office, Ferman recalled that her husband's friend had once hired him in a divorce. She asked Michael to call them . . . one of her daughters went to school with a friend of his son's. A call to the son's cell phone gave her his father's number.

They reached him while he was golfing at a Florida resort.

Once he understood the urgency of Ferman's situation, Shemtob recalled as much as he could without the benefit of his file. What he did remember confirmed, for Ferman, critical details that would help focus the investigation.

Yes, Ellen had recently come to him looking for legal help to get a divorce from her husband. He recalled telling her that she'd get a sizeable monthly amount to cover alimony and child support.

He even recalled having drafted a separation letter that he had been waiting on Ellen for an OK to send out. He had a whole file on the case that he'd be happy to go over with them when he got back.

Olivia gave police more confirmation of her parents' pending divorce.

In his thirty years of policing, Peffall had conducted lots of tough interviews. Telling Olivia that her mother had been killed rattled the veteran detective, who had four children of his own. Later that evening, Peffall and O'Keefe talked to Olivia again at the Upper Merion police offices. When asked how her parents got along, Olivia said that they were getting a divorce, that her mother had told her about it two weeks earlier and her father had mentioned it too, although she couldn't remember what he had said. "They both agreed to it. My dad was supposed to move out when they got separated. My mom told me that she was going to get a lot of money when they were divorced, because my dad had a lot of money in banks in other countries."

Olivia painted for investigators a portrait of a troubled home: She said her parents did not fight, but they slept in separate rooms; her father kept his locked. Her father didn't have a lot of friends, but he traveled monthly for his work as an economist to Japan and England, and would visit his family for ten days every year in Israel. Her mother, who took medication for depression, slept in most mornings until 11 a.m. On the day her mother was killed, Olivia's father had taken her to school because she had missed the bus.

CHAPTER 11

December 24, 2006

At their daily meeting the next morning at the Upper Merion Township Police Department, Marino got a call on his cell phone. Robb wanted to go home. The forensic team had finished their work and it was time to let him back into his house. They would do their usual, explain what had been taken for evidence, like the doorknobs and locks, and the four one-foot sections of the kitchen floor stained with bloody footprints.

They also needed to tell him about the services that he could hire to come in and clean the place up. The blood spatter and brain matter sprayed all over the kitchen was still there, but now it had dried and hardened.

Why not ask Robb to take them on a walk-through, so he could replay just what he'd done the day Ellen was killed?

The idea came from Nilsen, who had spent a lot of time working the evidence in the house, and had actually removed the floor tiles and sent them to the FBI for testing.

Would Robb do it? He was under no legal obligation to even talk to them. They knew that. Surprisingly Robb wasn't lawyered up, not yet, so there was no one around to tell him not to talk to the police. He had been cooperating on everything they had asked him to do. He had even given police saliva, skin and hair samples so they could compare them to what they'd found in the home, and he had given his written permission for police to search his car, his computers and his office at Penn. Why not act out what he had already told police in detail?

Marino and Gershanick got into Marino's unmarked gray Ford 500 for the ride to the hotel where Robb was waiting for them out in front. Nilsen would meet them at the Robb home.

En route, Robb told them he'd had a lunch date the day before at one of the chain restaurants nearby with Arnold Jentleson, a neighbor, and his son, Brett, a good friend of Olivia's. Robb had taken both children out to movies and dinner.

Gershanick and Marino exchanged puzzled looks.

Who was Jentleson? They made mental notes to talk to him.

The detectives hadn't really known one another before they were tapped by their superiors to play the lead detective roles in the case.

A cop for a decade, the 35-year-old Marino had worked for the sheriffs (warrants and on the bomb squad) and for the East Norristown Police before joining the county detectives in 2002. Stocky and dark-haired, Marino enjoyed big-game hunting and had photos of himself with a prize caribou in his office. Marino was one of those guys who'd always known he wanted to be a cop, just like his father, who'd spent several years in the FBI before returning to private law practice in Montgomery County. A hard-liner on crime and drugs, the senior Marino spent sixteen years as an ace criminal attorney before being elected district attorney. He is now retired.

Gershanick, a ten-year police veteran, had spent about half of his years in policing as a detective. Detective Nilsen had been an assistant with the district attorney's office for seven years. He'd previously spent seven years as a detective in Lower Merion Township, and six years in patrol and as a platoon investigator.

As they walked into the house—the last place Robb had seen his wife, pummeled to death on the kitchen floor—the professor appeared unaffected. The officers looked at each other as if to say, "Do you believe this?"

It seemed like a good time for Marino to ask if Robb would take them on a tour of the house. No problem, he told them.

As part of the walk-through, Marino was trying to account for all of Robb's time that day. They had a twenty-minute gap between the time he said he'd gotten home and called the police, and nearly an hour's gap from when he'd left Penn and arrived home. Could it be, they wondered, that Robb was waiting nearby, hoping that Gary would arrive and find Ellen? They were still trying to figure out why Robb appeared to have placed the call to police at 1:45 p.m., literally minutes before Olivia was due to walk in the door.

Just as he was about to ask Robb to do the walk-through in real time, Nilsen pulled Marino aside.

"Don't rush him through. Let him tell us what he did," Nilsen whispered out of Robb's earshot. Marino nodded in agreement.

"OK, Rafi, go ahead and take us through exactly what you did on Friday," Marino told him.

Starting from the garage, Robb retraced his steps from when he'd arrived home, opened the garage door, walked into the garage through the den and up the stairs into the kitchen, where he'd spotted Ellen's feet on the floor. He stood right where Nilsen had removed the floor tiles on which the killer had left his bloody shoe prints. He described his steps into the kitchen, his wanderings through the house looking for a phone and checking to ensure that Olivia wasn't with the family dog upstairs. When they got to his second-floor bedroom, Marino asked him why he hadn't used the telephone up there to call police. "There's a phone right there. Why didn't you call right from there?"

"Sometimes I unplug it when I want to sleep at night," said Robb as he crawled over the bed and plugged the power cord into the back of the phone. Marino reached for the receiver to check that the phone was working.

As they left the room, the detectives asked Robb about the lock on his door. Robb said the door was probably open when he'd left for Penn the morning of his wife's murder, and when he returned home to find her body. Asked whether he typically locked the door when he wasn't there, Robb said that "Sometimes I lock it." When the detectives asked what might prompt him to lock it, he said, "Maybe if I get into a fight with my wife."

Marino, Gershanick and Nilsen knew they were getting stuff—more than they would have gotten if they were sitting in a room and asking him to go over every step he took. When they got to another phone in the kitchen, Marino asked again, "Why didn't you call from here?"

Robb didn't answer.

He never did explain why he had waited nearly twenty minutes from when he'd gotten home to call police. He also couldn't explain the nearly hour-long gap from when he'd left Penn in West Philadelphia to when he'd arrived home and called the police. That drive, even in traffic, only took forty minutes.

As they made their way around the boxes and other clutter in the house, Robb ignored it and made no apology or explanation. He impressed the detectives with what he didn't say, and by acting like nothing unusual had happened in the house.

As Robb laboriously explained how he'd taken his laptop to his bedroom and then come back downstairs before calling the police, Marino couldn't help but ask, "With your wife dead, why did you go to your room to put your computer down? How did you know that there wasn't an axe murderer waiting in the closet for you?"

Robb had no answer.

Whenever Marino asked about a detail that the officers figured Robb didn't know or didn't want to answer, he would say, "I don't know."

He never got flustered. Never got angry . . . He gave as flatlined a response as the officers had ever seen.

Nilsen then asked Robb to describe exactly what his wife had been doing when he left for Philadelphia that morning.

Ellen had finished wrapping one package, but had not yet wrapped the second one, which was for Olivia's counselor, Robb told them. When he'd left for Philadelphia, the package had been on the table, unwrapped.

Robb probably had no idea how important his answer was to the next request: "Show us what you did after you got out of your car in the garage."

Robb led the way, showing the officers how he'd parked in

the driveway, manually opened the garage door and walked through the garage into the family room. He then went up the steps to the kitchen, where he said, "I could see my wife's feet."

The way Robb told it, the door from the family room to the kitchen had been open. That's the same door where the crime-scene specialists had found a spatter of Ellen's blood. They had found blood smeared on the floor in the area between the door and the oven, as if it had been smeared on the floor by the weather strip underneath as the door was pushed open.

Robb also showed how he'd walked out of the house, through the garage to his car, where he'd retrieved his cell phone to call Upper Merion police.

"How did you know the number?" Marino asked. He'd recalled seeing it on the side of town police cars, Robb said.

With that answer, the detectives exchanged glances again, as if to say to Robb, 'Is this really your story?'

The entire walk-through, even with their questions, had taken a little less than fifteen minutes.

Ellen's friends had already decided they knew who had killed their friend, but the police had to make the case and gather the evidence to make an arrest. All they could do was hope and pray that the killer would never get away with what he had done. As a group, they had worried about Ellen over the years, especially after they all knew that Ellen and Robb had been staying together only for Olivia. After two days of tears and sorrow, the women decided they needed to create a public display for Ellen. They wanted Ellen to know how much they loved her and missed her. And they wanted the community to know that everyone had lost someone special.

On Christmas Eve, Mary Beth Pedlow, LuAnn Dubin and Sharon Sellman gathered in front of the Robb home and assembled the items they had collected to create a memorial around a quiet spot on the front lawn in front of an evergreen tree and near a wooden bench. LuAnn brought the evergreen cross with a large red velvet bow, and Sharon and Mary Beth brought candles. They added a framed message:

ELLEN
MAY YOU BE AT PEACE,
LOVE,
YOUR FRIENDS

Alexandra McLean, a neighbor across the street, added a white ceramic vase with five crimson roses. As she told an *Inquirer* reporter later on Christmas Eve, the flowers were for Ellen. "We didn't even put our lights on last night, because we felt awkward. What are we going to do—put them on like it's a party?"

Mary Beth Pedlow, Patty Volpi, LuAnn Dubin and Sharon Sellman would form "Friends of Ellen," with its own e-mail address, to continue working to keep alive Ellen's memory. Their first project was to make sure that the memorial remained in front of the Robb house.

"People may not have seen her in the neighborhood a lot, but she was a caring person who would do anything for anybody," Sharon told CBS 3's Walt Hunter, pausing as she added items to the memorial. "She had a heart of gold. She wouldn't hurt anybody. It's senseless to think that someone would do something to someone who was so gentle."

CHAPTER 12

December 25–27, 2006

Gallen let the detectives take off on Christmas Day—except for Marino, who drove his county car into the city to check out a tip of a discarded crowbar. It turned out to be a bust. It was actually a metal part that had fallen off a moving truck. It was nothing like the weapon they were looking for. But just getting the call told them that the press release was attracting attention. The public also wondered where Ellen's killer had dumped the murder weapon.

Although he fully trusted Ferman to handle the investigation, Castor couldn't help admitting that he missed the action. He was taking a few days off to spend with family over Christmas, but his head and his heart were on what was happening in the office.

He made no apologies: "I'm a field man, not a desk man. I like running homicide investigations."

By the time he got back on December 27, he was ready for an update on the investigation, starting with an 8:30 a.m. briefing from Ferman. At 9:30 a.m. about thirty officers, along with Ferman and Gallen, filed into the Montgomery County detectives' conference room for their first full meeting with Castor.

Their plan was to fill him and each other in on what they knew, and map out plans for the next step in the investigation.

"OK, where are we with this Robb case?" said Castor, who was sitting at the conference table with Ferman and Gallen.

Marino and Gershanick joined in from their chairs in the first row. Other officers had filled in behind them. As the topic shifted, other voices joined in. Saville, Santarelli and Finor described the murder scene. Dinnell the autopsy results; Kuklentz and Lee the lengthy interview with Robb, with McGowan outlining the unsuccessful lengths they'd gone to to get Robb to take a polygraph. Minzola replayed the translated interview with the Chinese store clerk. He didn't need the translator to understand an adamant "No" when asked if Robb had been there the day of the murder.

Castor listened intently and asked questions when he needed to drill down for more details or to get them all brainstorming. The detectives had done a lot of work in four days, focusing the investigation and blowing huge holes into Robb's alibi and his story.

"Where do we go from here?"

By now, they all believed that Robb was their suspect, but they all also knew that their case was circumstantial. He'd had opportunity and motive, but police had no physical evidence tying him to the murder. Could they get Robb to talk or reveal a detail that could lead them to the murder weapon?

Castor wasn't worried that this could be a circumstantial case. As he had told the detectives on other cases, circumstantial evidence can be great if you have a lot of it. He reminded the team that they'd had a circumstantial case in 2001 when he successfully prosecuted Guy A. Sileo for the 1996 murder of Jim Webb, his partner in running the historic General Wayne Inn. In the end, the case turned on circumstantial evidence: the location of the gun wound and the fact that Sileo had told the family that Webb had been shot even before police knew it. Forensic evidence ultimately showed that Sileo had possessed a gun capable of firing the shot that had killed Webb.

The case, which had grabbed lots of headlines, was one of a string of high-profile prosecutions that solidified Castor's reputation as a tough and successful prosecutor. By the time the case came to trial, Castor had become DA, but he had promised the widow he would prosecute the case himself. He won a first-degree murder conviction against Sileo for the Christmastime killing in the office of the financially struggling inn so he could collect on a $650,000 life insurance policy.

Knowing all too well what he would be needing once they got serious about preparing for trial in this case, Castor ordered up both a timeline, so they knew how much free time Robb had actually had the day of the murder, and financials. Money was turning into a huge issue. They needed to know how much Robb was worth.

"What about Robb?" Castor asked the group. "How are we keeping track of him?"

They had already seized Robb's car and his passport. It didn't make sense to waste the time of an officer to track him, Marino told him.

"That works for me," Castor said. Once Robb gets his car back, "let's be clear that the minute he turns his car in the direction of the airport or onto I-Ninety-five, that we nab him. We don't want to risk the possibility that he tries to leave the country."

They knew that an escape attempt by Robb would actually bolster their case. It could only help to have to tell a jury that Robb had tried to leave the country.

To do it, he would need help. While at the hotel, Robb didn't have a car. His BMW was still in police custody so it could be closely examined for evidence, including any blood drops. One of the items inside was a plastic bag from King's Market in Chinatown, the place Robb had told officers he went the morning of the murder. But the fruit would be of little value to Robb in establishing any alibi, because there was no receipt in the bag. There was no telling whether the fruit had been purchased that morning or some other time. While they had the car in custody, Detective Bud Dinnell, a specialist in alternative light source testing, examined the car for any evidence. The ALS testing would pick up any stains on carpeting, walls, bedding or car seats, even if it had been cleaned. When that turned up negative, the officers also got a court order from Judge Paul W. Tressler allowing them to install a tracker. The officers were able to convince the judge that allowing Robb to move around freely was their best bet of finding the weapon or other evidence.

There was one problem. They didn't have the keys and didn't want to get them from Robb. So they appealed to BMW in Germany, which promptly got them a key by the next day.

Castor already knew from Detective Michael Gilbert's work on Robb's financials that he was worth some $2.3 million even without his $400,000 home. A sizeable chunk of Robb's money was in an Israeli bank. If he got out of the country, he'd have no problem finding resources to fund an escape. The reality, though, was that Robb wasn't going anywhere. He was preparing for his wife's funeral. And he awaited his daughter's return from Gary's house in Sherborn, Massachusetts, about 20 miles southwest of Boston.

Before he could settle back into the house, he had to get the back door fixed and get an attorney. Thanks to a neighbor and financial planner, Arnold Jentleson, Robb got connected to a Norristown law firm where Francis Genovese, a criminal attorney and former assistant district attorney, agreed to represent him. Police access to Robb had come to an end. They'd have to deal with Genovese now.

CHAPTER 13

December 27, 2006

While the detectives were meeting with Castor on December 27, a call came in from the Upper Merion police. Robb had hired a glazier and a locksmith to replace the glass and change the lock on the house's back door—the same door that Robb had told police had been broken into to by a burglar. Was it OK for them to do the work?

Castor grinned and didn't hesitate. "Sure, but they're going to have an assistant."

"Call them back," added Risa, looking at Gershanick. "This is a good opportunity that we can't miss."

Detectives who have worked with Castor know that he stops at nothing in searching for evidence. He's always working within the law, but he likes to get creative about doing what's legal.

Sending undercover narcotics detectives in to take one last shot at Robb was worth it. He knew just the pair who could do the job.

When he got back to his corner office in the imposing county courthouse, Castor called Detectives Tony Spagnoletti and Stephen Forzato and lined them up to come by his office. Between them, the veteran officers had logged forty-five years working undercover in narcotics.

For Spagnoletti, the assignment would be a finale to a thirty-four-year law enforcement career that included twenty-six years working undercover. During his fourteen years on the Montgomery County detectives' narcotics team, he had often teamed up with Forzato, a twenty-one-year police veteran. For the last three years, Spagnoletti had been running the unit as the lieutenant in charge. January 12 would be his last day.

Castor met first with Spagnoletti and Gallen and later with Forzato. Not only had they investigated scores of drug cases together, but Castor, as president of the state District Attorneys Association, had enlisted them to teach officers around Pennsylvania in the fine points of undercover work, including sophisticated wiretaps. One case that turned out to be financially rewarding for the county—to the tune of $2.7 million—was the arrest in an illegal bookmaking scheme of Joseph and John Mastronardo. Joseph was the son-in-law of legendary Philadelphia Mayor Frank L. Rizzo. Both ended up pleading guilty to misdemeanor charges and not contesting Castor's seizure of the money, which he claimed stemmed from their "multimillion"-dollar gambling network. Castor agreed not to file more serious felony charges. The Mastronardos decided not to fight the charges or try to get the money back after Castor's office threatened to arrest their family members, including the Mastronardos' elderly parents, Joseph and Lucy; their sister, Cindy; and Joe Mastronardo's wife, Joanna, and their 23-year-old son, Joey. Joanna is the daughter of the late mayor and Joey, his only grandchild.

"Some things are more important than money," Attorney Dennis Cogan, who represented Joseph Mastronardo, told *The Inquirer*.

Castor called the plea "a good deal for everybody involved." The county would be able to spend the $2.7 million on law enforcement. Castor defended his case against the brothers, telling *The Inquirer* that it was built primarily on wiretapped conversations. He also acknowledged the pressure of the threat of charging family members.

"There was some value in not having your wife and family members arrested," he told *Inquirer* reporter George Anastasia. The brothers were later sentenced to jail and probation.

A decade earlier, during another arrest of the same defendant, Castor recalled picking up the phone when it rang in the home and hearing Rizzo on the other end. After Castor told him why they were there, the former mayor, known for his tough law-and-order stance, replied, "If they're guilty, they should go to jail," before hanging up.

Castor enjoyed getting into the nitty-gritty of the undercover work and often came up with his own ideas on how to pursue the illegal drug trade that swept through Montgomery County, a hub in the region's illegal underground drug network, as a bedroom community to Philadelphia. Drug pushers may have focused their trade in North Philadelphia and Camden, but their tentacles reached deep into the suburbs, where many of their customers lived.

In Norristown, the run-down county seat, Castor approved the undercover officers' obtaining a court order to plant a bug in an auto tag business to get the dirt on Norristown Councilman Ernest W. Scott, Jr. and his three sons, who subsequently pled guilty to a criminal conspiracy that included dealing marijuana and issuing fake car insurance cards. On the day Scott was arrested in 2002, county and state police officers displayed what they said they had seized from Scott—bags of diluted marijuana, phones, guns, photos of houses, television sets, stereos and computers. With the television cameras capturing the scene, Castor said the arrest was a warning to all drug dealers: "When we find you, we're going to take your electronic toys."

The Montgomery County district attorney's wiretap evidence from Scott's case was subsequently turned over to the U.S. attorney's office, which used it to launch a wide-ranging corruption probe that produced additional tax evasion charges against Scott and corruption-related charges against other Norristown officials and businessmen. Scott was sentenced in 2003 to six and a half to twenty years on the corruption and fraud charges and an additional twenty-one months for tax evasion.

Castor knew all that Spagnoletti and Forzato were capable of doing. The pair enjoyed talking to strangers and getting people to trust them.

Castor wanted them to go over and see what they could do.

He was obviously amused at the prospect of these two guys taking on the professor. He gave them a brief overview and sent them on their way. They all knew there was no risk with this assignment. It was actually a win–win for Castor. Once the officers took up their friendly undercover characters, there was no telling what Robb could let slip.

Getting him to confess would be the frosting on the cake, but anything else could help shoot more holes into his alibi. "Just get him talking and let's see where it goes." The plan was for Spagnoletti to go in with the glazier and Forzato to follow with the locksmith.

They each contacted the companies and made plans to go in later that day. That would give them enough time to huddle with their colleagues in the homicide unit and read the affidavit prepared to obtain search warrants.

Marino, the lead detective, along with Finor, the ballistics expert, and Santarelli, the crime-scene specialist, gave them an overview of the case and the crime scene. Kuklentz, who knew Robb better than any of them after questioning him for more than twelve hours on the day of the murder, described him as tight-lipped and liking to control the conversation. "Was Robb streetwise?" Forzato wanted to know. "Would he have had any dealings with street people?"

"Not at all," said Kuklentz. Robb was an intellectual, a university professor for whom math was a hobby, and who lived in a quiet low-crime suburb: There was no indication that he had ever been in contact with criminals or anyone with close associations to criminals.

With that, Tony and Steve developed their plan for how to approach Robb. Tony would go in first as an assistant to the glazier for Burhans Glass Company. Steve would follow with the locksmith from Dayton Lock Company.

"Damn," said Spagnoletti as the Burhans Glass Company truck drove past the Robb residence. From his perch on the passenger side, Spagnoletti could see that three television vans were parked outside the Robb house. Both officers were well-known among reporters and TV camera techs, who would automatically start rolling on anyone going into the Robb house.

The last thing the detectives needed was for any of the reporters to recognize them, or for Francis Genovese, Robb's attorney, to spot them.

The vans appeared to be there for the long haul—a Robb
stakeout.

That wasn't going to work. Spagnoletti called Castor for
help. "I'll take care of it," he said, reaching quickly for his contacts at the television stations. Castor asked the vans to pull
back away from the house. He had his reasons, and they knew
him well enough to understand that it had to be important.

Castor came up with another way to make sure Genovese
didn't drop in. It just so happened that Genovese was representing another defendant whose trial was scheduled to start on January 8. One of the prosecutors in the case called Genovese and
asked him to come over to their office to review the exhibits
that would be submitted at trial.

As Castor teased Genovese weeks later: "You don't think it
was an accident that Jim McGowan and Steve Latzer kept running out of the room that day, do you?" Genovese didn't know
it at the time, but Detective McGowan and Assistant District
Attorney Steven Latzer, while meeting with him, deliberately
took their time coming up with the documents by taking turns
leaving the room as if to search for yet another folder.

Dressed in a Burhans Glass hoodie, Spagnoletti looked the
part as he accompanied Bob Rath, a company field supervisor,
who really did know how to repair the glass. They knocked on
the front door where Robb met them with handshakes. He led
them through the house to the back laundry room where there
was a door with a shattered window.

"This is tragic. Sorry to hear about your loss," said Spagnoletti, who had taken on his undercover persona of Tony Corelli.

"Yeah," said Robb.

After looking at the door with the missing glass, the worker
explained that he would put something temporary in for today
so the door would be secure, and they would return in a few
days with the full glass. Spagnoletti had set it up that way. He

wanted to make sure he could get a second try at Robb if he needed it.

With that, Tony slipped away to check out the house with Robb following him. He stopped when he got to the family room, which had boxes stacked to the ceiling, covering most of the floor.

"What the hell is this all about?" Tony demanded, turning to Robb.

"My wife liked to buy things."

"If that was my wife, she'd be buried in the middle of all of that rubble."

Robb said nothing, but gave Tony a knowing smile.

"So, what the hell happened here?"

Robb told him the whole story, the same he had told the detectives five days ago, how he had come home from dropping his grades off at Penn and found his wife dead in a pool of blood on the kitchen floor.

"They think I did it," Robb said to Tony.

Just that morning, *The Philadelphia Inquirer* had reported that the police believed Robb had faked the burglary of his home. What led them to that conclusion was that the burglar had never stepped on the glass after opening the door.

"Let me tell you about Castor," Tony said, digging his hands in the pockets of his jeans.

"What do you know about him?" Robb asked.

"If Castor is after you, he's going to get you one way or another."

Tony stepped closer to Robb, and looked back toward the other room, where his companion worked on the door. He kept talking, but in a hushed voice.

"Here's my deal. I don't know anything about setting glass and windows. My friend is the manager there. I know him. I grew up with him. I'm on parole, work release. I have to have a job to stay on parole. I have to be working, so he gave me a job. I go around with this guy and represent the company."

Tony let that set in before going at Robb again.

"Hey, Doc, who's your lawyer?"

"Genovese."

"Listen, Doc, I don't know who that is." (He actually did. Genovese is a former assistant district attorney in Montgomery County and a respected criminal attorney.) "You need a high-powered guy. Castor is ruthless. He's a no-good bastard."

With that, Tony had him hooked. Robb wanted to know more about Tony's situation and, about the crime that had landed him in jail. Robb even started showing him around the house and pointed out to him the spot in the kitchen where detectives had cut up a portion of the floor where bloody footprints had been found in the pools of blood around his wife's head.

After checking it all out, Tony continued his ruse.

"What was missing?"

"Nothing."

"Doc, something is missing. People don't break into a freakin' house and kill your wife and nothing is missing. Are you saying someone had something against her?"

"No," Robb said.

"Doc, you are not understanding me. You've got a lot of stuff missing here. You need to re-evaluate and find stuff that are missing. You get my drift? You find stuff that [is] missing. You call the lawyer and tell him you found stuff stolen in the house."

He hadn't been able to find his wife's purse, but he didn't think any valuables were missing, Robb told him. With that, Tony left, telling Robb he'd return when the glass came in. As he walked out of the garage and stepped into the driveway, he passed his colleague, Steve, who was wearing a dark blue Dayton Lock Company shirt with the name "Joshua" embroidered over the right side pocket. "You won't have any problem," Tony whispered to Steve as they passed each other. "He'll be easy."

After meeting them at the front door, Robb took them inside and showed them the doors where police had taken the knobs, and the lock on the back door that needed replacing.

While Kevin Traylor, Steve's co-worker, went to the truck to get some forms to fill out, Robb led Steve to the kitchen.

"Why did police take the doorknobs and locks?" Steve asked.

"Oh, didn't you hear what happened here?"

"I did read something in the newspaper, but didn't realize this was the house."

"Well," Robb continued, "the police believe I am the prime suspect. The police say in ninety-five percent of murders, the victim knows the killer. And they believe it is me. They say the house wasn't broken into, because the glass from the door wasn't found anywhere in the house."

Steve, promising to take a look at the glass later, added, "Well, whether you did or didn't do that is no business of mine. We're here to provide you with a service and to make you feel more secure."

Robb nodded.

Despite Steve's offer to help him feel more secure in the house, Robb never asked him for better locks or heightened security. Even when Steve flatly asked, "Do you want to feel more secure in your house?" Robb said nothing and nodded his head.

At another point, Steve said he knew of a security alarm company. Robb showed mild interest, but didn't want the work to be done right away. Robb said he had been living in a hotel and had just moved back into the house that day. He said his daughter would be returning today or tomorrow.

"You don't want them to get this done tonight?"

Robb answered: "No, that's not necessary."

While in the kitchen, as they stood in the same spot where Ellen Robb had been found brutally beaten, her husband offered Steve a soda. "No, thanks," he said as Robb led him to the laundry room to show him the door with the broken glass and how it had allowed the burglar to unlock the door and get into the house. Robb urged him to look for signs of a break-in and pointed to specks on the wood that Steve quickly dismissed.

Robb told him the police thought the burglary was a setup because the glass hadn't been trampled on. Steve told him he'd replaced a lot of locks due to burglaries because the burglars preferred to pry open the door at the deadbolt rather than break the glass.

"Really?" Robb said. "Why?"

"Because it is very loud when glass breaks, and you have neighbors around here." With that they looked for evidence that a burglar had pried open the door, and found none.

"It's obvious no one tried to pry the door," Steve told him.

As they walked back into the kitchen, Steve also mentioned that he was divorced and his girlfriend's brother worked at the Upper Merion Township Police Department.

"Hey, I think it would look good for your situation if there were a lot of break-ins in your neighborhood recently. Do you want me to check with her to see if she can find out if there were burglaries in your area?"

After asking more about his girlfriend, Robb responded, "Yeah, that might be good."

They left, but returned about ten minutes later after discovering that they had forgotten to give Robb his new keys.

Steve again asked Robb if he was serious about wanting him to find out more about the burglaries in the area.

"Sure," he said. "But I think the horse is already out of the barn."

"What do you mean by that?" Steve asked.

"Well, the police already think I did it."

CHAPTER 14

December 28, 2006

While away for Christmas, Castor conferred with Ferman and decided he would handle the Robb case himself. It was a high-octane case with lots of public attention, which is never a bad combination for a district attorney seeking re-election the following November—and having his eye on future statewide runs for attorney general, governor or even U.S. senator.

But the case also intrigued him. He knew it would be difficult, hinging as it did on creating a puzzle out of tiny pieces of circumstantial evidence. This wasn't going to be as simple as having some piece of forensic evidence pointing to the killer. And, he figured it was the kind of case that the public expected the DA to handle himself.

Ferman, who had the January Motel 6 murder trial to get back to, had been keeping Castor in the loop with daily updates.

In his office, Castor was studying the photos of Ellen Robb. "Her face has been removed from her head," he said to himself. "There must be some psychiatric component to that."

He called Dr. Timothy Michals, a Philadelphia forensic psychiatrist, and asked him for his opinion. Michals, who, with Dr. Steven Samuel, a psychologist, has conducted a study of some 300 murder cases, told him there was a legion of evidence that described this type of killings.

Their analysis confirmed for Castor that Ellen Robb had been the intended target of the beating and not a victim who'd just happened to be home when someone tried to burglarize the house.

Ultimately, the pair gave Castor a written opinion that the beating was "likely an enraged blitz attack which occurred without warning." They also called Ellen's murder "an overkill, excessive force type of crime where the obsessive intensity of force used against Mrs. Robb went beyond that necessary to cause her death."

They wrote to Castor after examining photos of Ellen Robb's body and the scene, and reviewing statements from her friends and family.

They theorized that whoever killed Ellen Robb had wanted to confront her up close. "She was so severely beaten, she appears more like an 'it' or a thing." The experts said Ellen's killer wanted to see her suffer and to control and demean her as she suffered.

"The killing has the signature of a need to depersonalize Mrs. Robb, such that she is hardly recognizable as a human being."

The opinion offered by Drs. Michals and Samuel would become a critical piece of evidence that would trigger a legal fight that ultimately revealed the identity of the killer.

Once he reviewed the case with the detectives, Castor also knew that the media would be pumping him for an update, and he could use that event to his advantage.

With the murder occurring two days before Christmas on a Friday afternoon, it got picked up, but didn't get the kind of attention it would have if it had broken in a normal week. The calls he had on his desk from just about every crime reporter in town told him that there was a lot of interest in it: A "cookie mom" in the suburbs found brutally beaten on her kitchen floor, her Penn professor husband the last person to see her alive and the first to see her dead.

The *Inquirer*'s first story on the killing was a 242-word short article that ran on the third page of the local news section under the headline "Penn professor's wife slain." The story, based largely on Ferman and Early's press release issued at the end of the first grueling day of investigation, detailed what was known at the time—that Robb had found his wife dead in their home, the victim of what the medical examiner said was blunt force trauma. She'd tried to fight back as she was "struck repeatedly with a long, solid cylindrical-shaped object."

For Wendy Ruderman, the Robb story at least gave her a good story on the front page of the "Local & Region" section for the Christmas Day paper. A tenacious reporter, Ruderman filled out the details by working the Montgomery County DA's office and going out to the neighborhood on Christmas Eve and knocking on doors on Forest Road. Her story described a chilly marriage between the games theory specialist and the former Brownie troop leader and homemaker who cared for the couple's 12-year-old daughter.

"They were still married, but they were living separately in the same house," First Assistant DA Ferman told Ruderman.

A neighbor said Robb was devoted to the family dog, Copper, and walked him at least three times a day, but rarely talked to anyone he saw. "He has a really flat affect," said Alexandra McLean, who lived across the street. "He's very serious. He doesn't smile very much." Several neighbors said Ellen hadn't been seen since the summer, and that it was Robb who'd taken their daughter around trick-or-treating at Halloween or selling Girl Scout Cookies.

The *Inquirer*'s coverage picked up on December 27 with a story by Wendy Ruderman and Keith Herbert, quoting sources that said investigators had concluded that the murder scene had been staged to look like a burglary. As evidence, the story cited the broken glass on the laundry room door that had not been trampled on. The story also disclosed that Ellen Robb had been planning to divorce her husband.

The story included a quote from Ferman: "We're looking into reports that she had recently retained a divorce attorney, and began moving forward with plans to divorce."

Prosecutors had previously said that the marriage was strained and the Robbs slept in separate bedrooms.

Ferman said Ellen Robb had not yet filed any divorce

papers. Information about her plans was coming to police from people they were talking to. Ferman did not identify a suspect and said an arrest was not imminent.

For several reasons, some of which had to do with his own strategy, Castor was ready to fill in some of the blanks on the Ellen and Rafael Robb story. By going public with some of the information being gathered in the investigation, he would show the public that Ellen Robb was not the victim of a random burglar and put added pressure on Robb and people who knew him.

Ellen Robb's murder would have hit the airwaves that day anyway. There would be a viewing that night, followed by a funeral the next day. But Castor's press conference ensured that the press had facts to push out there. There was no doubt where the investigation was heading.

Castor, who by now was fully briefed on every detail of evidence that the detectives were coming up with, wanted to start turning up the heat. If Robb—the master of strategy games— thought he was going to outsmart them, Castor needed him to know that wasn't going to happen.

Whenever Bruce Castor calls a press conference, the media show up. Not only does the county have its share of sensational cases, but Castor just gets it. He knows how to generate big headlines and television time. He knows the kind of information that the media craves. He knew that the Robb case had it all.

Summoning the press to the district attorney's conference room in his suite of offices in the county courthouse, Castor was on his turf. The room was equipped perfectly for this kind of thing with a county DA seal on the back wall draped on both sides by county and United States flags.

Castor asked for the public's help in solving the murder. He said someone could have seen or heard something that might help investigators. He was hoping that giving the public some of the details of what occurred would jog someone's memory. A window had been broken and there'd been a dog in the home—both of which can make noise.

"Anybody who saw anything unusual at that house between eight-twenty and about ten-fifteen a.m." last Friday should come forward, he said.

Castor performed just like reporters were used to seeing him. Camera-ready in a dark grey suit and orange-and-gold tie, Castor served up a lot of details, but also chose his words carefully. He called the murder an "exceedingly, exceedingly bloody attack, and her face was unrecognizable."

He called Ellen Robb "the specific target of this assault" and said her husband "is not excluded as the killer." He added: "We are trying to determine who would have a motive. The divorce context can be a motive for murder." The broken glass in the back door appeared to be the result of a staged break-in, he said. And while investigators looked into a murder-for-hire scenario, they are now "leaning away from that." They had also excluded the possibility that either Ellen or Rafi had a lover, or that Rafi may have hired someone to kill her.

Castor also made an unusual plea for information from Robb's friends and associates. "I'd like to hear from people who know Dr. Robb and can discuss with us his personality, his habits, the way he interacts with people, his affect and generally what type of man we are dealing with here."

In a KYW radio interview Castor put it like this: "I want to know if his reactions to law enforcement are appropriate, based on his previous affect with people and relative to our knowledge of how ordinary people react under these circumstances."

In other words, are the blank responses and lack of emotion the Robb that people knew? The detectives were still shaking their heads. If he really came home to find his wife dead on the kitchen floor, why didn't he run out of there screaming in fear? How could he calmly take his computer to his bedroom before calling the police? That was just the first of many oddities in Robb's behavior that struck Castor and his team. Now, the district attorney was ready to share it all with the public in hopes that someone would call them with information.

Responding to reporters' questions, Castor said Robb was

not being monitored. "We always have to be concerned that somebody might flee, but you don't restrict people's liberty unless you have probable cause. If I thought we had probable cause, he would be arrested," he said when asked if Robb, who is also an Israeli citizen, posed a flight risk. Castor said the Penn professor was cooperating by agreeing to have investigators search his Penn office and seize his computers and cars.

He said Robb couldn't be excluded as a suspect, but also said he did not have enough evidence to arrest him.

When asked about Robb's plans to return to the house where his wife had been murdered, Castor said, "I think it's creepy. That's all I can say about it. I don't know that it's indicative of any evidence of guilt."

At the same time, Robb and his attorney, Genovese, publicly denied that he had killed Ellen.

In an interview with NBC 10's Deanna Durante, Genovese said the Robbs' marital problems were not new and could lead people to think he had a motive and a reason to harm his wife. "It's no surprise to him all the talk about strife in the marriage. It's nothing new to him. Talk about divorce has been going on for some time, but of course, when that gets out, the thought is that he had motive and a reason he'd want to do harm to her. Absolutely not," he said.

Genovese told the media: "He understands why the focus of the investigation, at least at this point, is on him. Being the spouse, they always look closest to home first. But he's been cooperative with them—he's done everything they've asked of him as far as giving statements and giving them consent to search different things."

Genovese said his client was dealing with his wife's murder "a little better now, but says he's still very emotional."

He told the *Inquirer*: "He's confident that the police will find the person who did this and bring them to justice."

Outside the Robb home, where her friends tended to a memorial to honor Ellen, Sharon Sellman told CBS 3's Walt Hunter, "She had a wonderful laugh and she loved to laugh. And she would never hurt anybody, she had [a] heart of gold."

Added another friend, LuAnn Dubin: "We are hoping that

everyone who knew Ellen will personally pray for justice and for her daughter, who she loved deeply."

Ellen Robb's murder got immediate interest in cyberspace too, where crime bloggers took up every morsel of information to try to figure out the case.

They were especially intrigued about figuring out whether Robb was utilizing any of the strategies that he had mastered as a game theory specialist teaching at an Ivy League university.

On websleuths.com, postings ran the gamut from people on the other side of the country theorizing about the murder to writers who claimed they were neighbors.

Steve Huff on his blog labeled the story, "The Mysterious Murder of Ellen Robb" and gave readers links to documents and stories as the case unfolded. In an early posting, Huff pointed out that Robb spelled his name "Rob" at the University of Pennsylvania. Did it mean anything? No one ever answered the question.

Citing Robb's work in game theory and a recent paper on long-term relationships, Huff concluded:

I think some will tell you that marriage is a game. Two partners playing against life, and sometimes each other. . . . What happened in the professor's cool and mathematical mind when his wife Ellen finally told him it was time for her to opt out of this particular kind of "game play"?

One contributor, identified as CN, wrote:

This is an extremely quiet and safe neighborhood, and everyone is shocked and very tense about this, wanting some answers. However, Prof. Robb seems very calm and non-chalant over the whole thing. He has returned to the home and has been staying there, not easy for someone who cared at all for the fact that the mother of their child was brutally murdered in that house. Additionally, since returning the house has been left open, the garage door was up all night the other evening, and the outside lights (always on all evening while Ellen was alive) were all shut off. I know that if I came home to find a family member murdered I would be terrified to be in that house, and if I really thought it was a stranger I'd have my house locked up like a drum with every light on . . .

CHAPTER 15

December 25–29, 2006

For Ellen's friends and family, the Christmas holiday was a painful time of mourning. Instead of a joyous family gathering in Boston, the Gregory family arranged for Ellen's funeral.

Gary took Olivia back to his home in Sherborn to join his wife, Kim, and family. They would return for the viewing on December 28.

Mary Beth Pedlow, her husband Drew and their children went to Hammonton, in South Jersey, to visit Mary Beth's family for Christmas. She was supposed to return home with them the next day, but decided to stay a few days until the viewing, telling her mother and sisters that she just needed to be with family. The trauma of the last few days had left her shaken and overwhelmed with guilt. She needed a quiet place to grieve, so she stayed with her children while her husband returned home. Replaying continually inside her head was the same question: What could she have done differently to help Ellen? Mary Beth couldn't help thinking that there were three types of friends—friends for a reason, friends for a season and friends for a lifetime. She knew that Ellen's had been a lifetime friendship.

As she watched television reports of the police investigation into Ellen's murder, Mary Beth became more and more distraught. Why wasn't Ellen's family telling everyone about the Ellen they all knew? And why didn't the press have a better photograph? She packed up the car and headed home, thinking,

"I've got to go home and find another picture." After digging through her box of photos, Mary Beth came up with an old one that was at least better than what the media had. Ellen was wearing glasses, but it showed her smile, her great smile. It's what Mary Beth wanted everyone to know about her friend.

Mary Beth also waited for a call from Ellen's family to help with the funeral arrangements, but it never came.

So on the day of the viewing, Mary Beth, a short but spunky blonde, planned to get to the funeral home before the crowds of people who she knew would want to pay their last respects to Ellen. The viewing would only be held from 7 to 9 p.m. on Thursday, December 28 with the funeral the next day, starting with prayers at 8:30 a.m., at the Donohue Funeral Home in Wayne.

Outside, television trucks surrounded the funeral home as reporters did live stand-ups showing a steady stream of mourners entering the funeral home. Becky Best, a high school friend, in an interview with Angela Russell of CBS 3, described Ellen as a "great person who loved to party." Her killing and the excruciating wait for news of who did it "was like something out of a murder mystery novel. It's too weird."

When she arrived, Mary Beth quickly picked out Ellen's closest friends, who were also waiting outside the locked door. If nothing else, they would be able to support one another. When she knocked to get in, she was told they would have to wait, that the family wanted some time alone. Mary Beth respected the request, although she kept hoping that somehow she would be able to get in before Robb arrived.

The funeral home looked a lot like a suburban office building—one floor, red brick with maroon shutters and a center entrance on a well-landscaped lot on West Lancaster Avenue, a busy thoroughfare in Wayne, a few miles from the Robb house.

As the crowd waiting to get in clustered around the door, Mary Beth and the other friends got pushed to the end of the line that moved slowly into the building. In the viewing room, the casket was closed and encircled with flowers, including her favorite yellow roses. As mourners approached the casket, they viewed three big boards with photos of Ellen's life, and on the closed casket a portrait photo of a beautiful, smiling Ellen in a vibrant blue dress.

As she approached the casket, with five people in front of her, Mary Beth was horrified to see Robb arrive and take his place beside the casket between Ellen's mother and her brothers.

LuAnn Dubin saw him too. He arrived fifteen minutes after the rest of the family, looking disheveled and very out of place, dressed, not in a suit, but casually, in a multi-colored knit cardigan over a shirt and pants. The friends noticed that every man wore at least a sport coat except Ellen's husband.

As he acknowledged the condolences of people passing before him, Robb would repeat that a burglar had done this, a burglar had broken into their home and killed Ellen. Olivia alternately spent time in a nearby room with her friends and stood by the casket as her mother's friends and family came by, and extended her hand. "Thank you for coming." Mary Beth turned to her husband Drew, who stood behind her. "I can't do this. I can't go through that line," she said as she put her hand on the casket and stepped away and found a chair.

In hushed tones, her friends recalled how Ellen had touched so many. Her smile lit up a room. And, even if six months or a year went by between phone calls, Ellen would pick up the conversation as if they had last talked the day before. The three boards of photos reflecting Ellen's life helped them to remember all of those cherished moments.

As Gina Bacci reached the front of the receiving line, Robb extended his hand toward her as he mumbled, "It's truly tragic." Gina pulled her hand away and wiped it on her slacks as she quickly moved by. "That man killed my friend," she said to anyone within earshot. Robb just stared at her and nodded nervously.

"He acted guilty," said Gina, who first met Ellen through Mary Beth, and rented her an apartment in Wayne when Ellen, in her early 20s, first started working in retail sales.

Jan Hines, Ellen's high school friend, had never met Rafi,

and had no intention of meeting him now. Making her way with another friend, Jan decided she couldn't pretend. She knew she couldn't give him any condolences. "He didn't value her in life," said Jan, recalling what Ellen had told her friends about her marriage. "He didn't respect her."

Arlene Leib knew the Robbs because her daughter had gone to summer camp with Olivia. As she approached the casket, she asked Robb how he was doing. As Arlene later told police, Robb told her, "Well, you know, I am in double trouble." When she asked what he meant, Robb added, "There is no second suspect."

Arlene then inquired whether Robb had an alibi for the time when Ellen was killed. He responded, "Not really," and shrugged. She found Robb unemotional and detached, even disrespectful.

Perhaps it depended on who came through. When Brett Jentleson, a friend of Olivia's, came through, Robb hugged him and "cried like a baby," his father Arnold Jentleson told the *Inquirer*. The Jentlesons appeared to stand alone in defense of Robb.

When she got to Robb, Patty Volpi, who knew both Ellen and Rafi from activities at Olivia's school, tried to quickly give her condolences and move on. "Sorry, Rafi," she said as Robb squeezed her hand with a long, hard shake. His body language, his comments, his behavior—none of it looked to Patty like a husband in mourning.

To watch Robb, especially his demeanor, was one of the reasons Gallen had sent Detective Mary Anders from the major crimes unit to work undercover and blend into the crowd. From her spot among the mourners, the officer noted Robb's awkward behavior and how Ellen's family and friends avoided him.

At the end of the evening, Olivia insisted on going home with her father. Robb had returned home earlier that day, as CBS 3 television cameras exclusively filmed him as he pulled into the driveway, got out of his car to raise the garage door, drove his BMW into the garage and reached up and closed the door behind him.

As he disappeared into the house, Upper Merion police remained in view, holding metal detectors to scan the property and the woods behind it, searching for weapons.

Everyone steeled themselves for the funeral, which took place the next day in the Radnor United Methodist Church on Conestoga Road in Bryn Mawr. The historic stone church with adjoining hall was the place where Ellen had solidified her faith. It was also located close to the neighborhood where Ellen and her brothers had grown up. In many ways, Ellen was going home.

For many at the funeral, their first shock was seeing Robb, wearing a ski jacket and a knit cap, holding what appeared to be a paper coffee cup as he joined family and friends in carrying the casket into the church. Robb had not been asked to be a pallbearer, but had just grabbed the sides of the casket to the horror of everyone around him.

As they made their way into the pews of the church sanctuary, the assembled shunned him, leaving him to sit alone, with only Olivia by his side.

The minister's words fell heavily on the sobbing mourners as he tried to remind them that Ellen would enjoy everlasting life in paradise and urged them not to abandon their faith.

"When we gather for funerals, especially one as horrific as this, the question arises: 'Why did this happen? Where was God?' " he said. "I don't know why this happened, but I can tell you: God weeps."

In a move that surprised many, when it came time to give Ellen's eulogy, Robb walked up to the podium and unfolded a paper from which he read his wife's eulogy, much like he would deliver a class lecture. From the sanctuary, Ellen's friends and family showed disapproval. In his heavily accented English, Robb said he wanted to tell them about the Ellen he'd married and what had made him fall in love with her. As mourners continued to shake their heads and scoff out loud, Robb told how he'd fallen for Ellen despite their different "culture, religion and upbringing." He told how they had lived for a year in Israel, where she'd won over his family with her vivacious personality. Robb's mother, a Holocaust survivor who had worked with her husband to run a textile business, was touched when Ellen organized a birthday celebration for her. She was so impressed that she talked about it for years after.

But his words came out like he was reading a paper that someone else had written about a person he did not know. "It was just reading something, very detached, very unemotional, very cut and dried," said Patty. "There was no inflection in his voice, and no regret. It was odd."

Around her, mourners were stunned. "I can't believe he can talk about her that way," someone whispered.

Ellen's neighbor and close friend LuAnn could not bear to look at Robb. Clutching her coat, she sat still among the 150 mourners, her eyes shut tight, her head on the shoulder of her father, Bill Brunell. She was appalled and couldn't help thinking, "How could the family allow him to stand next to them?"

After all, the district attorney had just said the day before that he didn't have enough evidence to charge Robb for Ellen's murder, but he also could not exclude him as a suspect.

It fell to her brother Gary to describe Ellen in words everyone could recognize. The mourners touched their eyes with tissues and quietly sobbed as Gary made his way to the microphone to deliver a eulogy that he has since posted on a website in Ellen's memory.

To friends who had come from near and far, Gary thanked them and invited them to join him in celebrating her.

"So, where do we begin? How can you rationalize what happened?" Gary asked, noting that when someone dies from natural causes or in an accident, it can be said that it is God's will. "Yet I, we, have all been troubled because this is clearly not God's will."

He urged her friends to take comfort in knowing that Ellen rests with God and urged them to carry Ellen with them every day. Sharing with them a description of Ellen by her friend, Chris McGuire, Gary called Ellen an "amazing comet. They are exceptionally rare, and once you see one, you are touched and you will carry it with you forever."

Recalling anecdotes that her friends and family knew so well, Gary reminded them of Ellen's laughter, her kindness and how "she never said anything bad about anyone." How she always came with a gift even if she was arriving a little late and how her penchant for sending thank-you notes earned her the nickname "Miss Thank You" from an uncle. He described her "unparalleled politeness," her "spirit," and her family pride. "Once you were in the circle with Ellen, she would defend you forever and hold you so very high," he added. He noted her "contagious enthusiasm" for the simple joys of life.

He told how she worked three jobs to put herself through college so she could send her Social Security checks home to help her widowed mother and two younger brothers. And how she would always tip waitresses well, recalling her own stints as a waitress. In her own community, Ellen was an active volunteer "for and with her daughter." Gary also described how Ellen held her family and friends "close to her heart" even if she hadn't spoken to them for a while.

He said how so many people had told him "how she was the nicest, kindest person" they had ever met. He described one man who had come to the wake purposely to tell the family that while he had only known Ellen briefly, six years earlier when he worked on her kitchen, she "was truly one of the nicest persons [he] had ever been touched by . . ."

Added Gary: "How amazing is that—how amazing for a comet named Ellen."

In closing, Gary spoke the words Ellen had written to comfort a friend who had lost her mother in 1980 at Christmas: "I suppose the only thing that can get one through this is remembering the true meaning of Christmas—love, unity amongst all men, warmth and generosity. All of this symbolizing a beginning for all those who believe."

He urged those who loved her to carry "her kindness, laughter, grace, enthusiasm, generosity, dignity and love forward in our hearts—through each day—for as long as we are alive."

Patty couldn't bear to go to the burial site, which was in Valley Forge Memorial Gardens, not far from their neighborhood. She thought she'd be imposing, so she went only to the church and slipped out while the service was concluding, and drove with a friend into the cemetery, where she spotted three open graves, one with the flowers she had seen earlier at the funeral. It was enough for her to know that Ellen's final resting place near a duck pond was peaceful and beautiful.

Some mourners elected not to go to the burial and others passed on going to the breakfast afterward at The Radnor Hotel. Mary Beth went, not because she cared about Robb, but because she wanted to make it clear that she was there for Olivia. She told Robb to call if he needed anything. Two days later, he did, telling Mary Beth that he had car trouble and Olivia needed a ride to school. Thankfully, Mary Beth's husband Drew was able to take her. Mary Beth couldn't bear to be alone with him in the car.

CHAPTER 16

December 30, 2006

The case was a pressure cooker for Marino and Gershanick. Not only was it a first-degree murder case, but Robb's status had triggered a lot of media attention. And the boss had decided to handle the case himself in a year when he was up for re-election. With Castor's public comments that Robb was not excluded as a suspect, the detectives knew it would only be a matter of time before they would have enough evidence to charge him. Their job was to fill in the details as best as they could and as quickly as they could. They wanted their statement of probable cause to leave no doubt.

As they looked at the demands of motive, a key task was to nail down whether the Robbs had been in the process of getting a divorce, and whether one of them was moving out of the house.

The Robbs had talked about it a lot, and even filed papers in 1993, but nothing had happened. Was this time any different?

Ellen had told her friends the divorce was happening, but Robb sidestepped it, telling police in his interrogation only that the couple had talked about it a lot, but not recently, and not specifically.

What he didn't tell them was that a divorce had been in the works, and he knew it. Within a couple of hours after Ellen was found murdered, her friends and family told detectives that she had seen a lawyer and was planning to get a divorce.

For starters, the detectives needed to establish how far along the divorce plans had gone.

Ellen's brother, Gary, and Mary Beth, Ellen's friend, were the first to tell them that Ellen had seen a lawyer and was planning to leave Robb around New Year's Day. Mary Beth recounted her telephone call with Ellen two days before her death, in which Ellen had said she was finally going through with the divorce they had talked about for the past five years. Ellen told her that Robb knew about the lawyer and about her hunt for a place to live.

She said his response was that she was "just being emotional because she was going through menopause," Mary Beth told Detective Godby.

As she left the Upper Merion police office, Mary Beth bumped into Gary. They embraced and shared their loss. "Call me," said Mary Beth. "Let me know if there is anything I can do to help."

Gary also confirmed the divorce plans, telling Detective Glauner that he had known all about their marriage and plans to divorce. He said the marriage had been bad for the past thirteen years, and really bad for the last ten.

Having that much allowed Marino and Gershanick to dig deeper.

As the lead detectives, they were primarily responsible for fitting the puzzle pieces together. Looking at their list of people to interview—some had come on their own, others had information they needed to get—the officers focused first on those who knew whether a divorce had been imminent. The detectives also knew what they saw. "We knew right away. There was no love lost there," recalled Marino, noting that the Robbs had separate bedrooms. "It was clear something was wrong with that family," added Gershanick.

Sharon Sellman, a neighborhood friend whose son was in Olivia's class at Roberts, called Gershanick and told him he had to get to Josh Bowden, a friend of Ellen's from Radnor High.

Bowden's story would give them their first clue into the

depths of the emotional and verbal abuse that Ellen had been enduring for years.

Bowden, who lived nearby in King of Prussia, had graduated a year ahead of Ellen, and had kept in touch with her with phone calls at least once a year. He'd last spoken to Ellen almost a year before she'd been killed. At that time, she'd told him she was a "shut-in" and her marriage was "not good."

"She told me she wishe[d] that he would move out," Bowden told Marino and Gershanick. "She said she wanted a divorce, but did not have the money to initiate it."

Asked if she'd said anything else about Robb, Bowden then added: "She said, 'If something ever happens to me, he should be considered a prime suspect.' I told her that she needed to get out of there."

"Why didn't Ellen move out?" Marino asked.

"She said she didn't have the financial means to leave the house."

Back in the car, the detectives knew they had a breakthrough. Six days after the murder and they had solid information that Ellen had feared Robb. And with every person they spoke with, they learned even more about the emotional struggle going on in the Robb household.

Their day included talking to two other women who had called them. They'd known Ellen and had phoned wanting to help in the investigation. The first stop was at the home of Cheryl Friend, who had moved away from the Forest Road neighborhood several years earlier to Worcester, a town farther north, but still in Montgomery County.

During the half-hour interview, Cheryl told the officers that she'd gotten to know Ellen when their daughters were in the same class at Roberts Elementary. Cheryl described Robb as being good to himself and Olivia, but not to Ellen. She said that Ellen had told her in 2001 about an incident in which Robb grabbed her by the jacket and ripped it. She also said that Robb "would throw food on the floor just to watch and make Ellen pick it up." Robb "would do anything to demean Ellen," including urinating in the bathroom sink, she told the detectives.

When asked if there was anything else she wanted to tell them, Cheryl said, "I know in my heart he did it. Ellen told me once that she thought Rafael would like nothing better than to take Olivia to Israel with him."

From there, they headed to Wynnewood to meet with Arlene Leib, a self-employed writer who said she had met Ellen two years ago when their daughters had gone to summer camp together. She recounted Robb's conversation with her at the viewing the night before, when he'd lamented that police considered him a suspect. She went on to say that "Rafael treated Ellen as a possession, and he could never give her any money. Rafael controlled Ellen with money."

Even thinking how a defense attorney would view those statements, the detectives knew they were getting somewhere. Robb referred to himself as a suspect and lamented that he lacked an alibi.

"I know we've got the right guy," Marino said as they took their seats around midday at Angelo's Pizza Company, in King of Prussia's Sweet Briar shopping center, which was well known for its tasty cheesesteaks. "Yeah," added Gershanick. "Everything is pointing to him."

Marino ordered his cheesesteak with American cheese and sauce, no onions; Gershanick wanted his with provolone, mushrooms and onions.

Their last stop for the day would hopefully nail the fact that Ellen was planning to move out of her home in January.

Marino got behind the wheel for the fifteen-minute ride to Devon to see John J. Murray, the Prudential Fox & Roach realtor who had shown both Rafi and Ellen a townhouse a short distance from their home, on Susan Drive in Upper Merion Township earlier in December.

Murray said he vividly remembered talking to the Robbs. Ellen told him they were getting a divorce, but it was unclear which of them would be moving out of their home.

Ellen first called the office after seeing a For Rent sign on the property a short distance from their home. The two-story townhouse, which had three bedrooms and 2 ½ baths, rented for $1,550 per month. Ellen met Murray at the townhouse on

Saturday, December 9 and toured it with him while she explained that she was getting a divorce and wanted it for herself and her daughter. She hesitated about making a decision. Murray asked her if there was any reason, since she seemed to like it.

"No, it's perfect," she told him.

But, shortly after, Ellen called Murray back and asked if he could show the townhouse to her husband, Rafael. When Murray asked her why, she told him it wasn't clear yet which one of them would be renting the property.

Murray said Ellen had told him that she liked the property and intended to rent it, but was concerned that with the holidays, January 1 would be too soon. She asked if she could start the lease on January 15.

Murray told her the leases start on the first of the month, but the unit was empty, so she could take her time over the following two weeks to move in.

"Oh, that sounds like a good idea," Ellen told him.

Ellen and Rafi had each separately told him they planned to make a decision very soon, Murray said.

In fact, he had tried to get Ellen to give him a decision on December 21, the day before she was murdered. Murray told her he wasn't going to be in the office, and if she decided about the lease, she should call him on his cell phone.

With the holidays, there was a lot going on, but she knew she needed to make a decision, Ellen told him.

As Marino and Gershanick drove back to the detective bureau, they went over what Murray had told them. "Another time when Robb was lying," Gershanick said, recalling Robb's statement to police the week before. Ellen obviously couldn't lease the townhouse unless he said yes. The monthly rent had to come from him.

Back at the office, they began to analyze what they had learned. Robb had obviously not told the detectives all he knew about the couple's plans to divorce. Money was turning out to be a main issue between them. It was becoming all too clear what Ellen's family and friends meant when they'd said Robb had controlled his wife with money.

There was something else. It was almost a standard question

in an investigation like this one. Was there any indication either that Robb was having an affair or that there was some other person involved in their marriage? The detectives were also acutely tuned to the possibility that perhaps Robb had hired someone to kill his wife. As they worked through all of the interviews, the detectives asked questions about both points. And, repeatedly, they came up empty, except on one occasion.

A neighbor told police on January 2 that when Olivia was a baby, Ellen had suspected that Robb had someone in Israel, because he went there for long stretches of time. The suspicion was never confirmed by anyone. As far as the police knew, there was no girlfriend or lover lurking in the background.

While Ellen's friends and family were telling detectives about the problems between the couple, Genovese was proclaiming Robb's innocence on national television. In an appearance on January 2 on Greta Van Susteren's *On the Record*, Genovese backed up Robb's alibi that he had gone to Penn, e-mailed a colleague and stopped for a soda the morning Ellen was killed. "And, unfortunately, when he got home, he made the discovery of his wife's body and immediately called the authorities."

And when Van Susteren pushed on the reports of a pending divorce, Genovese repeated what he had been telling the Philadelphia media, that divorce was an old story between Ellen and Rafael. Ellen had filed back in 1993 "and then never went any further with it. So that's been hanging throughout for over a decade at this point."

Genovese made one claim that everyone acquainted with the couple knew could not be true. In an attempt to downplay problems in the marriage, Genovese emphasized that they did live in the same house together, "slept in the same bed together every night." They had a 12-year-old daughter "so for the sake of the family, they were trying to make things work."

He emphasized that Robb "had nothing to do with his wife's murder" and wasn't trying to establish an alibi in his travels the morning she was killed.

Castor's public plea for help was largely a bust. No witness emerged and those who knew Robb described the man detectives already knew: stoic, taciturn, reserved and controlling—especially toward his wife, although he clearly loved his daughter.

CHAPTER 17

January 3, 2007

How could Mrs. Robb be wrapping Christmas presents when she was murdered—*and* the last time her husband saw her?

Castor obviously enjoyed the question.

"You don't miss anything," he teased the reporter with a chuckle.

"The evidence says Mrs. Robb was murdered very shortly after he says he left her wrapping Christmas presents," Castor told the reporters. "It's a terrible coincidence for Dr. Robb if he's not the killer."

Six days after telling the press that Robb could not be excluded as Ellen's killer, Castor stood before them again to upgrade his status. Only this time, reporters got lots more, including a 19-page affidavit attached to a warrant asking that the court order Robb to submit fingerprint and DNA samples.

Reporters from every media outlet in the region squeezed into Castor's conference room on the fourth floor of the county courthouse for a press conference in a case that the district attorney described as being "of great public interest."

Castor opened by telling them that at 11 a.m. that morning, Robb had arrived with Genovese, his attorney, to give samples of DNA, blood and fingerprints.

His office had filed the search warrant and affidavit earlier that day for Robb to give up the samples, and Castor told the reporters he knew the information would become public.

While the warrant was routine, given the amount of blood at the scene, Castor knew that the filing would stir a lot of questions. And rather than talk to the reporters all individually over the next two days, he decided to make himself available to all of them at the same time.

Dressed in a gray pinstriped suit, crisp white shirt and purple dotted tie, Castor easily took questions for over an hour. He not only told the reporters a lot about the evidence the investigators had gathered, but indulged their questions about motive and even his possible prosecution strategies.

Flanked by First Assistant District Attorney Ferman and Assistant District Attorney Robert J. Sander, who would assume the second chair in the trial, Castor took the first question:

"Are you convinced Dr. Robb is the killer, and is he being evasive with the timelines to throw you off track?"

Castor paused before answering. "The evidence so far indicates very strongly, circumstantially, that Dr. Robb had some involvement in this killing. Circumstantial evidence is very good if there is enough of it. I am not convinced there is enough of it at this point to categorically say that I think Dr. Robb [committed] this murder."

By the end of the hour, however, Castor had described a web of suspicion spun by the evidence he did have. There was no doubt that the investigation was focused on Robb, and an arrest could happen soon.

But, first, Castor wanted Robb's samples to compare them to what had been found in the house, just to make sure that someone else couldn't have committed the murder. The forensic experts expected Robb's DNA to be in the house, since he lived there. Having his samples would give them a chance to exclude him as the killer.

As the reporters probed deeper about what he hoped the blood specimens would tell him, Castor moved them away from expecting a *CSI* ending to this investigation.

"I don't see the case being a forensic case. I see the case being a case that the skills of the investigator and the skill of the prosecutor hopefully will turn into a successful conclusion."

When asked what else he needed to make the case, Castor

ducked the question and returned to the subject of circumstantial evidence . . . "little pieces of evidence by themselves do not add up to a conviction, but when fit together like a jigsaw puzzle, create a picture of who did the crime and how it was done."

Castor revealed some of those details—evidence that he and the detectives found suspicious: Robb telling the dispatcher his wife's head was cracked, when veteran investigators looked at her and thought she had been shot; a timeline alibi that appeared to give him more than enough time to kill his wife and dispose of the weapon and bloody clothes before showing up at Penn, where he would be seen, photographed or time-stamped at various places, including getting a parking ticket; and a burglary in which nothing was stolen.

Castor did allow for the fact that the inside of the Robb house was cluttered and filled from floor to ceiling with all kinds of stuff, so that Robb might not know what was missing.

Castor dwelled on the psychiatrists' analysis that the person who attacked Ellen Robb was "trying to depersonalize her—wipe her off the map," not the act of a burglar who randomly picks a house on a quiet suburban street. "Mrs. Robb was targeted for murder," said Castor.

Castor called Robb's statement that Ellen's head was cracked a major point for him. "How can he know that if he's not the killer?" he asked out loud.

"It's similar to Guy Sileo knowing Jim Webb had been shot before we did," Castor reminded reporters of the famous local case—a decade earlier, almost to the day, December 26, 1996—concerning the shooting death of one restaurant partner and the conviction of the other for murder.

Despite telling reporters that the Robb case would not turn on forensics, Castor teased them by telling them that the interior of Robb's car had been searched.

"Did you find anything?"

"Yes."

"Blood?"

"Come on, David," he answered one of the reporters as

they all laughed at the suggestion that Castor may know something that he wasn't telling them.

Going public with the warrant also gave Castor an opportunity to aim squarely at the defense.

Castor said he had sent a letter to Robb and Genovese giving them the deadline of noon tomorrow to come up with the information.

"I was surprised to see Mr. Genovese on television and in the newspapers asserting Dr. Robb's innocence," Castor said, looking directly at the television cameras. "If he does have that evidence, he has until noon tomorrow to tell me about it, or we will make the next decision in this case."

And what was that?

"Whether he gets arrested or not."

Castor left no question that his sights were on Robb—and that he wasn't impressed with Robb's PhD or expertise in game theory—a discipline in which he analyzed strategy to determine how to take the most advantageous step.

"What I see developing here is a situation where a very bright man decided he was going to try to lead us down the wrong path. But remember, he's an amateur at this, and we are not. It may be we are going in the wrong direction and he didn't do it, but he is certainly making it look to us that he did."

He added: "He has motive and opportunity and I think, right now, he's got a great deal of explaining to do. I am willing to listen."

Anyone used to covering Castor saw the performance as vintage Bruce. Brash, confident and taking advantage of every opportunity.

Castor's deadline struck Genovese, who couldn't help picking up the phone and calling Castor. "I thought it was your job to prove my client was guilty, not my burden to prove his innocence," he told him. All Castor had to do was ask and Robb would have given him any samples he wanted, Genovese added.

But Genovese also recognized the strategy from his days in

Castor's office. The more paperwork you file, the more you can talk about what you have.

By the end of the evening, Genovese was barraged by reporters who wanted him to react to the evidence that the Montgomery County detectives had amassed against his client. He knew Robb was Castor's only suspect.

To Castor's challenge that he and Robb come forward with evidence, Genovese told KYW Newsradio's David Madden, "If there were, we would be the first to let Mr. Castor know about it. I guess, unfortunately for Dr. Robb, he's already told the investigators everything he knows."

Genovese was even more blunt to CBS 3: "He's professed his innocence to it. He told me he had nothing to do with the murder of his wife."

Castor's public theatrics around Robb were no surprise to Genovese, a former assistant district attorney who'd worked for Castor, and a veteran defense lawyer who focused his practice in Montgomery County, operating out of offices a block from the Norristown Courthouse.

When asked later to comment on Castor's remarks, Genovese told Margaret Gibbons of *The Times Herald*, the local Montgomery County newspaper, that the district attorney didn't have to file the warrant and detailed affidavit to get Robb to submit samples for DNA testing and palm- and fingerprints. Robb had been cooperating all along, and would have continued to do so.

"There are two sides to every story," Genovese said. "You can make something sound suspicious or nefarious, but that does not make it true."

Television cameras had earlier captured Robb and Genovese as they left the detective bureau at One Montgomery Plaza after Robb had given the required samples. Dressed casually and wearing a baseball cap, Robb made a first, brief public comment: "I'm just agitated. I prefer not to talk." When asked if he'd killed his wife, Robb replied, "No. No."

CHAPTER 18

January 4, 2007

As the Robb case heated up, Castor was also making plans for his own political future. After twenty-two years in the district attorney's office—two-thirds of it as the boss or the No. 2—he had decided to jump into county politics with a run for county commissioner. He had lost a 2004 Republican primary for state attorney general, but didn't lose his aspiration for political office, possibly even a statewide post. His first move was to step away from the district attorney's office and enter the fray.

On the same evening as the Robb press conference, Castor decided to run. He had reached out to Melissa Murphy Weber, an attorney who had formerly worked for him in the district attorney's office, to be his running mate. It was half-time at the Temple University basketball game when she called to tell him that she was in. She had been elected to the state House of Representatives in 2002, but lost her seat in 2004, and was now in private practice.

OK, they decided, they would run together.

Their next challenge was imposing their will on the county's Republican committee.

The race wasn't until November of 2007, but it wasn't too early in January for candidates to signal their interest. By the new year, there were already six potential candidates. Castor was ready to float his plan, not to run for re-election as district attorney, but to run for one of the three county commissioner jobs.

The three-member panel controls not only what occurs in Montgomery County, but the 3,300 jobs and millions in patronage contracts. In a story in the *Inquirer*, Castor told then–political reporter Carrie Budoff that he was "strongly exploring the possibility to run" for county commissioner.

Castor told her that a GOP majority in the county was threatened. "I see a train wreck developing in Montgomery County politics, and I am trying to do my best to stop it."

As Castor saw it, allowing the Democrats to take control of Montgomery County government not only threatened how the county functioned, but also threatened the financial support enjoyed by the DA's office and law enforcement in general.

As a lifelong Republican who came from a blue-blood family line of early Philadelphia leaders, Castor saw himself as the best candidate to lead the county government and hold back the encroachment of Democrats who had increasingly shown their political muscle in the suburbs around Philadelphia. Especially in races for governor and president, the suburbs had gone largely Democratic. And since he didn't care much for the two GOP incumbents already in office, Castor offered to campaign with his own running mate.

By releasing the political trial balloon, Castor unsettled the status quo. As Ken Davis, the county Republican chairman and a Castor opponent, told the *Inquirer*, "I don't know where it is going to lead. It's kind of a Pandora's box. Once you open it up, you don't know what is going to come out."

Davis said he was supporting the incumbents—Jim Matthews (brother of MSNBC's Chris Matthews) and Thomas Ellis—because of their "terrific records." He told the *Inquirer* that Ellis was electable despite his ex-fiancé's filing of a protection-from-abuse petition against him in 2004.

Ellis' legal problems with his ex-fiancé were exactly why Castor predicted that the Republican team would be trounced in November. As one of the county's top vote-getters, Castor figured he had a better feel for the electorate. The fact that he had done a good job as commissioner didn't matter. Ellis had no profile with the voters and, in a political race, the Democrats would define him by his personal troubles. It would be the first step in the party losing their stronghold in the county, Castor reasoned.

But the idea that Castor would walk away from the DA's office was unfathomable to many who worked for him and with him. He loved the work and had proven himself a highly successful prosecutor. Would he really be happy dealing with the minutiae of running a county, even the most populous suburban county in the state? Could he really walk away from being the county's most visible law enforcement officer?

And would he still run if he couldn't get his way on a running mate? Castor might succeed in pushing Ellis off the party's ballot, but what about Matthews? There was no love lost between the two of them, and a Castor–Matthews ticket would surely be a shotgun wedding. Just saying he was thinking about running set several political wheels in motion.

And that included Risa Ferman, who had to make her own plans. If Castor ran for county commissioner, she would be running for DA. She needed to shore up her own support among county Republicans so no one else could make a move to run. Castor had always told her he would give her first crack to succeed him. She just didn't think it would be so soon.

A change at the top wouldn't make a difference for Robb, however. Castor had already made it clear to Ferman that he would stay on to prosecute the case even if he was elected county commissioner. Ferman could always name him a special prosecutor. Robb would never be free of Castor, no matter what happened in November.

CHAPTER 19

January 4, 2007

The day after Castor fingered him as a suspect in his wife's murder, Robb had a return visit from "Tony Corelli," the alleged ex-con glass helper who came back to actually replace the glass on the back door.

Robb appeared glad to see him, and said he wondered if Tony would be returning. Corelli—Spagnoletti, actually—replied that they were there to finish the job, but that he too had been looking forward to seeing Robb again.

While the glazier readied his tools in the rear laundry room, Robb pulled Tony aside, telling him, "I found things missing and I reported them to my lawyer." Among the missing items were his wife's purse and the contents.

"That's a good thing," Tony said as Robb led him into his study, where he asked Tony questions about himself. From his years of undercover work, he not only had a name, but all of the identification to back it up, and a life story to go with it. There was a lot for them to talk about. "You can Google me and find me," Tony told Robb.

Tony got the conversation back to the burglary. "This looks bad for you," Tony said. "If you didn't report anything stolen, there was no other motive than to kill her. If there wasn't anything stolen in this house, it was a robbery that went bad. There's no such thing as a robbery and nobody takes anything.

"Listen very carefully here," Tony told him. "I read that your

Ellen Gregory and Michael Weaver at Stone Harbor on the New Jersey shore in 1973.

Courtesy of Becky Rector

Ellen and Rafael Robb at the 1991 wedding of Becky Weaver and Al Rector.

Photograph by The Photo Loft, Inc.

The Wayne, Pennsylvania, home of Ellen and Rafael Robb, where Ellen's body was found Friday afternoon, December 22, 2006. Investigators scoured nearby woods for evidence.

Photo by Michael S. Wirtz / The Philadelphia Inquirer

A memorial area created by Ellen Robb's friends with a wreath and flowers on the front lawn of the Robbs' home in Wayne, Pennsylvania. The sign says, "Ellen May You Be At Peace."

Photo by Michael S. Wirtz / The Philadelphia Inquirer

Ellen Robb's casket is moved at the end of her funeral on December 29, 2006, by pallbearers including her husband, Rafael Robb (second face from left).

Photo by Joseph Kaczmarek / Philadelphia Daily News

Dr. Rafael Robb arrives at an Upper Merion courthouse on January 8, 2007, to be arraigned for the first- and third-degree murder of his wife, Ellen, 49, while she was wrapping Christmas presents inside their Wayne home.

Photo by Ron Tarver / The Philadelphia Inquirer

Rafael Robb, pictured leaving the district magistrate after his arraignment. He is escorted by Upper Merion Detective David Gershanick, left, and Montgomery County Detective Drew Marino, right.

Photo by Alejandro A. Alvarez/ Philadelphia Daily News

Running a gauntlet of reporters, Rafael Robb leaves his hearing to go to Montgomery County prison, where he is being held without bail.

Photo by Ron Tarver / The Philadelphia Inquirer

Robb case prosecutors (left to right: Robert J. Sander, Montgomery County assistant district attorney; Bruce L. Castor, Jr., then district attorney, now county commisioner; Risa Vetri Ferman, then first assistant district attorney, now district attorney).

Photo by Joan Fairman Kanes

David Gershanick, Upper Merion police dectective, lead investigator.

Photo by Joan Fairman Kanes

Drew Marino, Montgomery County detective, lead investigator.

Photo by
Joan Fairman Kanes

Deputy Chief Samuel J. Gallen, Montgomery County Detective Bureau, Office of the District Attorney.

Photo by
Joan Fairman Kanes

Ellen Robb's brother, Gary Gregory, sits with her daughter, Olivia Robb (left), during ceremonies at Roberts Elementary School to dedicate a gazebo in her honor on Sept. 28, 2007.

Photo by Tom Gralish /
The Philadelphia Inquirer

The "Friends of Ellen" linger after ceremonies at Roberts Elementary School to dedicate the gazebo in honor of Ellen Robb, who was once named volunteer of the year at the school.

Photo by Tom Gralish / The Philadelphia Inquirer

Rafael Robb is led into a pretrial hearing at the Montgomery County Courthouse on Friday morning, Nov. 9, 2007.

Photo by David Swanson /
The Philadelphia Inquirer

Montgomery County Courthouse in Norristown, Pennsylvania, encircled by live broadcasting vans on Nov. 26, 2007, the date of Rafael Robb's guilty plea.
Photo by Rose Ciotta

Art Gregory (right), brother of Ellen Robb, and his daughter, Lauren, attend a memorial service at the gazebo named for Ellen outside Roberts Elementary School on Nov. 26, 2007, the day Rafael Robb admitted in court that he had beaten Ellen to death.

Photo by Michael Bryant /
The Philadelphia Inquirer

LuAnn Dubin, a friend of Ellen Robb's (right), reaches out to Lauren Gregory, Ellen's niece, after the memorial service held in Ellen's honor at Roberts Elementary School. The gazebo in the background was dedicated earlier in the year in Ellen's memory.

Photo by Michael Bryant /
The Philadelphia Inquirer

"Friends of Ellen" at an event to raise money for the gazebo that has been placed in Ellen's memory on the grounds of Roberts Elementary School in Wayne, Pennsylvania. (Left to right: Patty Volpi, Sharon Sellman, Mary Beth Pedlow, LuAnn Dubin)

Courtesy of
Mary Beth Pedlow

arrest is imminent," he added, referring to stories in all the media that day describing Robb as the suspect. The DA was coming for him.

"I can make bail," Robb responded. Robb didn't know that bail wasn't an option in a murder case.

"You're not going to make bail, not with Castor, you're not. This guy is not going to let you make bail. What you need to do, this has to happen again in the neighborhood." Tony told him he needed to take the suspicion away from himself.

"You mean kill somebody?"

"No, a house entry, a house robbery, burglary," Tony continued. "It doesn't have to be on the same street, but in a several-block area to make it look like this happened before."

"I don't know the first thing about that," Robb told him.

"You shouldn't be involved in it. Coming from where I am, I know people. This is what you have to do."

Robb looked at Tony and smiled.

"We should sit down and have a drink away from here. You're a neat guy," Robb told him. "I'd like to talk to you more."

When Robb asked how he could reach him again, Tony told him to call the glass company office and they would contact him. In both of his encounters with Tony, Robb said he worried about his daughter and what was going to happen to her. He never mentioned his wife.

Tony knew Robb was an expert in the art of strategy, of assessing what an adversary would do next.

Had Robb been playing mind games with him? He doubted it, but he never really knew.

One thing Tony did know. Robb had lied to him about reporting items stolen.

The list of items Robb told Tony he had come up with was never turned in to police.

Robb was Spagnoletti's final case, the last undercover job of his thirty-four-year career. He would be retiring in seven more days. He would have loved to have gone out with a murder confession to his credit. He begged Castor to let him go back in. He thought for sure he could get Robb to tell him what happened in that house on December 22.

Castor gave him one of his signature all-knowing smiles. He had worked with undercover guys long enough to know that they loved to keep the ruse going. What Spagnoletti had already gotten was helpful and was already being written by Assistant District Attorney Sander into the statement of probable cause that would have to be presented to the court to trigger Robb's arrest.

It was time to move on, Castor told him. There was enough tension over whether he would go for an arrest. Castor didn't want to risk that Robb would flee or get himself involved in other crimes.

Although Robb had turned in his American passport, he was also an Israeli citizen and could hold that country's passport.

Besides, what Castor really wanted from the undercover officers was their assessment. They were experts at reading people. Was Robb their guy?

"No doubt," they told him. "You have the right guy."

Before any arrest, however, also on January 4, Robb's brother-in-law Gary would make one last try at getting Robb to talk.

For a visit to Robb's home—and a return to the same place where his sister had been brutally murdered—Gary agreed to wear a police wire for a second time. The otherwise quiet Forest Road had become a gathering place for television vans. The police were there too in an undercover van parked around the corner. They were set up to listen as Gary made his way inside the home.

Gary told Robb that he had seen the news and it looked like he was going to be arrested. He appealed to Robb to think about Olivia and what she needed. She had already lost her mother. Did she have to lose her father too? Gary was willing to help him. But, first, they had to get their stories straight on what happened on December 22.

Robb gave up nothing. He walked Gary around the house, describing for him what he'd seen when he arrived home. He talked about how much he loved and cared for Olivia, but he never admitted to Gary that he had killed Ellen. Gary had gotten no further with Robb than the week before when he'd met him in the hotel parking lot with the police watching.

On both occasions, Robb had been careful not to say anything that would implicate him in the murder.

For Gary, the effort got him no closer to knowing who had killed his sister, but at least he had tried to help; he had done something that the police could not do without him. Castor wasn't disappointed. He had agreed to try it, even though he didn't expect much from it. It couldn't hurt.

By all outward signs, Robb was trying to get back to his routine. Robb and Olivia had returned to the Forest Road home, and a CBS 3 camera, in what it labeled "exclusive video," showed Robb wearing a parka jacket and cap arriving there in his BMW and driving it into the upper driveway. He got out of the car to pull up the garage door. He then drove the car into the garage before closing it from the inside.

Later that night, the case again caught the interest of Greta Van Susteren's *On the Record* only this time she quizzed Gordon Glantz, the managing editor of *The Times Herald* in Norristown. Once she got caught up on the day's developments, she asked about Robb.

"Do you know where he is?"

"He's at home," said Glantz. "He's in his home. He's been seen in his neighborhood walking his dog around. Their twelve-year-old daughter is, from what I'm told, home and back at school, and everybody is behaving normally, right now. He had until twelve o'clock today to come back to the courthouse with his lawyer and present anything counter to what the DA presented yesterday, and he did not show up and do that. And that's where we are right now."

Van Susteren then asked for an update on reports that Robb had hidden money.

Glantz recounted what was contained in the affidavit—that when Ellen had told her daughter of the pending divorce, she had said that they would be getting a lot of money from Robb that he kept in overseas accounts.

In her rapid-fire style, Van Susteren asked whether he was

still working at Penn (no one would comment and it was between semesters) and whether the murder weapon had been found.

"No murder weapon was found. It's been described as a cylindrical object of some kind. It has not been found," Glantz told her national audience.

Genovese also made Robb's case later that night (January 5) on CNN's Court TV, hosted by Nancy Grace, who, in her opener, bluntly described the world's fascination with the case: "Tonight, the Ivy League, the worldwide gold standard for education excellence, a highly respected Ivy League professor literally living in his ivory tower, pulling down nearly a quarter of a million dollars a year. One little problem—his wife found bludgeoned to death in their upscale home, and police say the killer took the time to stage the scene, posing it like a movie set. Now, let's see. Who would do that?"

She played a video clip in which Robb was interviewed by a television reporter as he came out of the courthouse two days earlier: "I'm just agitated. I prefer not to talk."

The reporter said, "The police think you killed your wife. Did you kill your wife?"

"No. No."

"Absolutely not?"

"Not."

Grace also opened the telephone lines for callers to ask about specific pieces of evidence. One wanted to know why Robb had called the ten-digit police number instead of 911.

Genovese took it on. "There has been some confusion about that. I think the latest I had heard was that he may have called a local police number, and that may very well be because, you know, he knew that number from living in the township for a number of years. So that wouldn't surprise me, if he called the police as opposed to 911."

Grace wanted to know why Robb had told the police he'd gone up to his bedroom and put down his laptop computer after seeing his wife bludgeoned on the floor.

Genovese explained that Robb's "first concern after seeing his wife, above and beyond calling the authorities, was for his daughter's safety. That's why he went upstairs to check the bedrooms, just to make sure that she hadn't come home and something had happened to her, as well. So that's why he went upstairs. He did have the laptop and the briefcase with him when he went in the house, put them down upstairs and came back down the stairs after checking on his daughter to make sure she wasn't home. And that's when he called the authorities."

Responding to various questions, Genovese said Robb had been cooperative, giving police a lengthy statement and permission to search his home, car and office. When Grace pushed him on why Robb had gone through the garage to his car to get his phone after finding his wife's body, Genovese, the former prosecutor, continued to defend Robb.

"Well, I think you have to put yourself in his shoes and you also have to remember if you put ten people in that situation, presented with the circumstances that he found, you'd probably have ten different reactions. So I think, while the DA is trying to make his actions look suspicious, not everyone reactions [sic] the same way under the same circumstances. . . .

"And that he walked through the garage to get his car, I don't find that unusual, certainly not suspicious enough to charge him with murder."

Later that night, Van Susteren took up the Robb case again on her program and quizzed Genovese, asking when he learned that Robb was a suspect.

Genovese said he learned it from Castor's press conference, but that was no surprise. "We had been operating under the assumption from the beginning of the investigation that he was the prime suspect."

Van Susteren responded that she was perplexed by Castor's moves. Police usually don't name someone as a suspect until they are ready to make an arrest, for fear they would flee. "Any sort of thoughts why he sort of made a public statement and your client's not under arrest tonight?"

Robb was home and free, Genovese told her. "And I am probably as perplexed as anyone as far as the district attorney's comments and what he said during the press conference and the fact that he still has yet to make an arrest in this case. I am frankly a little bit surprised at all the information he's released to this point without there being an arrest."

That day, as Marino and Gershanick were back at Angelo's for a quick lunch between interviews, Marino gave his partner a heads-up: "I know how he works," he said, talking about Castor. "He isn't going to let this go on much longer." Robb's arrest would happen any day.

The reporters also knew the case was heating up and took any opportunity to get comments from Robb. The latest report aired on Fox News where Rick Leventhal point blank asked Robb while he was walking his dog near his home, whether he'd killed his wife. Robb responded, "No, I did not. I did not kill her."

When the detectives from both Upper Merion and the county gathered in the roll call room with Castor on January 5, the group—all thirty of them—knew this could be their final meeting.

Gallen, with Marino and Gershanick, were at center stage reporting on what the group had come up with, especially over the last few days, to nail Robb's motive. He'd definitely feared losing his money and his daughter in the divorce. They painted a portrait of Robb as a cold, uncaring husband who had been mentally abusing his wife.

When it came to the physical evidence, the detectives explained what they had suspected: There were no one else's prints found inside the house. The DNA and fingerprint samples matched Robb's. The one blood sample they did have had come from Robb's hands the day of the murder.

When Finor had tested Robb's hands for gun residue, he also found a spot of blood in the web of the right hand. The blood tested as Ellen's, and explained to them why Robb had repeatedly said that he'd touched his wife's face with his hand. Nothing at the scene supported Robb's story that a burglar had broken in—the door glass hadn't even been stepped on, and nothing was taken.

"There was another one I need to tell you about," Marino began, referring to an interview the day before with Becky Rector, a high school teacher at Lenape Regional in Medford, New Jersey, who told him that she had called Ellen to invite her to her 50th birthday party, but she'd refused to go because she said her husband had given her a black eye. "She said Rafael treated her terribly," Becky told Marino, and it had been going on for about ten years.

However, Marino told Castor to be careful. They'd talked to scores of people and she was the only one who claimed that Robb had hit Ellen. When she'd first called, she gave the police leads on others to talk to. She then called again to talk about the black eye, claiming she had told Gershanick, but he said she had never mentioned it. The discrepancy in her story left Marino and Gershanick wary about her as a witness. In the end, never having seen the black eye herself, Becky could only talk about what she said Ellen had told her.

Becky insisted that she had told the police all about her long talk to Ellen, during which she had tearfully described her husband's abuse.

"I did tell them," she said, recalling how she had placed the call from Texas, where she was visiting family. "If they didn't write that down, they made a mistake." The police had recorded her information. They just couldn't verify it anywhere, making it unlikely that Becky would ever get to testify about it.

When it looked like they had covered it all, Castor, looking around the room, put out the question: "Is there anybody here who thinks we shouldn't arrest him?" No one said anything. "Is there anybody here who doesn't think he did it?"

Silence . . . except for Saville.

While he too believed Robb was the killer, Saville advised Castor to hold off just a little while until they completed the last round of testing. They already had Robb's samples— swabs for DNA, blood, and prints—and the lab was working overtime to get everything tested. They promised to have them back first thing Monday morning. "Let's just make sure there wasn't someone else in that house," Saville told him. He wanted to be extra careful that Robb hadn't hired someone to murder his wife. Castor agreed. The last thing he needed was to arrest the wrong man.

"OK," said Castor. . . . They set up to make the arrest on Monday, January 8, 2007. If the tests showed something to stop that, Saville would get in touch with him right away.

Marino turned toward Gershanick and whispered, "See, I told you."

They were all on board. The arrest was just a matter of time. Assistant District Attorney Sander went over all of the paperwork needed. The statement of probable cause would get one final update based on the information presented at the meeting. It was essentially the same information contained in the affidavit submitted to the court directing Robb to turn over samples of his DNA and fingerprints.

The probable cause document would have more information, based on final interviews and the last undercover visit by Tony Spagnoletti in his guise as a glazier.

Writing the document was a group effort and contained sections authored by Castor, Ferman, Sander and Nilsen—the detective who'd gone to law school while a Lower Merion detective, and was now also a sworn special assistant district attorney.

It was Friday. If all went as expected with the blood tests, the arrest would happen on Monday. But that information, Castor reminded everyone, was only for the people in that room.

On Sunday night, Gershanick called Ellen's brother, Gary, and spoke to his wife, Kim, alerting her to come for Olivia.

On Monday morning at 9 a.m., Saville called Castor. "It's all her blood. We don't have a third party here. We got the results we thought we were going to get. He was our guy."

CHAPTER 20

January 5–7, 2007

Tongues were wagging in Chicago. Robb and his pending murder charges became the topic of hot gossip when the world's leading economists met January 5–7, 2007, in Chicago. While Castor was laying out the gruesome details of how Robb had become the primary suspect in his wife's murder, Robb's colleagues from around the world were making their way to the Chicago Hyatt Regency.

For three days, the world's brightest minds in economics get together every year to share research papers and make presentations on a wide variety of subjects—everything from school performance to the history of money to whether working women are good for marriage. Robb had attended in the past and even presented on his own research.

But not this year.

Those who knew him couldn't help talking about the sorry state of his life since his wife's gruesome murder. While he was still a free man, the district attorney had set his sights on him, fingering him publicly as his primary suspect. That news, delivered to the press by Castor two days before the session, had instantly made its way around the world. Network television and newspapers worldwide reported on Robb, the Ivy League scholar who the prosecutor suspected of bludgeoning his wife to death and trying to pass it off like a burglary. If there was ever a man-bites-dog story, this was it. The idea that

Robb, a quiet academic respected by peers around the world, was suspected of killing his wife made no sense to anyone who knew him.

While he studied several areas of economics, Robb's primary interest was game theory, the study of decision-making. Economists use it to predict consumer behavior, military experts to develop nuclear war strategies. It's all about predicting what parties will do in strategic situations. It can be simple, like competitors setting prices, or complex, like countries waging war. Game theory gained prominence in 1950 through John Forbes Nash, Jr., a Princeton economist whose brilliance and struggle with schizophrenia was the subject of the book and movie *A Beautiful Mind*. Nash won a Nobel Prize in 1994 for his pioneering work in game theory as a graduate student. His work is regarded as central to the theory of games. In 2007, three other economists won for advancing the field of mechanism design theory, which stems from game theory. Their work aims to build better social structures, such as designing an economic system that results in clean air.

Robb was no John Nash, but his work in evolutionary game theory is known by other game theorists and studied by graduate students in game theory across the country. Dr. David Levine, a game theorist who teaches at Washington University in St. Louis, spends several classes on Robb's work when he teaches his graduate students the fundamentals of game theory. Robb's research has even had an impact on Levine's own research.

Robb's work was "very influential," added Dr. Roberto Serrano, a game theory expert at Brown University in an e-mail. He said he and others have been able to use the tool laid out in a paper Robb co-authored in 1993 to refine predictions in different problems. Robb's paper, "Learning, Mutation and Long Run Equilibria in Games," was written with George J. Mailath, now the chair of the Economics Department at the University of Pennsylvania and Michihiro Kandori from Tokyo, and published in the journal *Econometrica*. It has since been cited by over 200 other papers. Mailath, in an e-mail, described Robb as a "full and equal partner in that research."

One of Robb's last working research papers was also on game theory. In the last version, circulated on Dec. 15, 2006, and titled, "Long-Term Relationships as Safeguards," written with Huanxing Yang from Ohio State University, they study a prisoners' dilemma game in which individuals interact with varying partners over time.

Economists aren't big on writing books, but they do share their research by writing papers that are published in scientific journals. The papers with the highest value are those that are judged by other experts who determine whether the research adds to what is already known in that field. A measure of Robb's fame in his field was the papers he published. In the twenty-five years since he had gotten his doctorate from UCLA, Robb had authored or co-authored more than fifty academic papers, including at least thirty published in refereed journals.

His name appears in the world's most prestigious economic journals. At Penn, he was also listed as faculty at the CARESS—Center for Analytic Research in Economics and the Social Sciences—and published by the Penn Institute for Economic Research, a joint research institute of economics in the university's College of Arts & Sciences and The Wharton School. His co-authors were scholars from universities around the world: Israel, Brazil, Japan, Germany and France, to name a few.

In addition to game theory, Robb studied economic issues in consumer behavior, organizations and pricing. His résumé—since removed from the Penn website—listed his field areas as: game theory, industrial organization, law and economics, public economies.

One of his most recent studies, with Wharton Professor Dr. Joel Waldfogel, found that the more students at Penn download music, the less they buy CDs. Most of Robb's work is a lot more dense than that, however. A look at the titles of his papers offers a glimpse into the world in which Robb spent much of his time: "Product Innovations and Quality-Adjusted Prices"; "Social Capital, Corporate Culture and Incentive Intensity"; "The Growth and Diffusion of Knowledge"; and his first published paper in 1981, "A Condition Guaranteeing the Optimality of Public Choice."

Beginning in 1984 and over the next twenty-two years, Robb was also awarded $656,527 in six grants from the National Science Foundation to carry out his research. A 1989 award for $51,536 allowed Robb to study the investment decisions of firms in industries where new products are introduced; another for $93,780 in 1992 to study why spending money on research and development results in physical investments and another in 1998 which examined human relations in the workplace and how they affect the performance of firms.

His largest continuing grant gave him $264,493 in government funding from July 1, 2000, until June 30, 2006, to study the effects on companies, workers and the growth of a country by so-called distortions such as taxes and tariffs. He credited it with funding the research for his newest work in game theory.

The sad reality for Robb was that his professional life and his home life were tragically out of sync. As his marriage fell apart, Robb's professional life blossomed with foreign sabbaticals, published papers and recognition for his important work. His 1993 paper was published in the same year that he and Ellen each saw lawyers to get a divorce. While they reconciled, their marriage never got back on track.

Robb was also well known and well regarded as a teacher, leading him to accept invitations to teach and lecture at universities around the world. And he was also in demand as a consultant for companies and governments worldwide, including the Federal Reserve Bank in Philadelphia.

As homicide suspects go, Rafael Robb was nothing like the killers the Montgomery County detectives were used to dealing with.

During one of their brainstorming meetings, Gallen wrote down "Game Theory" on his to-do list. With Robb as their primary suspect, they needed to understand better who he was and what made him tick. It became Marino's job to do the digging, which began with the Penn website, where he easily came across Robb's take-home final for his graduate course in game theory. Marino read the exam and shook his head. Perhaps it made sense to economics students, but not to him. Given Robb's intellect and specialty, the detectives couldn't help but wonder if Robb was playing games with them. Why had he been so cooperative answering their questions and taking them on a tour of the house? Perhaps he wanted to keep track of what they knew? It looked to them like Robb was trying to outsmart them and lead them astray. Or was he trying to figure out his next move in a scheme to get away with murder?

Robb's expertise as a game theorist wasn't lost on Castor who told reporters he figured Robb deliberately tried to lead prosecutors astray.

Castor started from the premise that Robb had killed his wife in a rage and set out to create an alibi for himself. "Now she's dead, now his game theory mind kicks in and now he's going to concoct and create a false trail for the police to follow, and concoct and create an alibi for himself, and that's why we think he went to various places to make sure that he'd be on camera and make sure he'd be here, and there are records so he could prove chunks out of the day where he was and was not available to commit the murder."

The first thing detectives did was check out Robb's alibi. He had gone to the Penn campus—security tapes confirmed that, and his parking ticket proved his car had been moved from the ramp to the street space in front of the Wawa store, where security cameras again caught him buying a soda. What none of the records could explain, however, was whether Robb's moves were planned to create an alibi for his whereabouts on the morning of December 22, 2006.

CHAPTER 21

January 8, 2007

Castor arranged it with Genovese.

Robb would show up about noon at the Upper Merion police station to turn himself in. The media, which had also been alerted to a Castor press conference at 12:15 p.m. that day at the county courthouse a couple of miles away, covered their bets and also had cameras poised at the police building.

The image captured by photographers and videographers would be transmitted all over the world: Robb going into the one-story brick building and coming out in handcuffs, flanked by Detectives Marino and Gershanick, who each took him by an arm. Wearing jeans and a blue dress shirt, and sporting a black outdoor jacket with brown sleeves, Robb was holding between his fingers the black knit cap that he usually wore on his balding head. Wire-rim glasses sat atop his nose. His sneaker-clad feet were in shackles; his hands were cuffed in front and clipped to a leather belt around his waist. He would be taken to district justice offices nearby in King of Prussia for arraignment before being taken to the Montgomery County Correctional Facility to await the next step in the case.

In the district attorney conference room at the courthouse, in a move that had the feeling of being an anticlimax, Castor formally announced to the press assembled that Robb had been arrested and charged with first- and third-degree murder along with weapons possession, tampering with evidence and making a false report. If convicted, he faced life in prison without parole.

Flanked by Ferman and Sander, Chief of Detectives Oscar Vance and, from Upper Merion, Lieutenant James Early and Chief Ronald Fonock, Castor opened: "We are here to announce that a warrant of arrest has been issued for Rafael Robb." He was in custody and would be arraigned later that day.

Castor didn't mince words. "The efforts to throw police off were amateurish," he said, accusing Robb of staging a burglary to hide his wife's hideous murder.

"What has changed between now and last week?" a reporter asked Castor. Referring to the 24-page arrest warrant, Castor said there were many new details and cited the fresh evidence supplied by the undercover narcotics officer's encounter with Robb. By the second visit, he had Robb saying that he had drawn up a list of items missing from his house. This after the officer working undercover as a glazier had told Robb that police would finger him as the killer if he continued to say that nothing was taken.

Castor explained: "Clearly, we believe there is no burglary and this was showing consciousness of guilt by endeavoring to cover up for the burglary." Another significant development was Castor's receipt of a supplementary report from Drs. Michals and Samuel, a forensic psychiatrist and psychologist, respectively, in which they described their view "that Robb was threatened by his wife in so far as she was going to hurt him financially in the divorce and also hurt his relationship with his child," Castor said. "In their opinion, the brutal attack, the depersonalizing of the victim, fit within the theory, the parameters they set forth, that this was an attack designed to punish somebody who was threatening him."

Dressed in a crisp deep blue pinstriped suit, white shirt and red-and-gold–patterned tie, Castor dramatically acted out what he was accusing Robb of doing: Ellen Robb had been wrapping Christmas presents when Robb came from behind with a long crowbar-like object and smashed her skull. She reeled as he continued to swing at her, smashing her fingers as she tried to protect herself. The blows continued after she fell to the floor, spattering blood all over the kitchen.

Robb had told the truth about being home when his wife was wrapping Christmas presents, and about going to his office at the University of Pennsylvania. He'd lied about what happened in between, Castor told reporters.

With that, Castor took a series of questions that laid out most of the details of his circumstantial case against Robb: calling a ten-digit number for police and not 911; glass from a broken window had not been trampled on; the family dog, locked in a bedroom; and the details of Robb's alibi—that he was in Philadelphia—failing to clear him.

That the couple kept separate bedrooms wasn't so far out of the ordinary. Ellen Robb had reached the point where she couldn't take it anymore, and had arranged for someplace to live; she'd had some idea of the money she was going to get. "I don't think the living arrangements in and of themselves are suspicious, but it certainly was coming to an end."

Asked if the killing was premeditated, Castor drew a long breath and declared it a "closer call." Technically and legally, Robb's actions were premeditated, since the decision to kill her could have been made in a split second while he was swinging the crowbar-like object repeatedly over her face. But the "sloppiness" with which he came up with an alibi indicates to him that "maybe it was not planned way in advance" and "all of this was an afterthought to throw police off the case."

One reporter asked whether Robb, the expert in game theory, had outsmarted himself.

"He might have," Castor said. "He's an amateur at this sort of thing. Let's remember, he's assumed to be innocent. The evidence suggests there's probable cause he committed this killing. . . . We do this all of the time . . . His efforts to throw police off the case were amateurish."

Asked to comment on the victim, Castor noted the horrible timing of the killing: "What really struck me is the wrapping of Christmas presents; how ironic that in the Christmas season, when peace on earth and good will and all that stuff is the order of the day, this brutal attack occurs. This child is never going to think about Christmas in the same way, because Christmas is when her mom was taken from her." Castor described Ellen as a devoted mother who hosted Brownie meetings "and drove her around and make her look pretty, the sorts of things mothers and daughters do.

"This is a very, very sad case'. Those of us who do this for a living . . . here we have somebody to go get. It's a great motivating thing when we have a terrible tragedy like that [and] we can try to bring some measure of justice to this young girl."

Reporters told the DA that neighbors had been horrified to learn that Olivia was back in her home, living with her father. Castor said she'd spent time in a hotel with her uncle right after the murder, but had requested to return home with her father. Castor didn't think Olivia would be in any danger. All evidence pointed to Ellen as the target of the killing.

At about the same time as Castor was speaking, Detective Peffall was at the Upper Merion Middle School asking to see seventh grader Olivia Robb. This would be Peffall's fourth meeting with her since the murder. After telling school authorities why he was there, the young girl was called out of her classroom and escorted to the school's conference room.

"Olivia, I have to ask you a few more questions about your mom's death," Peffall told her. "I am showing you a picture. Is this your mom's pocketbook?"

"Yes," the child answered, closing one more door on Robb's story that a burglar had broken into their home. What Olivia didn't know was that police had found her mother's purse out in the open and undisturbed in their home. They just needed to make sure that it had belonged to Ellen Robb.

As he had in his prior visits with Olivia, Peffall was struck by how little she said, and by her lack of emotion. It was as if she didn't quite understand that her mother was dead.

"Does Copper [the family dog] have free run in the house?"

"Yes, most of the time."

Castor dominated the news and the airwaves for most of the day. Even though the story moved from the county seat in Norristown to South Henderson Road in King of Prussia where the district justice held Robb's arraignment, Castor and the case he outlined against Robb were at the center of the stories in print, broadcast and online.

Robb faced a string of charges: first- and third-degree murder, violation of Pennsylvania Crimes Code Section 2502 (a) & (c); Section 907, possessing instruments of crime; Section 4906 (a) (1) & (2), false reports to law enforcement authorities; Section 4904 (a) (1), unsworn falsification to authorities; and Section 4910 (1), tampering with or fabricating physical evidence.

When Robb's attorney, Francis Genovese, finally got his chance, he told reporters they would fight the charges. Just because the Robbs were getting divorced doesn't mean his client wanted his wife dead.

Robb looked bewildered as he entered the courtroom wearing jeans, sneakers and a black wool jacket. He carried a black wool cap.

The proceeding before District Justice William Maruszczak was pretty routine. Pennsylvania law does not allow for bail in a murder case, so Robb pleaded not guilty. During the appearance Robb gave his Social Security number, height, weight and home phone number. Otherwise, he sat silently and displayed no emotion.

After the judge read the charges against him, he looked at Genovese and asked, "Where am I going now?" Genovese didn't answer as Robb was led by police to the Montgomery County Correctional Facility, where he became inmate #07-0178.

Castor had already indicated that he didn't think that the murder met the aggravating standards required by Pennsylvania law to make it a death penalty case. If convicted of first-degree murder, Robb faced life in prison without parole.

Once proceedings ended, Gershanick lingered in the courtroom. He was standing near Genovese as the defense attorney thumbed through the arrest warrant and noticed the section on the undercover work. Genovese shook his head. He knew Spagnoletti. He had worked cases with him as an assistant district attorney and knew how good he was at getting people to trust him. He also knew that DA Castor's office was capable of doing something like this—sending someone in under-cover to get Robb to talk.

"I told him [Robb] not to talk to anybody," Genovese said out loud. "The locksmith and glass guy . . . aren't they any-body?" Genovese shook his head and walked away.

To the media, Genovese sent a jab at Castor and began lay-ing the groundwork for what he expected would become part of Robb's defense: "I was expecting I would see more hard evidence—maybe forensic evidence—come before pointing to Dr. Robb as the killer," he told the Associated Press.

Despite what Castor argued was a compelling body of in-criminating information, Robb maintained his innocence. "He had nothing to do with his wife's death," Genovese told the *Inquirer*.

Robb himself commented to NBC News, which aired it the next morning on the *Today* show: "I did not kill my wife. I think the police is [sic] doing their job, but they don't have a second suspect, so right now they are just focusing on me. As far as finding a second suspect, I have no suggestions. I'm not in the law enforcement business. I don't know about it."

With Robb safely in county jail, Castor joined Greta Van Susteren on her program that evening to talk about the case.

Asked about Robb's alibi, Castor said they were able to corroborate some of it—the time he spent at Penn—but none of that mattered because police figure Robb had killed his wife around 8:30 in the morning and left her dead on the floor.

Castor also described how it could be that bloody footprints were found going out from the kitchen and into the garage, where they stopped. "What we theorize happened is that the killer, after doing the deed, went through the house, going out a different door than the one that was set up to look like a bur-glary. And took off all the bloody clothes and shoes and what-not, and put them in something, along with the murder weapon, and eventually disposed of it."

Back in Upper Merion, Ellen's friends were relieved that police had finally fingered Robb as the killer. "While today's news bring[s] some measure of relief, it doesn't bring her back," Susan Gay told the *Philadelphia Daily News*. Gay's daughter had been in Olivia Robb's class.

Friends paid their respects around a memorial in the front yard of the Robb home with a sign that read, "ELLEN MAY YOU BE AT PEACE, LOVE YOUR FRIENDS."

But a police officer interrupted them to clear everyone away from the home. Olivia was going to stay with her mother's family and needed to return home to get some clothes. They asked that no one be around the house when she arrived.

In Israel, Robb's mother's neighbors in Jerusalem recalled his visits two or three times annually. His father was deceased and his mother continued to live in the family apartment. His sister, Ruth, also lived in Jerusalem.

Betya Moag, a neighbor who'd lived in the building for forty years, recalled Robb as "just a normal boy." She told the *Inquirer*'s Ned Warwick: "When I heard about it on the television, I was shocked."

Another neighbor described Robb as ordinary. "If his mother had not told me he was a professor, I would never have known it."

Despite the intense publicity, the University of Pennsylvania wouldn't talk about Robb or the charges except to say that someone else would be taking over his classes for the spring semester, which had begun the day he was arrested. He was a tenured professor in the university's College of Arts & Sciences, and doctoral students he had been advising would work with other faculty. He would remain on the payroll until the case was decided.

When the students returned to campus, they were welcomed with a story in *The Daily Pennsylvanian* giving them a timeline explanation of what they had missed while they were away for winter break.

The final entry: A professor who, before this murder, enjoyed a solid reputation on campus as an economist and teacher, was now behind bars.

When the campus daily asked whether Robb's case would hurt Penn's reputation or its ability to attract top faculty and students, university spokeswoman Phyllis Holtzman put it like this: "We're probably the size of a small city . . . and I think that every now and then, difficult situations happen."

But Robb wasn't Penn's only problem. Over the same year, the university had endured the headlines of two other professors brought up on sex-related charges. *Inquirer* reporter Melissa Dribben went back to 1994 and counted five disgraced faculty, including Robb. The two most recent: Tracy McIntosh, an internationally known brain-trauma specialist, had been sentenced in early 2008 to $3\frac{1}{2}$ to 7 years in jail for sexually assaulting a 23-year-old graduate student, the niece of a friend who had asked him to show her around campus. McIntosh assaulted the woman in 2002 after an evening of dinner and drinking that left her vomiting in the street. He took her back to his office, where prosecutors said he gave her marijuana and accosted her while she was barely conscious. He was charged with rape and related crimes, but later pleaded no contest to a lesser count of sexual assault.

In sending him to jail, Common Pleas Court Judge Pamela Pryor Dembe pilloried McIntosh for his pattern of sexually harassing women who worked for him. "I can think of no circumstance in which it was appropriate to victimize a child who was the next best thing to a relative," Dembe told McIntosh. "It was breathtaking in its vileness. It was vile. You went so far beyond the pale."

What made the McIntosh case so notorious in Philadelphia, was that it had actually taken two judges to get a jail sentence for him. A judge in 2004 had given him $11\frac{1}{2}$ to 23 months of house arrest, partly because of his reputation and research in treating brain injuries; but Philadelphia District Attorney Lynne Abraham appealed to a state court, which threw the sentence out as too lenient.

And retired Wharton Marketing Professor L. Scott Ward pleaded guilty in early 2007 in a federal courtroom in Virginia to a federal charge of producing child pornography in Brazil. He also admitted to videotaping children engaging in sexual acts. He was arrested at Dulles International Airport on a return flight from Brazil for excessive trips overseas. Authorities confiscated three mini DVDs of the professor performing sex acts with teenage boys, according to court documents. He was sentenced to fifteen years in federal prison for trafficking in child pornography.

Ward retired from Penn on July 1, 2005.

But he had continued on the Wharton faculty despite earlier cases.

He was convicted in Montgomery County in 1999 of two misdemeanor charges of propositioning an undercover state trooper who was posing as a 15-year-old, and sentenced to five years of probation and a $2,500 fine. Ward was acquitted in a 1995 trial in Montgomery County of charges stemming from accusations of a teenager who said Ward molested him six years earlier when the boy was thirteen.

Dribben asked: "Does Penn attract bad eggs, or just suffer the image problem when a rotten one splats on its public face?"

Referring to Robb, Neil Jokelson, a Philadelphia lawyer, told Dribben: "The anomaly of someone in such an exalted position doing what he's accused of doing perhaps accounts for the public fascination. If it was an ordinary guy, it would be just another wife-killing."

In reality, while Robb's arrest was tragic for him, it had no lasting impact on the rest of the 4,000-member faculty. It also did nothing to dampen student interest in one of the world's most elite universities.

CHAPTER 22

Ellen

With Robb arrested, the detectives continued working the case, trying to piece together the puzzle of the couple's life.

Ellen and Rafael Robb obviously had very different interests and personalities. What had brought them together, and what had driven them apart? The answers could elaborate on the motive for Ellen's murder.

Ellen Gregory's upbringing was far from Ivy League or even the Main Line. Ellen was born in Syracuse, New York, but grew up in a middle-class neighborhood in Rosemont which is partly in Radnor and partly in Lower Merion. Her heritage was Italian and Irish: Italian from her father, Arthur, and Irish from her mother, Mary Janette Bankhead Gregory. In a lot of ways, Ellen's childhood was very ordinary for a girl born in 1956, except for one major event—the sudden death of her father, 36, when she was a little girl while he was working for an American company in Bogotá, Colombia. Because of his work, the family moved first to Ann Arbor, Michigan, and then to Bogotá.

As the oldest of three, Ellen took on motherly responsibilities to help her widowed and sickly mother, but she always missed her father. Even in high school, she idolized him. When her teenage friends complained about their fathers, Ellen reminisced with, "My dad was wonderful."

Jan Hines also lived in Rosemont and, like Ellen, walked to school. They met in the 7th grade and remained friends through high school. They had a lot in common: both from Italian-Irish families and both pretty average in looks and in school.

For fun, they hung out, mostly at Ellen's house. Neither one cared very much about dating. Ellen, especially, didn't spend her waking moments pining for a boyfriend.

"She was fun. She had a good sense of humor," Jan recalled. "She had a sense of self about her." Soon, their group expanded to include Becky Best, who first met Ellen in Mrs. Gibbons' 10th grade English class at Radnor High School. They liked each other right away and became lifelong friends. "She was very loving, very giving, a fun person to be with," recalled Becky. In a class of 349—small compared to other graduating classes in the area—Ellen and Becky became instant friends, and as the years passed, more like sisters.

It was the early 1970s and Ellen especially loved to dance. When disco mania hit, the girls would gather at one friend's house and practice their dance steps to the radio.

Karen Schmidt (now Lander) was a senior when she met Ellen, who was a year younger. Despite their age difference, Karen was attracted to Ellen, who acted poised and mature. "I admired her," recalled Karen, who saw herself as shy, and Ellen as fearless and outgoing. Both girls enjoyed talking about big-picture, philosophical issues. When Karen went to Drexel, Ellen went to stay with her in the dorm to get a taste of college life. That summer, they became roommates while working as waitresses in Ocean City on the New Jersey shore.

While her classmates at Radnor, which pulled from some of the wealthiest areas in suburban Philadelphia, may have had a smooth ride, Ellen did not. She graduated from Radnor High School in 1974, and a scholarship enabled her to go to Mount Ida College in Boston. In letters home to Karen, Ellen told her she yearned to travel. But her grades were average and she struggled to stay focused on her studies. She preferred being social and working with people, and was eager to get started. Her interest in retail and design drew her to what was then Philadelphia College of Textiles & Science (now Philadelphia University) and she worked three jobs to put herself through, including a stint as a nanny. Ellen loved children, and the experience showed her how well she could take care of them.

The job market in the late 1970s was especially tight. But, Ellen came through, landing a prestigious job in the management training program at Bamberger's (a division of Macy's at that time) in King of Prussia. It's there that she met Mary Beth Campanella, a Villanova University grad who was hired to manage the lingerie department while Ellen managed housewares. Not only were they new at their jobs, but both had the same manager, so they found themselves spending a lot of time together. Soon, they were going out to parties too. Although Mary Beth only stayed for a year, she remained friends with Ellen and connected with her every six months. "Once she touched your life, you wanted to stay in touch with her."

On the job, Ellen developed her skills as the service-oriented manager who could solve problems and supervise others who reported to her.

Through Mary Beth, Ellen met Gina Bacci, who rented her an apartment on the third floor of a ten-unit building on North Wayne Avenue.

By then, Ellen had moved on to retail sales, working territories that stretched northwest to Reading for Hanes Hosiery, a division of Sara Lee. Ellen especially enjoyed the hours of retail, starting late in the morning and working into the evening. It seemed to fit her natural body rhythms. Gina saw Ellen almost every day, since she had to walk past Gina's apartment to get up to her own on the third floor. They chatted and visited and sometimes joined the other tenants for barbecues in the backyard. Sometimes Ellen would pick up supplies for Gina at the store. Many days, Ellen would visit her next-door neighbor, an elderly, sickly man, to ask how he was feeling and check on whether he needed anything at the grocery store. The gesture was vintage Ellen.

Ellen had boyfriends, but no one who stayed around too long. It was difficult for her friends to figure that out. How could someone so social and so pretty not have a long line of suitors? Ellen was always fashionably dressed and made up, with thick, nicely styled hair. She took a lot of pride in her appearance. And she was the life of any party. "She was incredible," recalled her friend Karen Schmidt Lander. "She made sure she greeted everybody, asking everybody how they were doing, asking about every relative they had that she knew about."

To her closest friends, Ellen confided that what she really wanted was to get married and have her own family. "The clock was ticking," her brother, Arthur Gregory, told the *Inquirer*. "Ellen really, really wanted children." She especially enjoyed spending time with Mary Beth, who by then was married and pregnant with her first child. "I can't wait to have my own," Ellen would tell her.

For Christmas one year, one of her presents was a subscription to a dating service. Ellen was skeptical at first, but decided to give it a try.

After her first date with Rafael Robb, she was cautious. She was intrigued that he was a world-traveled Penn professor, but apprehensive that they came from different worlds: He was a worldly academic who'd been born in Israel, the only son of Holocaust survivors who owned a tailoring shop in Jerusalem. She was a personality-plus retail manager who hailed from a middle-class suburban town. What they seemed to have in common was their mutual desire to have a home and family.

Ellen decided to give it a try and found that Robb was surprisingly comfortable and charming. They went into Center City for dinners at pricey restaurants and cultural events like the orchestra and theater. Robb eventually took her to gatherings at Penn, where she caught a glimpse of his world and his growing success as an economics professor.

"It's been eight months, do you believe it?" Ellen wrote to Karen. "I never dated anyone that long before."

Ellen continued living in the North Wayne Avenue apartment building and kept Gina up on the courtship. "She was swept off her feet by this guy. She was quite taken," said Gina. In less than a year, Ellen was moving into the Forest Road house that Robb had purchased.

The vivacious personality and the intellectual introvert. Could this marriage work? Her friends could only hope that opposites did indeed attract.

"At the time it seemed neat," recalled Karen. "She had found somebody. He seemed to adore her, and he had found somebody who helped him fit in."

Dating Rafi also gave Ellen a front seat on the world. As a couple they traveled to Israel and Europe, with Ellen sending a steady stream of postcards home to Karen, all extolling the joy of seeing new places.

The wedding ceremony was simple but elegant. On May 20, 1990, a sunny spring day, Ellen Gregory, 33, and Rafael Robb, 40, were married in a civil ceremony in a country inn in bucolic Chester County. Dressed in a white, beaded A-line wedding gown, the beaming bride was accompanied down the massive winding staircase at the Victorian Manor House at Springton Manor Farm by her younger brother, Art. Robb wore a tuxedo with a gray vest and ascot. Against the backdrop of an elegant Victorian home, they posed smiling for their formal wedding portraits. Most of the guests were Ellen's family and friends. Robb's family, who remained in Israel, did not attend. Robb's guests included a small group from the University of Pennsylvania, including best man Harold Cole. Becky, wearing a floral gown, was the maid of honor. Mary Beth, obviously pregnant with her first child, posed with Ellen for a keepsake photo.

CHAPTER 23

Rafael

The week leading up to December 22 was a busy time for holiday parties, including one organized by the Economics Department at Penn in a West Philadelphia restaurant. While the event was supposed to be festive, Robb appeared preoccupied as he drove to the party with fellow professor Jeremy Greenwood. Robb told him he was worried. He had a lump in his throat and the doctors suspected thyroid cancer. Once they arrived at the restaurant, Robb went off and mingled with the others there.

Robb's work face was much different from the one he showed neighbors and Ellen's friends and family.

Those who worked closely with Robb on research papers found him to be serious and scholarly. Even when working with junior partners, he was willing to accommodate their suggestions. He also had a good sense of humor, which, as one co-author put it, "makes working with him more entertaining." Cole, who got to know Robb when they were both assistant professors, described him as having a dry self-deprecating wit that made him fun to be with.

While working with one of his graduate students, Robb even showed compassion by helping the student and his wife through a tough financial time by hiring him onto a project and sponsoring him to attend a conference. "I am very grateful to him," the former graduate student wrote in an e-mail, asking that his name not be used. "I still couldn't believe that he did that [the murder], since he is such a nice guy, at least to me."

His pioneering work put him in touch with scholars all over the world, some of whom collaborated with him on research and articles for economic journals.

His most recent collaborator was Bruce Carlin, an economics professor from the University of North Carolina, who was working with Robb on a research paper on revolving credit.

Carlin had talked to Robb at 11 a.m. on December 21, the day before Ellen was found dead. That night, he'd called Robb at home and Olivia had told him that Robb had hurt his shoulder and gone to bed. On the day of the murder, Robb called and e-mailed Carlin at 11:36 a.m. from his Penn office, two time-stamped communications that police say he sent deliberately just so he could establish an alibi. The voicemail that Robb left on Carlin's phone was pretty innocuous: "Heading out to do errands. Talk to you later in the afternoon." Carlin called back and sent an e-mail, but could not reach Robb.

The next evening, Carlin got a call from Detective Peffall, who told him that Robb's wife, Ellen, had been killed. Carlin said he never knew her, that he and Robb communicated by e-mail, and Robb had never mentioned his family.

Robb's marriage to Ellen was his second. His first marriage in 1986, which ended in Philadelphia, had lasted less than two years. Robb's first wife, Bonnie Flood, of Minnetonka, Minnesota, told Montgomery County detectives that they'd married four months after they met. While they never fought, she knew right away the marriage wasn't going to work. He was meek and mild, but "consumed with money."

They'd met while Robb was a research visitor in residence at the University of Minnesota for a year ending in August 1984, after which he moved to Philadelphia to join Penn as an assistant professor in the Economics Department. His only other teaching position had been a two-year stint at Brown University right after getting his PhD from UCLA.

People who knew Robb say there was another side to Rafi.

They knew a quietly jovial guy who enjoyed sitting around and visiting with friends. Even LuAnn, one of Ellen's closest friends from the neighborhood, recalled a different time when Robb appeared jolly and happy, enjoying a tropical drink on a hot summer day while waiting for Olivia and LuAnn's daughter, Brooke, to get ready for an outing.

When Olivia was in grade school, Robb would join LuAnn for holiday time visits to school to share the Jewish traditions of Hanukkah. Robb wanted the children to know the story of the festival of lights.

As Olivia got older, Robb enjoyed taking care of her, or as his brother-in-law Art put it, "Olivia grew on him and he did take care of her. They would go on trips everywhere. They weren't normal trips though, they were like grown-up trips, where there wasn't a whole lot of fun kid stuff to do. Rafael did not do anything that he did not like."

Mostly, though, Olivia got what she wanted. As the child between two warring adults, she got what she asked for from her father and her mother. It was like they were both in competition for her approval, something that increasingly became a problem for Ellen.

LuAnn had also seen Robb get enraged with Olivia when she kept pestering him to allow another girl to join them for dinner and a movie. Going from an extremely calm and pleasant demeanor, Robb had turned beet red, his veins popping out of his neck. He took Olivia outside and they got into a heated argument.

Among neighbors, one stood out to befriend Robb after Ellen's murder. Arnold Jentleson, a financial advisor, obtained Robb's power of attorney and took on the maintenance of the Robb house. Jentleson got to know Robb through their children. Brett Jentleson, a friend of Olivia's, often went on outings with Robb and his daughter to the movies, dinner, amusement parks.

When asked by the *Inquirer*, Jentleson described Robb as, "a very nice guy. Warm, jovial, joking." Later, he declined to talk about Robb, insisting that everyone was innocent until proven guilty.

One thing Robb did like doing was going to the gym, and he regularly went to a local private facility. When it came to religion, Robb appeared ambivalent. While he was born Jewish and his upbringing was important to him, Robb allowed that Olivia would choose whether to be Jewish or Christian. At Christmas, the family had a tree, and celebrated Hanukkah.

Robb was born in Israel in 1950 to Holocaust survivors who had moved to Jerusalem. In 1976, he received an undergraduate degree in economics and math at Hebrew University in Jerusalem—the Harvard of Israel—and then moved to the United States, where he received a master's in 1977 and a doctorate in 1981 from the University of California, Los Angeles. His dissertation was titled "Essays on Public Choice." He served a stint at Brown University before joining the faculty at the University of Pennsylvania in 1984. Along the way, he became an American citizen.

At the University of Pennsylvania, Robb was a tenured professor in the College of Arts & Sciences, where he taught undergraduate and graduate economics courses in intermediate microeconomics, microeconomic theory and game theory.

In addition to getting research grants, Robb, in the spring of 2002, also won the prestigious Irving B. Kravis Award for excellence in undergraduate teaching. That he was respected by his students fits in with the view of Rafael Robb held by his best friend and Penn colleague, Dr. Harold Cole. Despite having tenure, Robb was generous with his time with students and colleagues, what Cole called "a generosity of spirit." Socially, especially during their early days as professors, Robb was fun to be with, a conversationalist on a wide range of subjects from his own work to world politics.

On campus, he was well-liked. "He was always approachable, accommodating," college junior Seungha Ku, who took an economics course with Robb in the fall of 2006, told *The Daily Pennsylvanian*, the campus newspaper.

"I thought he was a very nice guy . . . you could easily see yourself liking him outside of the classroom," added junior Dimitry Cohen, who told the newspaper he had nominated Robb for another teaching award in 2005.

CHAPTER 24

Early Years

As newlyweds, the Robbs socially kept to themselves. They seemed to drop away from Ellen's circle of girlfriends, who were now growing into a circle of couples.

If they did attend a party, Robb would come in, politely say hello and disappear. But they came in separate cars so Ellen could stay. Everyone who knew Ellen knew she was always late. So when she came to parties, as one friend put it, "She was the last to come and the last to leave."

Robb actually liked to cook, so they occasionally threw dinner parties when they proudly showed off their house and their plans to redesign it. Ellen, with her designer touch, was excited about being able to upgrade the interior. Even Robb pointed to areas in the split-level brick house built in 1959 that they wanted to change. For a home in an upscale neighborhood, it was modest in every way, with three bedrooms, one full bath and attached garage.

Money became a problem right away. When Ellen moved in two years before the wedding, Robb insisted that she write him a monthly check for half of the house bills—utilities, mortgage, everything—even though the house was in Robb's name, and she earned a lot less than he did. Ellen was still working at her sales job. When she left it in 1994, she was earning about $60,000 a year plus benefits. By then, Robb was a tenured professor at Penn. His most recent salary was about $200,000.

When her friend Mary Beth nudged her about the arrangement, Ellen tried to reassure her, "Don't worry, after we get married everything will change."

It didn't.

Even after the wedding, Ellen was writing Robb a monthly check for half the household expenses.

While starting a family had been important to both of them, Ellen had difficulties getting pregnant and staying pregnant. She suffered a miscarriage that deeply affected them both.

She feared that her dreams of being a wife and mother, and living in a nice house in the suburbs with a professional husband, were slipping away.

Before leaving for a teaching stay in Europe, Robb surprised Ellen by telling her he wanted a divorce. After the shock wore off, Ellen called her friend Karen to come over. It would be the last time Ellen would confide anything to Karen about her marriage. "Rafi wants a divorce," Ellen told her. "What am I going to do?"

After hashing over the details, Karen told her, "Ellen, you need a lawyer." Ellen went on to tell Karen that her husband had money stashed away in overseas accounts, to which Karen repeated that she "really needed a lawyer."

Ellen was obviously troubled. "I went through his office and found some information. I've never done this before," she said.

Karen couldn't tell how this was sitting with her friend. "Are you OK with him getting a divorce?"

"Yeah, yeah," Ellen responded. "It's for the best. I just want to make sure that I'm not screwed in the divorce."

When she left, Karen fully expected that her friend would move ahead. She was stunned to hear from Ellen a couple of days later.

"You're not going to believe this," Ellen declared. "I'm pregnant."

Before Karen could say anything else, Ellen continued. "I told Rafi and he wants to work it out, and he wants to stay together."

That didn't last very long.

For the duration of the pregnancy, Ellen sought refuge with

her brother, Art, who lived nearby in Haddonfield, New Jersey. Art and his then-wife, Mary Ann, helped Ellen by giving her a comfortable and secure place to live. They helped her get through what would be a difficult pregnancy.

In November 1993, when she was four months pregnant, Ellen, accompanied by her long-time high school friend, Becky Best, went to see Philadelphia attorney James Tyler to find out her options. She had been to Israel with Robb and worried that he'd go back there and leave her with no way to support her baby. Robb wanted her out of the house. She had no money. The accounts were in his name and he had already started taking money out of them, Ellen told Tyler. Ellen wanted to make sure she had somewhere to live and money to support her baby after the divorce.

"I sensed that he [Robb] was very controlling," Tyler recalled for police. "He wanted her out of the house even though she was pregnant at the time. She had no money. The accounts were in his name only and the house was in his name only."

Tyler also told police he saw no signs of injuries to Ellen and she said nothing about abuse.

Over a series of meetings and phone conversations with Robb's attorney, they worked out a written agreement of child support, and Ellen would get the house on Forest Road. Ellen's attorney filed a divorce action in Montgomery County Court, but nothing ever happened after that to finalize it. Tyler waited to hear from Ellen, who did not get back to him. The last contact was through Robb's attorney in August 1994. Tyler tried to reach out to Ellen the next year just to close up the case, but never heard from her again. The case eventually evaporated from the court file for lack of action.

Ellen's family, who knew of problems right from the beginning of their marriage, hoped he would never return. As Art would later tell Marino: "There were always problems."

When asked if Robb was ever good to his sister, Art responded, "No. I even tried to talk Ellen out of it, even on the day of the wedding."

"With him it was always work," Ellen's mother told *The*

Philadelphia Inquirer. "And when he was home, his face was in a book. She married the wrong man."

Mary Beth, who by then was married, living up the road and pregnant with her third child, saw Robb's attempt to leave Ellen as another side of the calm always-in-control Robb. Perhaps his father's death around that time had had something to do with it, coming at the same time as a new baby. Or, perhaps he had not gotten over the miscarriage they had recently endured. Whatever the case, Robb walked away, leaving Ellen traumatized, depressed and pregnant.

Karen saw it clearly at the baby shower that friends threw for Ellen. "I could see that all the fight and spunk had just gone out of her."

Robb stayed away for most of the year, teaching overseas, but returned in time for the birth of their daughter, Olivia, on April 26, 1994.

It was a rocky time. One day while visiting Ellen and her newborn, Mary Beth tried to help. "Do you still love him?" she asked Ellen. "Is this something you want to work out?"

"Oh, yes, I love him, but I don't know," Ellen answered.

Mary Beth knew how much Ellen loved Mary Beth's children and how much she loved caring for Art's daughter Lauren. She had waited so long for Olivia, and the prospect of raising her as a single mother was more than Ellen could handle.

Maybe there was a way to work this out, Mary Beth thought. To her friend, she offered this last piece of advice: "If you still love him and you can work it out, go back and work it out."

Ellen and Rafael agreed to reconcile. Robb would support Ellen so she could stay at home and raise Olivia. The house would remain in his name for another four years, a time when friends and family hoped that the marriage could survive.

Robb rented an apartment on the French Riviera while teaching in France, and wanted both Ellen and Olivia to come over to be with him. But, Olivia was colicky and Ellen didn't want to travel.

A turning point for Ellen came when she accompanied Robb on a sabbatical to Israel. Ellen was nervous about the trip because she didn't speak Hebrew and there was so much that would be new to her. While she had always wanted to travel, she now faced the scary possibility of being away from home for a whole year with a young child.

Ellen eventually took her friend Gina's advice: "Relax and enjoy it."

While there, Ellen appeared to have overcome the challenge of fitting in with Robb's Jewish family. But, it was formidable. She was Christian, did not speak Hebrew, and knew little about Jewish customs.

Facing those challenges, Ellen drew from her most powerful faculty, which had served her well in the past: her personality. She won over her mother-in-law with a surprise birthday celebration that Robb's mother would talk about for years afterward. And, even for her husband, Ellen threw a birthday party that endeared her to the family.

Despite those high points, her stay in Israel was difficult. She was forced to pretend she was happy even when she wasn't. She was every bit a stranger in a strange land.

Trouble followed them as they stepped foot back into their Forest Road home. The home that Ellen and Robb had turned into a showplace had been trashed by the tenants Robb had found to rent it out while they were gone. The state of the house deeply bothered Ellen, who was also miffed at Robb for not doing more to get the renters to repay them for the damage.

Soon after, they would retreat to separate bedrooms.

CHAPTER 25

Changes

During Olivia's primary years at Roberts Elementary, it was Ellen who became a celebrated volunteer, earning herself a plaque on the school wall as the 2004 Volunteer of the Year. Ellen did it all, helping the teachers with projects, raising money for the school parents' group or even year-long commitments such as being the Brownie troop leader.

Olivia was in third grade when Ellen went in to read stories to the children as part of their after-school Bear Program. Ellen didn't have to, but she brought along cookies—not only for the children but for the adults as well, earning her the nickname "cookie mom."

No matter what was happening at the school, Ellen was eager to help. "She was always there, always the first to volunteer," recalled Jovanna Bevilacqua, a Roberts teacher. "She was so happy, such a caring person."

Just watching Ellen and her young daughter, Jovanna couldn't help but think that they were so close, inseparable. "They were mother and daughter, but like best friends too. Wherever you saw Olivia, her mom was right behind her."

As the Brownie leader, Ellen pushed the cookie drive, making home deliveries of orders if the buyers couldn't pick them up. She did the same thing for the school's major fundraiser which Ellen ran by herself. Parents put in orders for weekly groceries, including frozen foods, and the school group would get a cut of the purchase price. If they didn't pick up their groceries, Ellen would load them up in her car and run them around to people's homes.

She would even pay the bill and wait to get reimbursed. Ellen went over and above what anyone expected her to do. Patty Volpi, who was an officer in the parent group during those years, worked closely with Ellen on any number of school functions—field trips, gift wrap sales, spring fairs. For all of it, she could count on Ellen to work wherever she was needed—in the kitchen with food, on crafts, on raffle tables and on pony rides.

"She would go above and beyond for other people no matter what sacrifices it took from her."

Like the semester when Ellen loaned her car to Olivia's babysitter, Nina Ravolaharivao, so she could get to her college courses in nursing at Neumann College in Aston. "She would do anything for you," recalled Nina, who has since graduated and started working as a nurse in Philadelphia.

Around school, Ellen became affectionately known as "the bag lady."

As homeroom mother, Ellen was always bringing something into school for the kids, and she always needed plastic bags.

Ellen told them it was easier for her to show up for after-school and evening activities. Her friends knew that she suffered from colitis, a bowel disease that caused diarrhea and cramping. She found it difficult to be anywhere first thing in the morning.

Even among her neighbors, Ellen was generous and considerate. She and LuAnn, who lived three doors from the park, would meet at the playground for lunch with their daughters, and Ellen would typically bring along some extra goodies for LuAnn's daughter Brooke. Ellen clearly relished her role caring for Olivia. It was all about her little girl.

As a stay-at-home mom, LuAnn found it refreshing to share a few moments talking to an intelligent and thoughtful adult. While they both loved caring for their daughters, they also enjoyed the private adult time they shared. While the girls played in the sand, the moms found common ground talking about fashion. LuAnn had worked for a modeling agency as a make-up artist, and Ellen had put in a dozen years in retail sales. They discovered they knew the same people.

LuAnn, who was having her third child, had already been a homeroom mom, and tried to warn Ellen how much work she faced if she took on the cookie sales project. Ellen laughed. She wasn't afraid.

Indeed, LuAnn marveled later watching Ellen volunteer for everything and doing it well. She obviously enjoyed being around people and being needed.

While serving as the Brownie leader, Ellen noticed a tiny, shabbily dressed little girl who quickly ate any treats Ellen put in front of her. Ellen would deliberately arrange playdates for the girl to come to her house so she could make sure she got ample food and leave with at least one extra piece of clothing. She did it that way because the girl's mother resented any attention, and didn't want anyone to know how poor they were.

As Olivia completed 4th grade, Ellen's friends started noticing changes. Rafi attended more school activities. Patty Volpi noticed that Ellen wasn't volunteering anymore, although she would still attend school open houses and musicals. It was like Ellen was pulling away. Friends from all segments of her life—childhood, high school, college, neighbors—they were all experiencing the same thing, but they didn't know it. Individually, they figured Ellen was just really busy.

Karen Lander was among the friends who got a cold shoulder from Ellen, but she had no reason to think there was anything wrong. She tried to rekindle their friendship after seeing her at a friend's father's funeral, but Ellen never responded. "I kept calling and calling, and sending her notes," said Karen. "I thought she didn't have time . . . I thought she was probably on a million committees. 'She has a new life and new friends,' I'm thinking, 'she doesn't have time to keep up.'"

Mary Beth, who stayed close to Ellen the longest, knew when to back off to keep Ellen from shutting her out as well. They knew how proud Ellen was and how difficult it would be for her to tell them how bad things had gotten with Rafi.

CHAPTER 26

Trouble

The fragile arrangement Ellen and Rafi had worked out a decade ago was no longer working.

The cracks had been visible to Ellen's family and friends for at least three years, they told the investigators.

Ellen's friends knew her as a kind person who wrote thank-you notes, remembered birthdays and hosted play-dates for their children. They also watched helplessly as Ellen descended into darkness, becoming increasingly withdrawn and depressed. They saw Robb as distant and unavailable, and had little contact with him. Mostly their view into the home was from their children's contacts with Olivia. And they were worried.

LuAnn Dubin saw her friend deteriorating physically and emotionally. Finally, in 1999, when Ellen was in the hospital at Easter time for an asthma attack, LuAnn figured maybe she could get her to talk.

She encouraged her to leave Rafi, telling her she could get a part-time job and Olivia could see her father on weekends. "You could work this out. It's not undoable," LuAnn told her.

Ellen too knew her marriage had become dysfunctional and that she was better off if they were not together—but he wasn't willing to leave.

"LuAnn, this is not working," Ellen told her. "It's getting to the point where this is affecting my daughter. I don't want her to believe that this is how life really is, or that any family should live like this."

Olivia was in 4th grade and old enough to notice what was happening in her home, and Ellen worried that she was learning the wrong lessons.

But, as reflected in so many other conversations she'd had with her close friends, though Ellen knew her situation was hurting her and her daughter, she wasn't able to change it. Robb wouldn't leave and she was afraid she couldn't support herself without him.

LuAnn's view into the Robb household included her daughter Brooke's experiences. On one occasion, Olivia had invited Brooke to sleep over. Around 11:30 p.m. that night, Ellen called saying she was bringing Brooke home. LuAnn figured her daughter, who wasn't a good sleeper, had woken up and wasn't able to get back to sleep. What she found out later was that the Robbs had been quarreling and Brooke had been so upset by the yelling that she'd asked Ellen to drive her home.

Ellen never talked about it.

It wasn't the first time. Brooke, who had been friends with Olivia since they were in preschool, spent a lot of time at the Robbs'. "Sometimes they would fight," she later told police. When asked if it got physical, she replied, "No, they were just, like, yelling at each other."

Ellen's friends learned not to push too much. When they did, Ellen would retreat and refuse to answer their telephone calls or even come to the door.

Something was terribly wrong.

CHAPTER 27

Darkness

A darkness had fallen into Ellen's life, robbing her of joy and the will to even leave the house. Even when her old high school friend, Josh Bowden, called her in early 2006 for their annual talk, Ellen told him she was a shut-in. Neighbors on Forest Road told reporters after she died that she'd been a recluse, because they never saw her outside. Instead, they saw Rafi taking Olivia trick-or-treating or to sell her Girl Scout Cookies.

What very few people knew was that Ellen was suffering, emotionally and physically. Rather than admit to anyone that her marriage was a sham and increasingly unbearable, Ellen avoided the encounter. She turned inward and stopped going out for anything. She ignored friends who called or sent notes. While she was seeing a doctor and taking medication for depression, none of it seemed to help her cope with what had become an untenable situation—a husband and wife leading separate lives in the same small house with their 12-year-old daughter as the only lifeline between them.

Both took prescription drugs for depression. When she died, Ellen had been taking Zoloft and an amphetamine.

As Ellen's depression deepened, she did more and more hoarding and shopping online. And as the boxes arrived, they took their place on top of the ones delivered the day before.

Three years before her murder, Ellen showed signs of her

emotional problems. Ellen had put up the Christmas tree in December only to have it still up in March. When she realized Ellen couldn't handle it by herself, Mary Beth and Nina Ravolaharivao, Ellen's babysitter went into the house, put away the tree and helped clean out some of the clutter that had accumulated in just about every room in the house. They filled countless black trash bags with garbage. Ellen at first looked embarrassed but welcomed the help. She headed upstairs to work there. Among the boxes, Mary Beth found unopened orders of Avon that Ellen had purchased from her. She decided she would cut her off. She didn't want to enable Ellen's shopping mania.

Her penchant for collecting plastic bags to take treats into Olivia's elementary school had grown to the point that there were plastic bags all over the house, and the family had nicknamed her "the bag queen."

There was no dearth of people to talk to the detectives about the Robbs. Friends and acquaintances called them wanting to tell what they knew. The challenge facing the detectives was simple. They needed to keep blowing holes through Robb's statement to the police. That's what would help prove that he had killed her. As Castor planned to ask the jury, why else would he be lying unless he'd done it? Robb himself raised suspicions when during his first talk with police he failed to come clean on their plans for a divorce, and downplayed that they had had a stormy marriage.

The detectives needed to find out why Robb would have wanted his wife dead.

Almost immediately, they learned just how bad the Robbs' marriage had become. That they'd kept separate bedrooms was just the beginning.

The question still remained, however, whether Robb had previously beaten his wife. Castor wanted to know what Ellen had told others. He wasn't sure whether the information would make its way into the trial testimony. Whether a defendant had previously beaten his wife had resulted in reversals in convictions elsewhere in the state. He wasn't going to take the chance. It was one thing for a friend to hear about Robb hitting

Ellen, but she would have to see it or see bruises to be able to testify about it.

As Marino and Gershanick dug deeper into the Robb marriage, they found that no one around Ellen Robb could clearly answer that question—but many could tell them about troubles inside the Robb household.

There were no records of police calls to the Robb house. No one from the county's domestic abuse agencies or Laurel House, the safe house for abused women, came forth. And there was nothing on file in court indicating that Ellen had gotten an order of protection.

Yet, as they would soon learn, the Robbs existed in a darkly troubled marriage in which Ellen suffered silently and a lot of people around them knew that they fought bitterly.

As they got to Ellen's closest friends and family, Marino and Gershanick heard unequivocally that there was no one else who could have killed Ellen except her husband. When it came to physical abuse, however, Ellen's friends said they repeatedly asked her if Robb was beating her, and she denied it.

"I asked her many times," said LuAnn. " 'Is he hitting you? Is he touching you?' "

"No," said Ellen, adding, "A couple of times we shoved each other."

"Ellen, no one is allowed to touch each other. You're not allowed to do it to him and he's not allowed to do it to you. Things escalate. That can't happen."

"Oh, no," Ellen responded, waving her friend away from the possibility that she was being beaten. "It's more mental. It's the anguish. It's the belittlement."

LuAnn pushed her friend to do something. "Who's to say that he's any better than you are? Why are you allowing him to make you feel this way?"

Ellen always ended things the same way: "I know. I know, LuAnn. I know."

If she was seeing her friends or answering their calls, Ellen usually avoided talking about her marriage. As a friend looking in, Patty saw the Robbs as co-existing. At times they could do it and other times they couldn't. Ellen never told her friends or family that her husband was violent toward her, but she did communicate a fear that she wasn't free to talk or have people stop over when he was there. At a Brownie troop meeting, sometime around 2000, Patty noticed Ellen with a black eye, but Ellen dismissed it, telling her she had walked into a kitchen cabinet.

Her friends knew that Ellen would be more open when Robb left on a teaching trip or during the six weeks in the summer when Olivia went to camp. That's when Robb usually went on a trip as well. At first Ellen hated the thought of Olivia going away for so long, but both she and her daughter got used to it.

As Robb told officers the day she died, the couple lived separately in their own home. While Robb at first told police there was fighting, he later changed his story to say they didn't get along. He said they fought often and he would lock his bedroom door to shut her out. But he then corrected himself to eliminate the words "we have fights." Rather he said, "We sleep in different bedrooms. We have slept in different rooms for many years. We don't get along . . . We don't see eye to eye."

And he dodged their questions about divorce, telling the police that he had talked with her about it many times over the years. Even when they went back at him after they had specific information that a divorce had been underway, Robb continued to avoid answering the question.

"Did your wife tell you recently she was serious about a divorce, and she was starting the process by hiring a lawyer?"

Robb's answer: "She said it many times. It was always the same thing."

Only one, Becky Rector, a high school friend of Ellen's, told police that she had called Ellen on October 27 to invite her to her 50th birthday party, and Ellen told her she couldn't go because Robb had hit her and given her a black eye. Becky tried to convince Ellen to come, telling her she could wear make-up or sunglasses, that it would especially be fun for Olivia because the party spot was a resort with an outdoor pool.

Becky recounted to others that she'd been driving when Ellen called, and had pulled over so she could spend time talking to her. She told the officers that Ellen tearfully told her that the physical abuse had been going on for about ten years, since the couple's trip to Israel.

But Becky told no one else.

"She told me she couldn't come to my birthday party because she had a black eye and she was embarrassed," Becky said. "I kept going on, 'You've got to get out of the house.'"

Ellen wouldn't go, telling Becky, "I'm OK. He's not going to do anything."

Becky kept pushing for Ellen to come to her home for refuge. Ellen's response was that her brother Gary and her neighbor, Mary Beth Pedlow, knew about the abuse and "[Gary] was handling it," said Becky. They didn't know.

After Ellen's murder, when her close friends heard that Ellen had told Becky about a black eye, they were devastated. Mary Beth sat and cried for twenty minutes. How could Ellen not tell her, especially when she had asked her repeatedly if Robb hit her? How could Ellen tell Becky, a high school friend whom she hadn't spoken to in years? Did she tell her specifically because she knew Becky lived in New Jersey, away from everyone else, and didn't know the other friends? Did she tell her because she knew no one else would find out?

Months later, Mary Beth finally met Becky and learned that Becky had told Ellen to tell her brothers and Mary Beth. "You've got to tell people. You've got to let people know what's going on," she said. Ellen assured her they already knew. "I told my brothers and I told MacBeth."

That news brought back all of the pain for Mary Beth. "She didn't . . . she hadn't told us. She hadn't told Gary or Art that he had hit her. She hadn't told me. It was very discouraging for us."

"I thought I was a lot closer to Ellen. I thought she would have told me," said Mary Beth. If only Ellen had, Mary Beth would have done something.

Mary Beth and LuAnn recall repeatedly asking Ellen if

Robb had hit her. She always said no. "I told her I'd be up there in a minute with the police," Mary Beth recalled.

That's the last thing Ellen would have wanted, they realized after her murder. Ellen never told any of them enough to take action. It was only after she'd died that they were able to put the pieces together and realize how much pressure she had been living with.

"Ellen only let little bits of the puzzle out to each of us," said LuAnn, a petite mother of three who has a reputation for being outspoken. "If we all had put the puzzle together, it would have been acted on much sooner."

Even Ellen's brother Gary told police that Ellen had endured heavy verbal abuse, while denying any physical abuse, "but I am not so sure about that." When reporters asked, Gary and Art would only say that they knew their sister had suffered from verbal and emotional abuse.

Ellen's friends told police that Robb would verbally demean her about her looks and her weight and their cluttered house, calling her stupid and reminding her that she couldn't work or earn a living.

Through his attorney, Robb denied ever hitting Ellen and painted himself as a victim of Ellen's depression and shopping disorder. He specifically denied giving Ellen a black eye and pointed to Olivia's statement to police, which the defense submitted to the court, that said she did not see her parents fighting. When asked by Detective Peffall if her parents fought, Olivia responded, "No, not really." She went on to say that she'd heard her parents talking about the divorce, but "they never argued about it."

Although the probable cause document that led to Robb's arrest detailed allegations that police had gotten from Ellen's high school friend Becky Rector that Robb had given Ellen a black eye, no one was expected to testify to it during the trial.

Castor didn't have anyone who could testify to having seen Robb hit his wife, and there were no police or hospital records.

For Becky Rector, who remains overwhelmed with guilt

for not doing more to help her friend, Castor's decision not to have her testify was devastating.

"I'm not lying," she said. "What would I have to gain by making it up?

"Ellen did reach out to me. She told me he was abusing her, not only mentally but physically."

They had been on the phone for nearly two hours with Ellen sobbing as she recounted how painful her life had become and how she would hide the bruises to keep it all from Olivia. When Robb came home, Ellen retreated to her car and talked to Becky from her cell phone.

Ellen's deepest source of emotional abuse stemmed from money, her friends said.

As the detectives heard repeatedly, Robb controlled his wife with money.

When asked by Detective Les Glauner to describe his brother-in-law, Gary put it like this: "Intelligent, cold, he loves his work and his daughter, money is everything to him."

Robb gave Ellen a credit card, but it could only be used for household items, including food. Anything else she wanted had to come out of her own inheritance, Art told the police. Ellen had spent about $40,000 from an aunt whom she was very close to, and other money from her own 401(k) account on purchases Robb wouldn't pay for. It was her aunt who had given her the money to buy the Subaru Legacy that she drove around.

"Everything had to go through that card," Art told the *Inquirer* in a piece by Kathy Boccella entitled, 'Portrait of a Doomed Marriage.' "He would ask her, 'Why did you buy this? Why did you buy that?' Bills would come in and he would go ballistic."

The more Robb tightened the money and leaned on Ellen to return what she had bought, the more Ellen would binge buy and then, out of remorse, take everything back. In the months before she was killed, there had been a big blowup over her purchasing, in which Robb had refused to pay, requiring Ellen to withdraw funds from her dwindling private account, Mary Beth told police.

Art said he'd tried to give Ellen a car to replace her clunky Subaru as long as she paid off the loan and the taxes, but Robb didn't want her to do it. And if she did, the car had to be titled in his name. Art dropped the idea and Ellen continued driving the wagon, which lacked air bags.

CHAPTER 28

Love and Money

As Castor built his case against Robb, he put loss of money and his daughter as the primary motives for the killing.

In putting together his witness list for the trial, Castor included two of Ellen's friends, along with her brothers and the two men who could testify that the divorce had clearly been underway—Ellen's attorney and her realtor.

Castor's witness list would include Ellen's women friends and family members who could drive home his case—that Robb's motive for killing Ellen was to preserve the money that he feared he would lose in a divorce, that money was a continuing issue in their marriage and that he feared losing Olivia. Her brothers would be able to underscore that Robb was verbally abusive and controlling, especially when it came to money.

Castor also planned to enter into evidence that Robb knew all about the divorce. He had been previously divorced in 1988 and he and Ellen had considered divorce in 1993 when they had negotiated a settlement before deciding not to go through with it.

In his statement to police, Robb said it was upsetting to him when his wife talked about getting a divorce. "I don't know what would happen to my daughter. It is a traumatic event." And while he could not see her after he was arrested, on the first night, Robb called Ellen's mother to ask about

Olivia. After that, he called Olivia often from jail to check on her and reassure her that things would work out.

Robb had gotten increasingly close to Olivia, especially now that she was an adolescent. As Ellen sank deeper into her depression, Robb would take over some of the duties at home, like taking his daughter to school or selling Girl Scout Cookies. Especially in the year before Ellen's death, it was Robb who would show up to meet with teachers or attend school functions.

Two years ago, he had taken her to his class at Penn for "Take Your Daughter to Work Day." He also spent generously on Olivia and her friends, inviting them along when he took her to amusement parks or movies or even to dinner. After Christmas, they had plans to go to New York City and see *Wicked*, the musical. Since Robb only taught on Tuesdays and Thursdays, he was generally available to do whatever Olivia wanted or needed.

At the same time, Ellen repeatedly told her friends that Robb had threatened to take Olivia to Israel. When Detective Godby asked Ellen's best friend, Mary Beth Pedlow, if Ellen had any fear or concerns about her husband, she told him, "She worried that he would take Olivia from her or that he would have her declared an unfit mother."

Ellen's closest friends could see problems developing between Ellen and Olivia—flare-ups when Olivia repeated some of the digs that she would hear from her father.

Despite all of that, in making plans for after the divorce, Olivia had already told her mother that she wanted to live with her.

Among the items seized from the Robb household the day of the murder was a black computer bag found on the bed in Robb's room, stuffed with financial records. In the drawers of a cabinet in the same room, they found the couple's income tax returns, the same documents that Ellen's lawyer had asked her to come up with. There were other financial records inside the desk drawer. For Detective Gilbert, the treasure trove of documents allowed him to give Castor the information he needed. Ellen had told her family, friends and lawyer that

Robb had a lot of money, some of it in banks overseas. Now, Gilbert could prove it. He put Robb's personal worth at $2.3 million, about half of that in retirement accounts. Some of it was being held in an Israeli bank. All financial records were in Robb's name.

Even at the $2.3 million, and not counting his home or his Penn pension, a divorce would have been financially punishing to Robb. Ellen's attorney had estimated that she'd stood to get $600,000 over the next ten to fifteen years. She had not been working and had no immediate prospect of work, so Robb would have been required to pay for her support.

Gilbert also found out that Ellen had had very little. She'd used her own money from her 401(k) to pay household bills. There were a few credit cards with modest balances in both of their names. She had $80,000 in a pension plan, $11,000 in Sara Lee stock; $60,000 in Vanguard, of which she'd inherited $25,000 in 1993 from an aunt.

In charging Robb, Bruce Castor painted a picture of a husband enraged over the prospect of sharing his millions with Ellen and losing his daughter. As Castor told reporters after Robb's arrest, the prosecution's psychiatric experts would be testifying that Robb had felt threatened by his wife insofar as "she was going to hurt him financially in the division and also hurt his relationship with his child."

Because money loomed large in the Robb marriage, knowing how much Robb was hiding from her became an obsession for Ellen. "Rafael locked his bedroom door and closet doors all of the time. She was almost obsessing about finding out all about the money," her brother Art told Detective Marino. "Every time they would get into a fight, she would bring up that she knew Rafael was hiding money from her."

Years before she'd started the divorce proceedings, Ellen told friends and family that Robb had money stashed away. She told them a friend who worked in investments was able to find evidence of money transfers. As recently as two weeks prior to her death, when she'd told her daughter about the divorce, Ellen had said she expected to get a lot of money "because my dad had a lot of money in banks in other countries," Olivia told police.

Once she consulted an attorney, Ellen appeared to have had a game plan for getting into Robb's personal papers. She'd talked it over with Gary and planned to bring in a locksmith while Robb was in New York City with Olivia after Christmas.

In earnings, Robb would have approximately $200,000 in salary plus other money that he earned from speeches and consulting. But, whatever he had, he considered it his alone and not something he wanted to share with Ellen, friends and family say. He'd bought the home where they lived in 1988 for $181,000 and put down $70,000. During their courtship, but even after they married, it remained in his name. It wasn't until 1998, after a lengthy quarrel, that Robb agreed to add Ellen's name as a co-owner. He remained alone on the mortgage.

CHAPTER 29

Courage

By the fall of 2006, Ellen had summoned the courage to end her marriage.

She found a lawyer, Al Shemtob from a friend, whose husband had hired him in their divorce, and she told Ellen that she had been impressed that he could be tough but fair.

Ellen liked the sound of that and called his office for an appointment. Gary had promised to pay the $5,000 retainer she would need to hire Shemtob. While she was worried about how much money she would get and the custody arrangement for Olivia, she knew she had to move forward.

She would cancel four times before showing up on October 13. She was finally ready.

To friends, Ellen sounded upbeat, happy and determined to go through with the divorce. She was finished with the talking and analyzing. There would be no more worrying about how it could work out. Her first step was meeting with the attorney.

Ellen got herself ready, organized her papers and drove herself over to Shemtob's offices in nearby Blue Bell.

For the next two hours, Shemtob explained to her the steps they would take that would lead to the divorce and answered all of her questions, many of which were about what she would receive, and custody of Olivia.

Ellen gave Shemtob a summary of the couple's finances: They literally lived separate financial lives. While Robb was the primary breadwinner with his $200,000 Penn salary plus bonuses and pension plans, Ellen had to dip into her own pension funds just to pay the household bills. She figured she had spent $10,000–$15,000 because Robb had refused to give her money.

She explained what she knew about Robb's other assets, including her suspicion that he was hiding money in foreign bank accounts in Israel, England and Germany, but she had no proof. She did know that Robb had sold a house he owned in Ardmore in 1988 before they were married, and invested the money in Israel.

Ellen had stopped working when Olivia was born in 1994, but before that, she earned about $60,000 as a retail manager. They jointly owned their home, although the mortgage was only in Robb's name. The house, which was worth about $375,000, had a $75,000 mortgage.

A lawyer for twenty-three years, who had done a stint in the district attorney's office, Shemtob and his firm concentrated on family law, which included divorce and all issues related to custody, support and equitable distribution of property associated with divorce. (He has since moved on to do finance work, but his wife Lori Shemtob continues in family and divorce law.)

Knowing the law and what usually happens, Shemtob was able to tell Ellen that she could expect to get 50 to 60 percent of everything Robb owned.

That included their house, which Ellen was now listed as a co-owner of on the deed, a pension from Penn and all of his investments both foreign and domestic.

Since Ellen didn't work and had no income of her own, Shemtob told her she could expect to get anywhere from about $3,700 to $4,500 per month. He was basing that on Robb's Penn salary. If Ellen had 100 percent custody of Olivia, her monthly income would be about $4,500 and the lower amount if the child lived with her father.

Custody of Olivia was a big issue for Ellen. She had lived in fear for many years that Robb would make good on his threat to take Olivia away from her to live in Israel.

Ellen knew there was a lot about her situation that her husband could use against her to try to get custody of Olivia. He could try to say that she was too depressed to care for her. She was under heavy medication for her condition. When she felt the worst, she was cutting her hair and cutting herself. She also suffered from stomach ailments that incapacitated her, especially in the mornings. She knew that her hoarding and excessive shopping could be an issue too. She also worried about the house and how they would deal with the mess left behind. She needed help.

Shemtob acknowledged that custody of Olivia could be an issue, but, at the very least, he figured that the custody arrangement would be 50–50.

Ellen was ready to move ahead. She didn't know if Robb would fight her for custody, but even if he did, she knew he was a good dad.

They made plans for Ellen to return on October 30 with her brother Gary. At that time, Shemtob went over much the same ground, but also advised that they begin looking for assets, that she identify bank accounts and verify income, that she collect their tax returns and get as much financial information as necessary.

After that meeting, Shemtob received a retainer check from Gary, and Ellen signed an engagement letter signifying that he was now her attorney.

Shemtob also prepared a separation letter addressed to Robb notifying him of Ellen's desire to separate. "She has advised me that she considers the marriage to be irretrievably broken and the parties to be separated," he wrote. He also told Robb that Ellen wanted to work something out "to minimize the stress on Olivia." He agreed to wait for Ellen to tell him when she wanted the letter to go out.

Just visiting Shemtob appeared to give Ellen confidence that the divorce was going to happen. She began telling friends, even acquaintances, of her plans. Just after Thanksgiving, she encountered Gina Buffa, the custodian at her daughter's school, and told her that she had finally gathered up the courage to leave her husband.

"I am so happy for you. It's about time."

Over the years, Ellen had befriended Gina, who worked evenings cleaning the school. The first time they met was when Olivia was in second grade, and they had hugged hello. Especially during her volunteer days, Ellen would visit often and would always stop and talk, even offering to help Gina do her chores.

Over the years, she had confided in Gina that she was miserable and tried to stay out of her husband's way. Ellen told her he put her down and degraded her verbally. When Gina, who told Ellen that she had gotten out of an abusive marriage herself, asked if Robb was hitting her, Ellen had grown silent and walked away.

Gina told police that she sensed Ellen was afraid, but she never told her why.

Gina's last memory of Ellen was the evening of November 2006 when she saw her parked near the school waiting for Gina to leave work at the end of her shift. Ellen beeped the car for Gina to come over. "I had to get out of the house," Ellen told her. "I came here to hide."

Gina noticed what looked like burn marks on Ellen's arm and asked her about them. Gina said Ellen told her that she picks at her skin when she gets depressed and upset. "I don't feel anything," Gina said Ellen told her. Hearing the words disturbed Gina, who saw Ellen as a sweet, loving lady with a "beautiful laugh" who "didn't want to be rude to anybody." All Gina could do was urge Ellen to leave. "Pick up your daughter and leave," she told her. "I'm working on it," Ellen responded. "When I get the courage to do it I'll let you know."

When Ellen came back after Thanksgiving, she told her she had finally gotten the courage and was planning to get an apartment. "She was under the impression that he [Robb] was going to give her the money to pay for an apartment."

Around the same time, Ellen bumped into LuAnn at the Acme grocery store up on West Lancaster Avenue. They both laughed at themselves and how awful they looked in their sweats. But Ellen looked and sounded happy. She told LuAnn that she was doing it. She had seen a lawyer and was planning to go through with the divorce. She had gotten financial help from her family and would be moving out right after the holidays.

There was always the threat of a fight over custody of Olivia, but Ellen told her friend she was ready. "You go, girl, you fight," LuAnn told her. They hugged goodbye and agreed to get together right after the holidays. LuAnn was struck by her friend's demeanor. She had snapped out of her depression and the physical problems that had kept her hidden. "She was the old Ellen again."

Shemtob next heard from Ellen in a December 1 phone call when she was seeking advice about moving out of the house. If she decided that she needed to leave the house, she needed to come to some sort of agreement with Robb over custody of Olivia. They both had to come to an understanding of where the girl would live and when she would see the other parent. He even suggested a schedule they could follow. While she liked it, she didn't know if Robb would agree.

As Detectives Marino and Gershanick put the pieces together, not only their interviews, but the information flowing into them from the almost thirty investigators working the case, it became clear that the Robbs' marriage had reached a crossroads.

Around the end of August and into September, the Robbs were looking at homes in their area. Robb showed up at an open house in late August for a large old two-story Colonial with a big yard that was selling for $749,000, and on September 10, went to another open house for a $339,000 Cape Cod. Ellen followed up on the Cape Cod and took a careful look at it. She especially liked that the house was in the Upper Merion Area School District, so Olivia could stay in the same school. While she liked the house, she told the realtor that she and her husband were divorcing, but he would not leave their home, so she would have to leave. She said she was worried about money because she didn't work and she didn't want her daughter to change schools. The realtor didn't hear from either one again.

On December 20—two days before Ellen's murder—she called her lawyer back to tell him that she had found a townhouse. She asked if he would write a letter to the landlord specifying how much money she was expected to get in alimony. Shemtob said he couldn't write to the landlord, because he couldn't promise anything, but he could write to her outlining the parameters of how much he expected her to get in alimony and child support.

Shemtob repeated to Ellen how important it was for her to work out a custody arrangement with Robb and not leave that up in the air. It would be best if he knew what to expect. She promised to get back to the attorney.

Talking to Shemtob sealed the motive they needed, Marino and Gershanick agreed.

"Here's our motive," they told each other. "He's not going to want to pay her. He's not going to want her to take his money," added Marino.

"Absolutely," agreed Gershanick. "Two to four thousand dollars a month is a lot of money. Plus there's this other money over here, and who knows what Shemtob can find?"

CHAPTER 30

January 2007

If there was a way to find something positive in Ellen's murder, her friends—known as the Friends of Ellen—were determined to make that happen. They didn't want their friend to be remembered as a crime victim.

They decided to attend the January meeting of the Parent Teacher Club of Roberts Elementary School, where Olivia had attended, and Ellen had been honored for her extensive volunteer work.

They went in asking for permission to plant a memorial garden for Ellen. Others suggested a bench or wishing well. Then one of the parents suggested that they build a gazebo instead. The gazebo idea stuck and soon took on a momentum of its own. They won the support of Principal Sharon Kuznick, who enlisted Fred Remelius, the school groundskeeper, to work with them on selecting the site and doing the preliminary work for it.

They especially liked that the gazebo would be located in a serene corner near the school and the wooded area known as the McKaig Nature Education Center. Now all they had to do was find a structure and figure out how to pay for it.

CHAPTER 31

January 9, 2007

The murder investigation didn't stop with Robb's arrest. As Castor told reporters that day, "We are now on day one of the charges. Detectives will now tie up loose ends as we move to trial."

One of the biggest loose ends was a murder weapon. Hood's autopsy had revealed that Ellen had been bludgeoned by a narrow, heavy object that caused horrendous damage with repeated blows.

Finding the weapon proved difficult. The December 23 press release from Ferman and Lieutenant Early asking for the public's help brought in lots of crowbar sightings, but none that panned out.

Castor repeated his call for the public's help when he announced Robb's arrest. He also described what the evidence showed: that Robb had likely put the weapon, his bloody clothes and shoes, and anything else in a big plastic bag that got dumped somewhere. And there were lots of places where that could have happened between the Robb home on the Main Line and his office in West Philadelphia.

That same garage had a rack with places for eight tools—but one spot was empty, between a shovel and a rake. It was there, Castor demonstrated to reporters, where he figured the murder weapon came from—something long and narrow, not a shovel or a rake. "It's quite obvious when you look at the wall."

If nothing turned up, Castor told reporters, he could always get Dr. Hood to accompany the detectives to Home Depot and select the kind of weapon he thought had been used.

The day after Robb was arrested, Castor got something better. Ellen's brother, Art, came to the detective bureau in Norristown from his home in Haddonfield, New Jersey, for an interview with Detectives Marino and Gershanick.

Art described helping Ellen clean the garage five years earlier and attaching a tool rack to the inside garage wall. He recognized the tools that were up there, and told police there was one missing. It was either a crowbar or a military shovel. The crowbar was about three feet long, the one end was curved to pull out nails and the other end was like a pry bar with a bent angle. The military shovel was green and about four feet long with a folding blade and a spike on one end which could only be seen when the shovel was in the half-folded position.

He was able to point out the shovel in a catalog and accompanied the officers to a Home Depot store, where he picked out a crowbar that resembled the one that was hanging on the garage wall. The one in the Robb garage was older and unpainted. "The last time I saw it, it was hanging on the wall."

Art, who worked for an engineering and contract management firm based in New York City, said he last saw Ellen when he stopped by in the middle of the summer of 2006. He last talked to her the week she was killed, and recalled teasing her for sending Christmas presents to his ex-wife's house. Broad-shouldered and wearing glasses, Art resembled Ellen, who was two years older than him. Although she was only six years older than their youngest brother, Gary, Ellen had played little mother to them as they were growing up and was credited by her brothers with helping them by working three jobs to put herself through college so she could send home her Social Security survivor benefit checks to help her widowed mother. While she was close to both brothers, Ellen spent more time with Art, since he lived nearby in New Jersey, while Gary lived outside Boston.

When asked by Marino if Robb had anything to do with

Ellen's murder, Art didn't mince any words: "There is no one in our circle of friends and family that would do this besides Rafael Robb."

It was clear from Art's descriptions that he had literally tolerated his brother-in-law for many years. He told police of inviting him to his home because of Olivia and Ellen, even though Robb often "would talk over our heads like we were all idiots and make us feel dumb."

He described other transgressions, like Robb eating a meal at Art's house and then going up to his bed and taking a nap without asking, or filling a fine china cup with coffee and walking out of the house with it. Or when he would peel oranges and throw the peels onto a good Oriental rug or crack peanuts and toss the shells on the floor.

On the Penn campus, there was doubt among some of Robb's friends and colleagues who knew a person very different from the murder suspect sitting in jail. At least two of his academic colleagues, one from Penn, visited Robb while he waited in jail for the trial to begin. One was Dr. Harold Cole, who is known to his friends as Hal. In their brief visit, Robb didn't talk about Ellen's murder but appeared to Cole to be dealing with the tragedy that his life had become.

"He exhibited a great deal of grace," Cole recalled.

From jail, Robb was free to use the telephone as long as he kept money supplied to feed the jail's phone meter, which charged $2.00 for every fifteen minutes for local calls. He regularly phoned Olivia, and his family in Israel. On one of those calls, Robb learned that his mother had died from her long illness. He was forced to mourn her by phone with his sister, Ruth. There was no way he would be able to attend her funeral.

CHAPTER 32

Castor made it official. Around the same time as his office was stepping into gear to prosecute Robb by presenting evidence at a preliminary hearing, Castor was making a life decision.

He was giving up the DA's office to jump into county government, trading a high-profile job that paid $137,000 for one that paid $85,000. And that wasn't the only difference. In the DA's office, Castor was the indisputable boss, who directed fifty attorneys and other staffers, and who decided whether to arrest and even whether to seek the death penalty. "I always liked wearing a white hat, doing the right thing," he said. As a county commissioner, Castor would be one of three to run Pennsylvania's most populous suburban county. They would decide how to spend a half-billion-dollar budget, which included raises for 3,300 county employees, and contracts on an array of services. But there would be a lot of mundane tasks too, like voting on bond issues and buying salt for the county roadways.

He'd be going from the black-and-white world he loved to the murky world of local politics, where three people running the show—even if two were from his own party—would require compromise and deal-making.

To understand why is to get a glimpse into the Castor personality.

As Castor saw it, "I'm not a very complicated person. I do

what I think is right, all of the time, personal considerations aside."

Politically, Castor looked statewide at the office of attorney general, or possibly even lieutenant governor. He'd tried to run for attorney general in 2004, but lost in the primary to a party insider.

In his pitch to run this time, Castor—a top vote-getter twice for DA—painted himself as the savior of the GOP, which was being challenged by the growing strength of the Democrats. After more than a century of Republican dominance in the Philadelphia suburbs, the Democrats had made inroads by electing a Democratic governor in Ed Rendell and voting Democratic in the last two presidential campaigns. Al Gore may have ultimately lost the White House, but he won big in the suburbs of Philadelphia. Their real aim was to take over a county courthouse, and Montgomery, with its history of electing Democrats to higher offices, seemed like the best target.

To hear Castor tell it, a Democratic takeover threatened the way of life as he knew it. And it was he who could preserve the status quo so Republicans could continue to run the county and maintain its fiscal conservatism, the quality of life and good schools. The GOP had held the courthouse offices for the past 140 years, but politicos were giving Democrats an even chance of taking over.

Meeting the media for a public announcement, Castor called the election "the most important one in recent memory."

As a proven top vote-getter, Castor said it would be "selfish" of him not to run. Besides, in his twenty-one years in the DA's office he had done everything he wanted to do. He needed a new challenge, and the politics of running the county would give him one.

But he faced a couple of important stumbling blocks. Ken Davis, the county GOP chairman, didn't want him to run and preferred that he seek re-election as DA. And there were two other Republicans already in office who also were seeking re-election.

Once he made the announcement that he wasn't running for DA, Ferman immediately announced her intention to seek the office as the Republican candidate. She had already lined up her own political support, so there was no question that she would be the candidate. She also had Castor's strong support as someone "who could do as good a job as I did."

That ensured that no matter how the Robb case ended, it would be Bruce Castor's finale, his last major prosecution, the case that would most likely seal in the public's memory his legacy as a hard-nosed prosecutor.

In fact, there was no change publicly in how the DA's office was pursuing the case. In preparation for the February 1 preliminary hearing, the DA filed for a warrant to get internal and external laser measurements of the Robb home so artists could produce a sketch for the judge to help him envision how the killer had made his way around the split-level home. They also got back a key DNA crime lab report. All of the blood in the kitchen belonged to Ellen, and Robb's DNA had also been present elsewhere in the house. Just what detectives had expected. Nothing that would exonerate or incriminate Robb. He lived there, and his DNA would be expected to be there.

So his memory would be fresh for the preliminary hearing, Castor wanted to take a look at the house while the detectives took the laser measurements.

As he walked through 670 Forest Road, Castor was thinking of the kind of evidence he wanted to show at the trial to help a jury see not only the layout of the rooms, but the pattern of the blood. The laser measurements would result in accurate sketches of both the interior and exterior of the house, and an animated graphic would show the blood spatter and its location around the door. The graphic would illustrate in 3-D color that the kitchen door had to have been closed when Ellen was murdered, and not open as Robb claimed. Whether the kitchen door had been open or closed was a critical piece of evidence and one that would undermine Robb's version of events. It would have been impossible for Robb to have seen her feet as he entered the house through the garage, as he'd claimed.

As they made their way out of the house, Gershanick noticed paperwork on the kitchen table that had not been there on his earlier visits. On top of a realtor's folder there was a handwritten list of household items and furniture with this note: "Rafi, you can have the following things. I'm taking these."

The day before the court hearing—the first in which the defense would get a crack at Castor's case—the *Inquirer* ran a major story, stripped across the top of the front page, by reporter Kathy Boccella titled, "Portrait of a doomed marriage."

The story, which detailed the Robbs' troubled and loveless marriage, quoted friends and family accusing Robb of emotionally abusing his wife by hiding money from her and using his power as the family breadwinner to control her. It went on to tell of Robb's love for his daughter, Olivia, and how he'd spoiled her with clothes, dinners and New York shows.

Castor couldn't help noticing the article as he prepared for the next day's court appearance. It couldn't hurt, he figured. Its color photos of a smiling Ellen Robb and the Robbs posing on their wedding day would help him make his point to the judge that their marriage had turned sour and Rafael Robb was the only one who'd had a motive to kill Ellen.

CHAPTER 33

February 1, 2007

From where Castor sat in the courtroom of Justice Maruszczak, Robb was the equivalent of the big spender buying a round of drinks. Robb had brought in the legal and technical power to fight the charges at the first step—the district justice level. In the Pennsylvania court system, even felonies like murder must first be heard at the lowest court level, which is presided over by district justices who do not have to be attorneys. If that judge determines there's enough evidence, the case gets kicked up to the Court of Common Pleas, and the judge there takes it for the rest of the way, including a trial. A defendant who is serious about fighting felony charges would take a first strike at the district justice level, regardless of how impossible it appeared.

Robb did just that, bringing in three lawyers, two from Philadelphia, and three technicians. The courtroom, which was the town hall meeting room, was wired for video monitors to show photos—one at the defense table, one at the prosecutor's, a third at the witness stand and a fourth for the judge. There were power cables everywhere.

"I had never seen anything like it," said Castor, who had tried cases in Montgomery County for twenty-two years. "It was a circus."

As he sat at the prosecutor's table, Castor couldn't help thinking that Robb was playing an away game. He'd brought in out-of-county lawyers who thought they would impress the judge with their gadgets and legal muscle. Didn't they know there was no chance this case was going to be thrown out at the preliminary hearing?

Joining Genovese for the preliminary hearing were two attorneys from the Philadelphia firm of Levant, Martin & Tauber, Robert J. Levant and Alan J. Tauber.

Getting a first glance at their set-up put Castor in a fighting mode. He knew what he had and he doubted the defense had anything he didn't already know. In fact, since the murder weapon had never been found, the defense would probably be surprised when he showed them what it looked like.

But first the defense had its opportunity to grill prosecution witnesses, starting with John Finor, the Philly ballistics expert whose initial opinion was that Ellen had been shot in the face.

The opinion was critical to the prosecution because Robb had called in the death and told the dispatch officer that his wife's head had been "cracked." How did he know that, if police experts, looking at her wounds and the surrounding blood, had opined that she had been shot?

In his questioning of Finor, Levant quizzed him on his credentials and experience and what he'd seen when he first viewed Ellen Robb's body—why he believed she had been shot.

When Arthur Gregory took the stand, he was asked to point out his brother-in-law from the five men sitting at the defense table. Robb was the one without the necktie.

Gregory repeated a lot of what he had told detectives on January 9, but with one difference. Shown a photo of the garage, he said there were tools missing—a crowbar and a folding military shovel.

He was able to confirm that the crowbar weapon that Castor held aloft and submitted to the court for evidence was the same size and description as the one he remembered putting up on the wall rack in the Robb garage when he had helped his sister clean up five years earlier.

The only difference was color. The crowbar in court was new and shiny; the one he remembered seeing in the Robb garage was unpainted and rusty. Even under Levant's questioning, showing him photos flashed on a video screen, Art insisted that the tools had been there even when he returned for visits. "I can say that I don't ever recall seeing them moved off the wall," he said.

The defense had shown photos depicting the Robb household as disorganized and cluttered with boxes and personal belongings—all of which police said they'd searched for any evidence, including a murder weapon.

There was one more thing Castor wanted to establish.

Ellen Robb loved to shop. Her brother told the court she "was known as a shopping bag queen," in response to questioning from Castor.

"She had bags everywhere throughout her house, but there were quite a few garbage bags kept in the kitchen, in the garage, in an area that we could call the family room." Castor successfully established that the killer had easy access to plastic bags—the kind that would allow a murderer to dispose of a weapon, clothing and anything else tied to the killing.

Drs. Michals and Samuel didn't appear in court for the preliminary hearing, but their written report to Castor was submitted as evidence, giving the DA the ability to comment on its contents in his summation, and denying the defense the opportunity to question them in person. It's the right to challenge their conclusions that Ellen was targeted in a "blitz attack" that loomed large as the case made its way toward a trial.

But before that could be dealt with the defense would have its first chance to try to undermine Castor's case.

Levant, insisting that the prosecution's scenario was a "fairy tale" with "not a stitch of evidence here for Your Honor to bind that man over," gave the court another view of Castor's circumstantial evidence.

He challenged how Robb could have beaten his wife to death and somehow not leave behind any blood—not a drop in his car, at his office or in the drain traps of his home. "So, he gets himself, the clothes, the mystery murder weapon out of the house into a car, goes about his business, not a speck of blood, not at the University of Pennsylvania, where he worked that day, nowhere in between is there a trace that that man took one speck of forensic evidence out of that house. It is completely implausible."

Next he challenged Castor's claim that Robb's motive for killing his wife was the pending divorce. Castor had said Robb feared the divorce would cost him his fortune and threaten his relationship with his daughter.

Levant mentioned neither, but said no one had been preparing to move anywhere—not on January 1 or on January 15. There was no paperwork indicating that Mrs. Robb would be moving out.

The prosecution had come up with a hole in Robb's alibi—he claimed he had visited a fruit and vegetable stand in Chinatown, but the clerk there gave police a statement that, while Robb was a regular customer, he had not been there on the day of the killing.

Levant asked why Robb would lie about that when he'd fully cooperated with police on everything else they had asked for. "He admits to them at every turn that he had opportunity."

Rather, Levant offered another version of events—that the Chinese clerk who spoke through three translators looked at a head shot photo and hurriedly answered their questions to get them out as quickly as possible. Having the police there was "bad for business, let's tell them what they want, and let's get them out of here."

Levant pressed on, challenging the prosecution's evidence. Regarding the shards of glass, Levant said it was possible Ellen Robb didn't hear the glass shatter as the burglar broke in. There was a television on, a washer was running around the time of the killing and the breaking glass would have landed quietly on a floor rug.

And Robb was justified in telling the police dispatch that his wife's head was cracked. That's what he saw, Levant told the court.

Levant even suggested that police purposely decided to offer that the wound was created by a gunshot: "So, at some point they say, 'Well, we will say it was a shotgun.' 'How did he know the head was cracked? He must have killed her.'

That's what's going on here, because a shotgun blast to the face at close range doesn't produce that crime scene. It does not produce that crime scene. Absolutely, positively not."

None of that surprised Castor. But it didn't bother him either. He knew the defense didn't have any real evidence to prove that Robb did not kill his wife, and he planned to have a little fun with the scenario they did present.

When he got his chance to address the judge, Castor asked that Maruszczak focus on three things: motive, opportunity and behavior exhibiting consciousness of guilt.

One thing Castor enjoyed was performing in court, especially when the facts were in his corner. He buttoned his jacket and rose to address the judge, and, in the most respectful of performances, mocked the defense's position.

If a burglar had killed Ellen Robb, he would have had to break the glass panes on the back door, come into the kitchen, close the door, and lock the dog away upstairs before surprising her from behind and repeatedly mashing her, Castor told the court.

And after, he would have exited covered with blood through the garage to the outside, where he would have stepped directly into public view.

"Now, it could have happened that way. And pigs might fly one day, but I doubt it.

"What happened here is, you have a man who knows that not only is a divorce coming, it is imminent. It is imminent. There's no forms filled out yet, but—you think it's an accident that the very night before Ellen Robb is murdered, she's on the phone with the real estate agent working out the final details about leaving the house and then moving in the following month? It's not just speculation. It's happening, and it's happening right now."

He drove home that the burglary scenario was "a little farfetched" and that money was Robb's motive for murder. In a divorce, Ellen would get 50 to 60 percent of Robb's assets. "Big, big motive for murder. And then every month for years on end he's going to have to pay $3,700 to $4,500 dollars every month for this woman who he clearly does not have any love for."

Castor notes Robb's affection for his daughter, whom he takes to school. On the day of the murder he gets home before she returns from school. "Is it because he wants to make certain that the child does not discover her mother dead?"

He then offered another scenario for how Ellen Robb had been killed: Robb takes his daughter to school, returns home, grabs the crowbar from the garage and "mashes her face in, and he keeps mashing it and mashing it and mashing it, so much so, that it is an overkill situation where the experts tell us that she was specially targeted to be depersonalized, to be turned into somebody—some*thing* other than a human being, an 'it.'"

Covered in blood, he goes out to the garage and puts everything—clothes, boots, weapon into a plastic bag. It just so happens that the crowbar from the garage wall was missing and the boots he was wearing were missing—Robb told police he used to have Timberland boots and then changed his statement to say that he had gotten rid of them.

"Now, his clothes are off and everything, all the blood and everything is in the bag, all wiped off. He can go back in and change his clothes and put on clothes from up in the bedroom, circumventing around the obvious blood, and he goes off to work."

Castor also belittles Robb's claim that he'd spent forty minutes at a tiny fruit stand in Chinatown, and underscored that the Chinese clerk was adamant that she had not seen him that day. And no one calls a full police number when 911 works faster and easier. Even Robb had known that the summer before, when he'd called 911 for help with a nosebleed.

Robb's bizarre behavior indicated that he knew he was guilty, Castor said. Robb told police he had arrived home, seen his wife on the floor, touched her face and gone upstairs to put down his computer, come down, gone outside to call police from a cell phone.

"Is that reasonable behavior? Or are you going to have a freak-out and become—go running out of there screaming for help? Very unusual behavior—unless, of course, you knew when you got home that she was going to be there dead."

He then chided Levant for misunderstanding the evidence from Finor. He was not suggesting that Ellen Robb was shot—rather that people who do this every day thought it was a gunshot case. While Robb, with no training, had called police and said her head was "cracked." "That is something only the killer could know, I suggest."

Castor allowed that his case was circumstantial. "But, just like with any puzzle, one piece doesn't give you the picture, two pieces [don't] give you the picture . . . in this case, you put the pieces together and the picture emerges."

Maruszczak didn't need much time to decide. Shortly after Castor concluded, he declared that "all of the elements have been established for first-degree murder" and the other charges. Putting an end to the four-and-a-half-hour hearing, the judge found "a prima facie" case and ordered that Robb be held over for the county court, where he would stand trial. The first step would be an arraignment in Court of Common Pleas on April 4—a routine court procedure that Robb would not attend.

Outside of the courtroom, the lawyers put their own spin on the day.

"We exposed for the first time today the theory that it was a crowbar that was used to commit the killing," Castor told reporters, adding, "especially a peculiar set of injuries on the forearms that matched up to the striations on the crowbar."

Robb's attorney said the case was still weak.

"The crowbar that the relative last saw approximately five years ago [on] a wall of garden tools is, to us, better evidence for the defense. If that's what the prosecution is going to reach for, then we welcome anything else that they have to bring on," Levant told reporters.

And, in a foreshadowing of arguments to come, Levant told *The Daily Pennsylvanian* that he gave no credence to evidence presented by Castor from a forensic psychiatrist and psychologist that Ellen had suffered a beating intended to "overkill."

Levant called the argument "a complement to junk science," adding that "No court in the land would let that in."

In court, Levant objected to Castor questioning one of the

detectives about the psychiatrists' opinion on the motives for Ellen's murder. The testimony "would not, in any court in Pennsylvania, meet the standards of expert testimony."

The hearing gave Ellen's family a preview of what they would face at trial. Ellen's brother Arthur told reporters it was difficult for him as he sat on the witness stand to look at his brother-in-law. "It's a mix of emotions," he said. "He's the father of my niece," referring to Olivia, who did not attend the hearing.

And stating what had now become painfully clear: "Olivia loved both her parents," Arthur said. "But she had to learn to love them separately."

Many of Ellen's friends came to the hearing. They not only wanted to see Robb up close and in handcuffs, but they wanted to make sure that the DA's case was solid enough to convict him. Even though they weren't asked to testify, they were satisfied that they were able to give police information that helped them zero in on Robb.

Shortly after the court appearance, as if keeping busy would help them ease their pain, the Friends of Ellen started working on a fundraiser for April 29 to collect money for Laurel House, a local women's shelter. During the event, they were also able to raise their first $1,000 toward the gazebo by raffling off three high-end items: a day of beauty at Neiman Marcus, an Avon gift basket, and a Hermès tie. They didn't know if they could get to the $6,000 goal, but they knew this event, at the Viking Cooking School in Bryn Mawr, was a good start.

CHAPTER 34

February 2007

When Tony Corelli, the undercover-cop-turned-glazier, was freely giving Robb some advice, he said Robb needed a good lawyer, one of those expensive Philadelphia guys, somebody like Frank DeSimone.

Robb seemed to be listening closely. Tony had no way of knowing, but he smiled to himself later when he heard that Robb had done just that—hired DeSimone to defend him.

DeSimone's reputation clearly preceded him. Anyone in Philadelphia legal circles knew DeSimone as a top Philadelphia homicide prosecutor who'd become a defense attorney, taking on some of the area's highest profile homicide and white-collar state and federal cases.

Just before taking on the Robb case, DeSimone had been tied up defending the owner of a nightclub who was criminally charged after the collapse of Pier 34, a popular Delaware River nightspot, that killed three young women in 2000. A 2006 trial had ended in a hung jury. Just before a new trial was to begin in 2007, DeSimone negotiated a plea that spared his client, Cherry Hill businessman Eli Karetny, 66, prison but sentenced him to a combination of house arrest, community service and probation. He pleaded guilty to three counts of involuntary manslaughter and forty-three counts of recklessly endangering other people. The district attorney argued that the men were more interested in making money than in safety, and sought a state prison term for each of three to fifteen years.

"This doesn't call for the death penalty . . . a prison sentence, I think, would end Mr. Karetny's life," DeSimone told reporters about his client, who suffered from diabetes and had health problems. To the dismay of the victims' families, Karetny and his co-defendant, the pier owner, were released from house arrest after serving their minimums. For Karetny, freedom came after spending nine months at home, half of his nine to eighteen months' sentence.

In her defense, Philadelphia Common Pleas Judge Sheila Woods-Skipper noted that Karetny had been a model prisoner and had even begun serving his community service working with a nonprofit to teach teens about the restaurant business. Releasing him was "standard."

Family members were stunned, with one mother declaring, "They were getting away with murder." But DeSimone told reporters that Karetny was getting just what he was supposed to get. "He didn't get away with anything. He did what he was supposed to do. . . . He's still on parole and still has to do community service."

DeSimone is picky about the cases he does take—no Mafia, no drugs. His most notable clients include Philadelphia Councilman Jim Tayoun, who pleaded guilty in 1991 to racketeering and other charges; Philip "Crazy Phil" Leonetti, an organized crime figure cooperating with the government; and former Common Pleas Judge Joseph Braig, whose name surfaced in a union scandal for receiving gifts. Judicial investigators determined that Braig had given a silver bowl and pewter ornament worth sixty-four dollars to the union's leader, who gave him five hundred dollars in cash and about two hundred dollars in horseback-riding lessons for his daughters. His lawyers said they were old friends exchanging Christmas gifts. Braig was ultimately cleared by the state Supreme Court.

A devout Catholic who goes to Mass daily, DeSimone doesn't curse, smoke or drink. When retired Cardinal Anthony J. Bevilacqua, himself a lawyer, needed personal legal help, he called on DeSimone. Bevilacqua testified before a grand jury that spent three years investigating priests accused of molesting children. In the end, the statute of limitations prevented any charges from being filed, but the grand jury issued a blistering report that accused the cardinal and his predecessor of protecting priests accused of sexually abusing children.

A native of South Philadelphia, where his father operated a cheesesteak shop at 15th and Morris, DeSimone dreamed of becoming a lawyer and then a prosecutor. Fresh from Villanova University and Villanova law school, a 25-year-old DeSimone interviewed first with an assistant in the office of District Attorney Arlen Specter, who told him they liked him, but couldn't hire him for several months. The next day, he interviewed with Vincent Ziccardi, the public defender. As he walked in, Ziccardi was reading DeSimone's résumé.

"Where are you from?" he calls out to him.

"Eighteenth and Ritner," DeSimone answered.

"You're hired. We hire guys from corners. I'm from Passyunk and Moore."

"But I'm waiting to hear from the district attorney's office in a couple of months."

"Forget about them. You are going to have fun here. You are going to love it," and he offered him a salary of $9,500.

Three years later, after winning his share of jury trials as a public defender against the DA's office, DeSimone would become the first assistant district attorney sworn in by incoming DA Emmett Fitzpatrick. The newly elected DA said he had been checking around the courthouse, and the judges kept pointing him to DeSimone. He had finally gotten his dream job where he continued to make a name for himself for taking cases to trial and getting convictions. It's where he honed his courtroom skills and his reputation for withering cross-examinations. In his summations, he's known for quoting Shakespeare or anyone else who will help him make his point.

One case he won't easily forget from his prosecutor days is the 1975 conviction of Philadelphia Black Mafia founder Robert Mims for the bloody 1971 robbery-murder at the former Dubrow's Furniture Store on South Street. During the trial, while DeSimone was questioning a witness, Mims shouted out at him, "I have the power to make your heart stop."

Mims was convicted of murder and given a life sentence.

In 1976, a witness who testified against Mims was murdered, and another defendant was murdered execution-style in his home. His wife was also killed.

Those murders remain unsolved.

DeSimone stayed in the DA's office for six-and-a-half years before declaring that he had had enough of the homicide grind and struck out on his own as a defense attorney.

When his name surfaced as representing Robb, veteran court watchers immediately recalled that DeSimone and Castor had their own history as rivals and anticipated a lively courtroom rematch between the classy, smooth DeSimone and the brash, driving Castor. That DeSimone, 62, had sixteen years more experience in handling courtroom drama than the forty-six-year-old Castor didn't matter. What he lacked in years, Castor made up for in confidence. Besides, Castor would have liked nothing better than a rematch with his longtime adversary.

The feud between Castor and DeSimone dates at least to February 2, 1994, the day a jury brought back an acquittal for Patricia Swinehart on charges she murdered her husband David, a flamboyant and well-known local developer.

It was a case that Castor had counted on to win even though he was fairly new to his job as assistant district attorney. DeSimone and another former prosecutor, Jeffrey Miller, defended Swinehart, who was a suspect in the murder for a dozen years before actually facing charges.

David Swinehart was murdered outside his home by a group of men as he walked to his car. He was clubbed in the head, repeatedly stabbed and stuffed into the back seat of his car, a trademark red-and-white Cadillac with Rolls Royce trim. Police later found bloodstained ice and snow in the driveway. The car with Swinehart's frozen body was found three days later outside a local alley.

Four men were charged, three convicted, including two of Swinehart's nephews, one of whom was having an affair with his wife and is now serving a life sentence for the killing.

Patricia Swinehart was charged after the fourth man, Terry Lee Maute, who was acquitted by a jury, but serving 20 years on unrelated charges, decided to change his mind. He testified that Swinehart had arranged the killing by recruiting three of the men, including himself. He said she'd paid him $3,000 for his role in the murder and promised him the maintenance contract on her husband's extensive property holdings.

The career criminal and former drug addict became Castor's star witness, an outcome exploited by DeSimone, who railed against Maute in a five-hour closing, calling him a "predator," a "beast," and a "savage," who'd lied so well in 1985 that a jury acquitted him.

"He's raping you from that witness stand," DeSimone thundered. "He raped one jury already. Don't let him rape you."

Castor, equally intense, appealed to the jury to see things another way: The Swineharts were in the middle of a divorce and Patricia had just learned that her husband, who she had counted on to give her $10,000 a month, was literally broke. The best she was going to get was $150 a month.

"She goes into the divorce thinking she will take him to the cleaners, make a ton of money and be done with the SOB," Castor said. "Then she decides that the only way she's going to get any money is through the life insurance. And the plan to commit the murder is made."

After the acquittal, Castor said he had been hamstrung by a judge's ruling that he could not tell the jury that David Swinehart had died the night before he was to change the names on an insurance trust agreement worth more than $500,000 from his wife to his children, which turned out to be the only real value in the estate. The judge refused to let Castor tell the jury about the switch plan, saying there was no evidence showing that Patricia had known about it. The ruling struck deeply at Castor's case. He had planned to drive home to the jury that Patricia had had to arrange the murder to happen on that Friday because she would be out of money by the next day. He'd be able to refute a point that DeSimone had hammered repeatedly to the jury.

Why would Patricia Swinehart arrange her husband's murder in her own home on a night when her house was full of people?

"The decision to exclude the imminent change in the insurance was devastating to our case, absolutely devastating," Castor told reporters at the time.

DeSimone disagreed, of course, and blamed the prosecution's defeat on a weak case that hinged on a lowlife. "They didn't have anything," DeSimone told reporters. "They had Terry Maute, who was nothing, and whom the jury chose to disbelieve. That's it, clear and simple."

But what Castor remembers is that he could have appealed the judge's ruling and didn't. He recalls visiting then–District Attorney Marino and talking about the ruling. The judge said the conspirator had testified that Swinehart planned to change his will, not his life insurance. They are different, and the prosecution couldn't suggest that Patricia knew about it. Marino asked him if he thought he could win without it. Castor said he did, a decision he came to regret. One of the facts weighing on him was that the murder had happened twelve years before. In retrospect, he believes that if he had appealed the ruling, he would have won the case.

In the days after the acquittal, Castor heard from eight of the twelve jurors in person or in writing, apologizing to him for their decision. They had been sequestered and, once they were home and catching up on the newspapers, they learned what the judge had not allowed them to hear.

With Swinehart burning in his memory as the only homicide case he'd lost as a prosecutor, Castor vowed never again to let an adverse ruling lie unchallenged.

It turned out to be a vow that would have an enormous impact on Rafael Robb's life. One of the issues key to the case was whether Castor could tell the jury about a psychiatric analysis of the killing.

Swinehart wasn't the only dust-up between DeSimone and Castor. Their most recent big case was in 1997 when DeSimone represented Craig Rabinowitz, the well-liked, seemingly successful Main Line businessman who was accused of strangling his young attorney wife, Stefanie, in a scheme to collect on her life insurance policy.

With the jury, which had been selected from another county, seated, and Castor literally minutes from calling his first witness, DeSimone tapped Castor on the shoulder and whispered to him that the day's proceeding would be short. When Castor asked why, DeSimone told him that Rabinowitz had decided to plead guilty.

The plea, which Rabinowitz said had come after he'd had a dream in which his slain wife, his father and father-in-law told him, "It's time to do the right thing," ended one of the most sensational murder cases in Philadelphia history. What gave it front-page headline status was that Rabinowitz had needed the money to pay off debts piled up from his relationship with a gentlemen's club stripper, who was known as Summer. The smoking guns that Castor, who was trying the case with Ferman, had ready to present at trial were that Rabinowitz had left behind papers that listed, in his own handwriting, $671,000 in debts and $1.4 million from his wife's insurance, and selling his car and her stock.

When asked in court by Castor why he had murdered his wife, Rabinowitz said there was no easy answer. "My life has become such a sham and a fake and a fraud."

In talking to his lawyers, Rabinowitz credited DeSimone, who was known for his religious devotion, with giving him the words to describe himself as having a "moral disconnect." He added, "I lost my ability to know right from wrong. Right became wrong and wrong became right."

While DeSimone described Rabinowitz's plea as "the day of reconciliation," Castor refused to give the defendant credit for any remorse.

Speaking to a crush of reporters outside the courtroom, Castor declared: "From what I know of Craig Rabinowitz, his only attribute that he was ever given by God was that he was a con man and a swindler and a faker and a liar. I didn't buy a word that he said . . . I think he was playing to the family . . . and to the other people in the courtroom to try and give them some feeling that maybe he isn't the monster that the commonwealth intended to portray that he is."

Rafael Robb knew all about the Rabinowitz case, as well as many of DeSimone's other big cases, before the two men met in the county jail. Robb knew he wanted DeSimone on his team.

Robb also knew that there was bad blood between the defense attorney and the prosecutor. He wanted someone who would fight for him, and DeSimone had obviously shown he was good at that.

DeSimone blames the Swinehart case for his rift with Castor, saying Castor is still smarting from losing to him. By blaming the judge's ruling, Castor is coming up with an analysis "that doesn't allow you to improve yourself."

DeSimone won't say he doesn't like Castor; just that he respects him and has found him to be honest, and his office good to work with; while Castor openly admits, "While I don't particularly care for the guy, the bottom line is, he knows his business."

To remind himself of his own defeat against DeSimone, for seven years after the trial, Castor kept in his office a courtroom sketch from the Swinehart case. Also hanging there, were drawings from two other cases in which he had been victorious—the Rabinowitz case and another, a famous local jury trial, in which Guy Sileo was convicted of the shooting death of his restaurant partner, James Webb.

In the Swinehart case, Castor looked every bit the part of the successful prosecutor, standing in front of a jury box, ready to argue why the bad guy should go to jail. "I needed to remind myself I wasn't perfect," Castor told an *Inquirer* reporter in 2002 about why he kept the drawing hanging in his office.

As it turns out, Robb had enlisted help from jail to research the area's best attorneys. He had already assembled a team of Francis J. Genovese, Alan J. Tauber and Jules Epstein. Shortly after hiring DeSimone, he pared his dream team down to DeSimone and Epstein, who together expected to take the case to trial. In Epstein, Robb had a Center City lawyer and

Widener University professor who was an expert in the fine points of criminal law and evidence. A University of Pennsylvania law school grad, Epstein was a partner in the highly respected criminal law firm now renamed Kairys, Rudovsky, Messing & Feinberg before becoming a law professor. He also wrote articles, a chapter in the book *Proving Criminal Defenses*, and did training for lawyers and judges in capital murder cases. Among his cases are appeals for death row inmates.

As a veteran litigator who had taken and won scores of homicide cases, both as prosecutor and defense attorney, DeSimone preferred defending a suspect who had said nothing—one in which he starts with a clean slate. That wasn't the case with Robb.

By the time DeSimone got the case, a lot of damage had been done from Robb's point of view. He had voluntarily given a 29-page, single-spaced interview to police without a lawyer present. He had taken detectives on a walk-through of his home, during which he'd acted out a lot of what he had already told them the day of the murder. He had unwittingly talked to undercover detectives who'd acted sympathetically, but gotten him to talk and make statements that Castor would surely use against him. His alibi had problems, because he'd claimed a stop at a Chinese fruit market that the clerk told police he didn't make. And there had already been a preliminary hearing where the judge had ruled that there was enough evidence to hold Robb over for trial.

Taking a look at all of that, DeSimone initiated a series of legal maneuvers aimed at improving Robb's position as they prepared for trial. He started by asking the court in a July 29 filing to re-open the preliminary hearing and challenge the basic evidence holding Robb. While the move was routine, it gave DeSimone the option of submitting new evidence to clear Robb if he came up with it.

He also started laying the groundwork for issues that would become more important closer to trial. It was a time for typical pre-trial motions—the kind of back-and-forth between defense and prosecution that allowed both sides to line up their evidence and to put issues on the table.

In one filing, he put Castor on notice that he was opposing the use of statements from friends and family impugning Robb's character as evidence. Their comments regarding what Ellen had told them about Robb's treatment of her or what they had observed of the couple's marriage were hearsay and inadmissible, DeSimone argued to the court.

DeSimone and Epstein also zeroed in on one piece of evidence that they figured could help them undermine Castor's case. During the investigation, the detectives cut out a piece of flooring from the Robb kitchen to preserve bloody footprints.

It was just the kind of evidence that DeSimone figured could help him argue that someone else could have killed Ellen Robb. The footprints could exonerate Robb because they were smaller than Robb's size 12 foot.

On April 12, a *Philadelphia Daily News* headline summarized the dispute: Will FBI tests wreck DA's slaying case? The story hit during a time when the footprints were being analyzed by the FBI, but no report had yet been issued to the defense.

The headline didn't matter to Castor.

He already knew from a verbal report from the FBI that the footprints were leading to a dead end. After an exhaustive search, the FBI could not find a boot manufacturer to match the prints, and could only conclude that they must have come from some foreign source not registered in available databases.

They also couldn't come up with a specific size, because the prints didn't show a complete foot. All they had to do now was wait for the FBI report to arrive. When it did, Castor told the court, DeSimone would have it. The fact that Robb wore a size 12 wasn't going to matter, Castor figured. Someone could wear a size 12 for the inner part of a shoe, but a boot could leave a much bigger footprint.

The defense hired their own expert—the Henry C. Lee Institute in Connecticut, the same consultants who'd worked on the O. J. Simpson case—who also could not come up with a size or make on the prints. While the shoeprint was not conclusive for either side, both sides planned to use it at trial.

DeSimone would argue that the fact that the FBI couldn't establish that the footprint belonged to Robb created reasonable

doubt as to the identity of the killer. If the footprints did not belong to Robb, then who did they belong to? Why not the real
killer? Why not someone other than Robb? DeSimone would
also ask why the country's premier investigative agency could
not match a footprint. What was so unusual about it that the
FBI couldn't even tell which company made it?

The government could not prove that the prints belonged to
Robb, but they could use them to hammer away at the boots.
Robb admitted owning them, but where were they now? Why
weren't they in Robb's closet as he told police they should be?

Robb initially told police he owned two pair of Timberland
boots. The boots "should be upstairs in my bedroom closet. I
haven't worn them in years." A neighbor had even given police a photo showing Robb in tall Timberland work boots on a
school outing. After he reread the statement, Robb changed it
to say, "I don't have them anymore."

Castor would also point out that the FBI had concluded
that the boots were likely foreign-made, although he had
hoped that the FBI would at least identify the heavy-lugged
tread shoe pattern. Robb traveled to Israel, Europe and Asia
regularly. He had the opportunity to purchase foreign-made
products.

A stretch? Perhaps. But both planned to use the bloody
footprints—Castor to tie Robb to them and DeSimone to argue
that there was nothing about them that Castor could tie to Robb.
The prints had begun in the kitchen close to the body, continued
out of the kitchen, across the lower level den and into the
garage. That's where they'd stopped.

For the prosecution, the story would continue like this: The
prints stopped at the spot where Robb could have stepped into
a huge plastic bag—one of the many that his wife left lying
around the house—and stripped himself of bloody clothes,
boots and the murder weapon. That's why police never found
any physical evidence tying him to the murder.

There was another scenario.

Castor had one other item he could have shown to the jury.
In Robb's trunk, police found an unopened package of a full-

length protective coverall suit—the kind that zippers up the front and allows you to easily step out of it.

Could he have worn a similar suit when he attacked Ellen? If he did, that would explain why cleanup was seemingly pretty complete. Also in Robb's car, police found a package of face masks and a realtor folder about the townhouse that Ellen had found and wanted to move into after the holidays.

From his first public comments, Castor had told reporters not to expect the case to turn on forensics. There wasn't going to be a DNA match that revealed Robb as the killer, or a fingerprint. That void of evidence gave the defense an opening. For DeSimone, all of the physical evidence—or lack of it—helped him give credence to the possibility that someone had broken into the Robb home and killed Ellen. All DeSimone had to do was create a reasonable doubt that Robb was not the killer, and the fact that there was no physical evidence tying him to the murder was a big help.

With the killing scene so bloody, how was it that Robb had no blood on him—not on his clothes or even his car? And the only blood on him—the small amount on the web of his hand—Robb explained by saying that, when he'd gotten home and discovered Ellen sprawled on the kitchen floor, his first reaction had been to touch her face with that hand. If Robb was really the killer, DeSimone planned to argue, then why wasn't there blood somewhere on him or his car? Could he really clean himself off so completely and not leave even a drop of blood anywhere on him?

CHAPTER 35

March 2007

Frank DeSimone's first meeting with Castor came when he and Francis Genovese met with Judge Tressler to set a date for Robb's arraignment in the Court of Common Pleas. The meeting with the judge was routine. He asked about the parameters of the case, their plans for evidence and pre-trial issues. He wanted it all taken care of before the trial.

But as the attorneys moved out to an adjoining room, Castor floated a trial balloon. Castor was convinced, he said, that Robb had killed his wife, but wasn't sure about Robb's state of mind. He was opening the door for the possibility that Robb had not planned Ellen's murder as was charged, but that it had happened during a blow-up between them, or, as the law states, as a crime of passion.

If Robb would admit to the killing, Castor "wouldn't rule out" allowing him to plead guilty to voluntary manslaughter.

Both were taken aback. Genovese especially, having worked for Castor as an assistant district attorney, knew he didn't offer pleas easily in murder cases. All the attorneys could say was that Robb had been adamant that he was innocent. They would tell him about the offer.

In the meantime, both sides agreed that for now, they were moving toward a trial. The first appearance was on April 4, when Robb was to be formally arraigned before Tressler.

After Castor walked away, DeSimone and Genovese, who

were both former prosecutors, savored the moment. They took the prospect of the DA agreeing to drop the charges from first-degree murder to voluntary manslaughter as a signal.

"It told me he wasn't convinced of the strength of what he had," said Genovese, who had prosecuted homicides and major crimes under Castor. He and DeSimone agreed on something else. As Genovese put it: If the deal stayed on the table, "this is as good a result as this guy is going to get."

Although Castor didn't personally like DeSimone, he respected him enough to know that he had already sized up the case. Castor figured that DeSimone saw the case the way he did, but he also knew that the defense attorney could not say anything yet—not until his client authorized him to.

As Robb's lead attorney, DeSimone was obligated to tell Robb about the DA's offer. During a visit at the county jail, DeSimone reviewed Robb's options with him.

It would be the first of many discussions with Robb on Castor's plea deal and their chances of winning at trial.

Castor could see what was coming in the Robb case. With the help of Epstein, DeSimone would attack one of Castor's central pieces of evidence—the report from forensic psychiatrists who, as expert witnesses, had concluded that the killer targeted Ellen Robb with overkill just to watch her suffer.

In his first pre-trial motions, DeSimone revealed that his defense would include a vigorous challenge to the notion that Castor's experts could characterize why and how Robb would kill his wife. The issue would be the driving force in the case in the months before the scheduled November 26 trial.

Meanwhile, Ellen's friends worked to keep her memory alive. An evergreen memorial that they had built around a tree in front of the Robb home had disappeared by early March. A group of a dozen friends met at the now–snow-covered site to rebuild the memorial with a cross of stiff yellow ribbon attached to the tree, surrounded by stuffed animals, candles, colorful silk flowers and a photo of Ellen with the inscription: In Loving Memory of Ellen Gregory Robb. You Will Always Be Remembered.

"We don't want her to think we forgot about her," an unidentified friend told CBS 3's Walt Hunter.

Dressed for snow in a heavy jacket, snug black hat and sunglasses to shield her eyes from the sun on snow glare, Mary Beth led a prayer as the group formed a circle and held hands. "We grieve at her loss. We thank you for the time we had to know her and love her and enjoy her company."

The memorial "allows us to do something for her when we couldn't do anything before," added Patty Volpi. "We feel helpless [about] what happened to her."

Behind the scenes, the friends were also raising money. They needed to come up with $6,000 to buy the gazebo they had decided to put on the grounds of Roberts Elementary in Ellen's honor. Some of it came from fundraisers and personal donations and the rest from selling pizzas through the school.

Whenever they ran into trouble, something came along to help them.

"This is very strange," Mary Beth told the others. "Every step along the way, it's like Ellen is inspiring us."

Six weeks after starting their project, they had enough to call Sam Zook, the Amish contractor, and arrange a June delivery.

By spring, Roberts Elementary had something to celebrate. On May 18, the third-grade students were among the guests at Valley Forge Presbyterian Church for the wedding of their teacher, Karen Faix, and Upper Merion Detective David Gershanick. About one hundred fifty people, including their colleagues from Roberts Elementary and the Upper Merion police force, celebrated with them at a reception at the Radisson Hotel Valley Forge.

CHAPTER 36

July 2007

Much of DeSimone's ammunition was aimed at keeping the jury away from Castor's key evidence—a report from forensic psychiatrists who characterized Ellen's murder as a "blitz attack" by someone who'd known her and wanted to see her suffer.

The report by Dr. Michals and Dr. Samuel concluded that Ellen Robb had been targeted for "overkill" by someone who wanted to dehumanize her and reduce her to an "it."

In court, Castor called the report "devastating evidence."

The only way DeSimone could attack it was to make Castor jump through legal hoops before he could present it to a jury. Castor had already talked about it publicly and had been quoted widely in newspapers and television news shows describing how and why Ellen Robb had been killed.

DeSimone first gave legal notice of his position to challenge Castor's use of the expert witness in legal papers filed in July. Citing nine Pennsylvania Supreme Court decisions barring expert testimony, DeSimone concluded that the court has "consistently and unequivocally rejected expert testimony that relies on profiles and typical or specific behavior patterns in criminal cases." This type of expert testimony "simply is not admissible in this Commonwealth."

For the August 27 hearing, DeSimone was joined at the defense table by Jules Epstein, who helped present to Judge

Tressler what the defense had already begun to lay out in their papers.

Such profiling can be helpful to police during the investigation stage to narrow their search for a suspect, but not in court to be used against an individual defendant, DeSimone and Epstein argued.

They called Castor's move "novel evidence," and asked that the court hold a hearing on whether the experts' opinion could be heard by the jury.

Castor didn't want the issue to go to a hearing. That would require him to lay out the heart of his case and allow the defense to question his experts—all before the trial even began.

His plan, he added, was for the experts to render their opinions of Ellen's murder, not offer a profile of a killer. "Rather, Dr. Samuel and Dr. Michals will testify according to their report describing the manner in which the murder was committed, using the evidence and their experience as guideposts," Castor wrote to the judge.

During the October hearing, Assistant District Attorney Sander pointed out that the experts are needed to "exclude burglars as being the individuals that would commit this type of murder . . ." It was Robb who had said that he had discovered a broken back door window when he arrived to find his wife dead on the kitchen floor.

If Castor planned to call the expert testimony psychiatry, it would be "on the fringe," countered Epstein.

In another filing, DeSimone challenged as inadmissible the testimony by Detective Finor at the preliminary hearing that he had initially thought Ellen Robb had been shot. Castor's point was that if experts thought she had been shot, then Robb's description to the police dispatcher that her head had been cracked showed that he was the killer. DeSimone wrote to the court, ". . . the real question is did he [Robb] see it differently than a layperson?"

Castor wasn't worried. He didn't think DeSimone would be able to keep out testimony from police on what they'd found when they arrived at the scene and what they'd told the district attorney. At trial he would bring in the pathologists to testify about how Ellen Robb had died. That would negate any issue about whether Finor could be challenged as an expert.

But first Castor would have to convince Judge Tressler, who had heard arguments on all of the pre-trial issues during hearings in August, October and November.

Arguing for Robb, Epstein said the DA should not be allowed to conclude to the jury that Robb had "insider knowledge" about Ellen's murder because he told the dispatcher her head was cracked. Connecting what Robb had reported seeing and a presumption of his guilt "doesn't compute," he argued. The jury might easily see the situation as he did.

Castor said Finor didn't need to be classified as an expert. The bottom line was that the jury needed to know how Robb had described the scene and how police had described it: "So that when Robb then says that her head was cracked, that's totally at odds with what all of the people working on the case had thought."

As Castor told Judge Tressler, the defense was worried that Robb's knowledge that Ellen's head was cracked would be incriminating and "they are afraid that they will not be able to make the argument sufficient to counter that. You know what? That's the breaks. That's the way courtroom proceedings operate. The police come in; they saw what they saw, and they say the conclusions that they drew, and what they did as a result of those conclusions."

CHAPTER 37

September 2007

While the attorneys traded strategy moves toward a November trial, Ellen's friends and family gathered on a sunny, warm evening in late September to dedicate the gazebo built in her honor.

Programs with a bright yellow rose on the cover and bouquets of yellow roses—Ellen's favorite—greeted friends and family as they arrived for the early evening ceremony in a shady area next to the school on Croton Road in Wayne.

Ellen's brothers, Gary and Art, wore miniature yellow roses on their lapels. Olivia wore a delicate wrist corsage with a bed of tiny roses encased in lace. Dressed in a black sundress, she sat quietly, her uncle Gary's arm around her shoulders as they listened to Ellen's friends talk about her and the project that had given them a way to remember her. The "Friends of Ellen" had selected the gazebo and its location in the grassy garden next to the school so it could become a quiet place for students and teachers to reflect and find peace. More than anything, they wanted the gazebo to be enjoyed.

There were many other days for tears. This would be a day to celebrate the Ellen they had known and loved, the Ellen who'd made herself so indispensable at Roberts Elementary that she had become a Volunteer of the Year, the Ellen who had so touched teachers and other parents that many of them came to help dedicate the gazebo in her memory.

Principal Sharon Kuznick, who was recovering from a broken leg, hobbled to the microphone to let everyone know that the gazebo would become part of the school's program.

"This gazebo will be a place to reflect on Ellen's life and the immeasurable contributions she made as a parent for the benefit of the students of Roberts Elementary School. Ellen loved nature, and this gazebo is a perfect location for reflecting on nature's beauty, for you can rest in it and view, a short distance away, the McKaig Nature Education Center.

"When you have the opportunity to stand or sit in the gazebo and gaze at the beauty of the surrounding gardens and nature center, you may ask the same question that I asked earlier today as I stood in the gazebo: Why?"

The question hung in the air, reminding everyone that they were there because Ellen had been brutally and senselessly killed.

"We are here tonight to dedicate this gazebo to a very special person—Ellen Gregory Robb," began LuAnn Dubin, one of the organizers. "Ellen gave us so many things. She gave us the gift of laughter that will fill our hearts and our memories forever." And a lot more, she added, as others in the crowd happily nodded in agreement, Ellen's endless phone calls and thank-you notes and simple gifts. "She continues to share her spirit and give her spirit from above."

The gazebo was built only because so many people had come together to help make it happen, Mary Beth Pedlow told the crowd. "Anyone who knew Ellen knew she would have loved the bargain." As the person who had coordinated the project, Mary Beth described how so many had volunteered to help. Paul and Patty Volpi had planted the flower beds around it; the structure itself had been made possible by Sam Zook, an Amish contractor who had replaced the roof at the Robb house and remembered Ellen as someone who was nice to him. When he'd heard about the killing, he'd asked Mary Beth how anyone could have hurt her.

To help the effort, Zook negotiated a $6,000 price, which the group had been able to raise, for the maintenance-free white structure. Paul Volpi had also worked with John and

Michael Hopson to prepare the site and lay the foundation to meet the town's code. The one thousand-pound structure was put in place in June.

"This was truly a community project to show that this woman was a beloved member of our society," Mary Beth said.

When he rose to thank the "Friends of Ellen" on behalf of the family, Gary repeated a description of his sister that he had shared during her eulogy. Recalling a comment from Ellen's friend Chris McGuire, Gary described his sister as "an amazing comet. They are exceptionally rare, and once you see one, you are touched—and you will carry it with you forever."

Gary described how Ellen had had a knack for being able to stay in touch with people even if she hadn't spoken to them in a while. "Once you were in her circle, you would not be let out," he said, choking back tears.

A plaque attached above the gazebo entrance said nothing about how she had died, only how she had lived:

This gazebo is a gift from the community in memory of Ellen Gregory Robb who loved children, nature and Roberts Elementary School. May all who come here remember her in love September 28, 2007.

The other plaque with Ellen's name on it hung in the school's front hall on the Parent Teacher Club Hall of Fame in recognition of her volunteer work at the school.

CHAPTER 38

November 2007

The issue of whether the psychiatrists' analysis of Ellen's murder would ever be heard by a jury came to a head at the November 9 court hearing. Not only did Castor reiterate that the testimony would be critical to his case, but he let it be known that he would appeal if the judge ordered a hearing. It would become a key development.

Robb came to court that day looking clean-shaven and sharper than he had the day he was arrested. He greeted his lawyers and chatted briefly with DeSimone and Epstein, listening intently as both sides took their turns addressing the judge.

Epstein stood first, telling Tressler that prior cases supported the defense's request for a hearing.

"The case law supports our request for a Frye hearing," said Epstein, who looked collegiate with his longish hair and wire-rim glasses. A so-called Frye hearing would air whether Castor's expert witness report met the allowed definition or not.

Castor disagreed, saying that his evidence was not subject to Frye.

"The reason for Frye is so you never have to do it again," he said, noting that such a hearing had to be held when DNA evidence was first used in a trial to establish it as reliable science.

And in a reference that Castor knew the judge would understand, he added, "This case is no different than the Guy

Sileo case," alluding to the testimony in that trial of the pathologist, Dr. Ian Hood.

"I am so convinced that this is a critical point in this case that the Commonwealth intends to appeal if it goes against us," Castor told the judge, as he stood at the prosecution table in his signature pinstriped suit, Assistant DA Sander sitting beside him.

Castor was actually repeating in public what he had already signaled to the defense and the judge privately.

Tressler replied, "I agree this is a substantial part of the case, and you are substantially handicapped if it goes against you. Frye applies to novel evidence. Are you not arguing this is not novel?"

"No," Castor responded. "This is not novel."

Tressler agreed to make a decision the following week.

In Judge Tressler, both parties had a wily veteran—a former prosecutor and criminal defense attorney who had presided over one hundred murder cases in his twenty-five years as a criminal court judge, including high-profile ones like Sileo, who was convicted by a jury trial and sentenced by Tressler to life in prison.

He was known for being tough but also highly skilled in the fine points of criminal and courtroom procedures, subjects he often taught to judges and lawyers across the country. He reserved a special place for juvenile court where he knew he could "make a difference" by being the authority figure they often lacked at home. He had won national kudos for innovative programs.

Outside the courtroom, Castor and the defense attorneys took turns explaining what was at stake.

"This is important to me now, because you have the obvious defense [that] the burglar does the killing. This evidence debunks that," Castor told reporters. "Believe me, I understand why the defense is upset. This piece of evidence really crushes their case."

The defense argued that Castor's approach was novel and smacked of junk science. If he wanted to use it, he was subject to proving its scientific basis in a court hearing. Epstein told reporters that Pennsylvania courts haven't yet decided the issue, which has been rejected around the country. "If you look around the country, courts say, 'No, you can't,' and that's the issue that's before this court," he said.

Under Pennsylvania law, only the prosecutor could appeal an order that would deny his use of information in the trial. The defense could only appeal later, after a verdict.

If Castor did end up appealing over this issue, it would delay Robb's murder trial for several years as the issue made its way through the Pennsylvania courts.

The result for Robb would be to sit in jail and wait for an outcome of the evidence issue before a trial.

That development would have a dramatic impact on the outcome of the case.

Before launching on this strategy, Castor had analyzed the move every way in discussions with Assistant District Attorney Sander. He wanted to make sure there were no flaws in the idea before he carried it out.

Castor asked himself, Is there something I'm not thinking of?

In the end, they agreed that they had to do it. If the strategy worked, Robb would plead. "We want Robb to know that no matter how the hearing goes, either way he's going to jail for a long time," Castor said.

For Castor, the situation reminded him of the Swinehart case, only this time he wasn't going to hesitate. He would use his power to appeal to protect his witness. In Swinehart, Castor blamed himself for losing the case because he'd failed to appeal a judge's ruling that had been won by DeSimone.

With a November 26 trial date looming, the judge's decision would be key and begin a delicate phase of Robb's case.

Castor had first floated the possibility of Robb pleading guilty to a lesser charge than murder early on, before Robb was even arraigned.

At that time, Robb was focused on beating the charge and on assembling a legal dream team to help him do it.

Although the possibility of a plea deal was out there, there wasn't any action on it all summer and into the fall. DeSimone was focused on preparing for a trial. Castor, too, worked with the detectives to fine-tune the evidence they had.

All of that changed when Castor let it be known that he would appeal an adverse ruling from the judge on the experts' testimony.

The prospect of waiting several years for a trial was real, DeSimone told Robb.

On November 6, Castor was the top vote-getter to win election to one of three seats on the county commission. He immediately made it known that he would stay with this case to the end, whenever that would be. Risa Ferman, the newly elected DA, had appointed Castor a special prosecutor so he could follow the case even if it didn't go to trial for several years—another step for Castor to put pressure on Robb. As Castor saw it, Robb had virtually no choice but to plead. Would he?

In every meeting he had with DeSimone, Robb asked detailed questions and analyzed his lawyer's responses. Robb had backgrounded DeSimone and had spoken with him about how he had won an acquittal for Patty Swinehart, who was charged in the contract murder of her husband. The Swinehart case was also the only one in which Castor had lost a murder trial. As Robb would learn, there's one major difference between the Swinehart case and this one: Castor was offering Robb a plea. There was no plea offer to Swinehart.

As DeSimone patiently explained, he was prepared to put on a vigorous defense, but there were no guarantees he would win. If he lost, Robb faced prison for the rest of his life.

Or he could plead guilty to a lesser charge. The likely possibility would be voluntary manslaughter, which—while it carried a maximum prison term of up to 10 to 20 years—the standard amount under the state's sentencing guidelines for someone like Robb, with no prior conviction, would be a minimum of 4 ½ years and a maximum of 6 years.

If the case went to trial, Castor figured Robb would testify, that he couldn't resist trying to outsmart the prosecutor from the witness stand.

DeSimone had another plan. He didn't expect to have Robb testify. He would never be a sympathetic witness, and he would be subjected to Castor's brutal cross-examination.

Castor had carefully thought through the details of the case before letting on that a deal was possible. He certainly believed Robb had murdered his wife. But he also believed that the evidence, especially the way she was brutally killed, pointed to a crime of passion, a rage killing with a weapon of opportunity. A guy who'd suddenly lost his cool and grabbed whatever he could to act on it. He didn't tell DeSimone this, but Castor saw a conviction of first-degree murder as a potential injustice. Technically, Robb was guilty of premeditated murder. As he'd delivered the blows to his wife's face, at some point, he must have become aware of what he was doing—that he was delivering blows to her face that would kill her.

For Castor, the difference was that murder required malice as the law defined it. First-degree murder required malice, meaning that the murder was premeditated and the killer had a specific intention to kill. That's not what the evidence showed.

It's an analysis that he thoroughly discussed with Assistant District Attorney Sander, who would be assisting him in the trial. As if he were giving a lecture, Castor explained his reasoning:

"It's a more severe crime to kill someone with reason. In other words, you have all of your faculties and you go kill somebody, as opposed to you fly in a rage and kill somebody.

"Both result in somebody being dead, but the law considers the mental state of a premeditated deliberate killing worse than killing in a rage. The circumstances of this killing, then, cry out for the conclusion that this is a rage killing."

When someone is killed by a knife or gun, the killer usually uses just enough force to bring about death. But, as the forensic psychologists had concluded, Ellen Robb had suffered many more blows than were needed to bring about her death. They called it overkill.

The repeated blows to her head and her face created a psychological component to the murder. The killer had literally obliterated her face. The killer wanted *her* dead. She'd died at the hands of someone who had gone out of control, who had gotten so angry that he lost control of himself.

Castor knew enough about the Robb marriage and household that he could envision a scenario where they had a fight, and the years of pent-up frustration, coupled now with the fear that he would lose not only his financial fortune, but also his daughter, threw him into a rage.

He could just hear Robb say, "I went into the garage and grabbed the first thing I saw and I beat her to death."

Castor could also see how Robb's attorney could argue on his behalf—to explain why he'd lost control. One reason was the conditions he lived in. The house was stuffed floor-to-ceiling with mostly new merchandise, much of it still in boxes. There was a pathway leading from one room to another. Not that the cluttered house could justify killing anyone, but it could partly explain why Robb had become so angry.

Castor also figured that the case could never get to a plea. He figured Robb was stubborn enough and controlling enough that he would refuse to admit what he had done. Castor saw Robb as arrogant, thinking that he was smarter than the prosecutors. He could see the game theory expert wanting to testify just to prove how smart he was. And Castor would be prepared. As he put it, "I have been doing this job a long time and I know how to do it. I think that his mouth will get him convicted of first-degree murder."

The closer they got to a trial date, the more intrigued DeSimone became.

He didn't quite know why Castor was floating the idea of Robb taking a plea. Was it that he had won the election and was moving on to his new career as a county commissioner? Perhaps he didn't really want to go to the trouble of preparing for a murder trial in the last month of his term? Or, DeSimone figured, Castor had to worry about the prospect of losing the case. Whenever a case goes to trial, it's a roll of the dice for both parties. Surely, Castor didn't want Robb to walk away a free man after all of the publicity and detailed filings by the prosecution that laid out nearly all of its circumstantial evidence against his client.

With the guilty plea, Castor would have something. Robb would get some jail time to ponder how he had fallen to this, a convicted felon, from his perch as an expert economist at the top of his game at one of the world's premier universities. A plea would resolve a case that was built on circumstantial evidence. There was no physical evidence that connected Robb to anything, and the weapon had never been found.

And Robb had insisted to his attorney that he had never hurt his wife.

"This guy never hit her," DeSimone said in an interview, challenging the notion raised by Ellen's friends that Robb had been physically abusing Ellen and had given her a black eye. DeSimone had put together a different view of the Robb household and Ellen. "People would have seen it, but nobody saw it. She told somebody she had a black eye because she didn't want to go to a party.

"The victim needed help. She was crying out for help, and nobody helped her—nobody." He acknowledged that Robb had tried to limit her spending, because she already had purchased too much.

And he wondered why no one intervened—not family, not friends.

"Why didn't they do something? You couldn't walk into the house. I would agree ten thousand percent if everything on the surface seemed perfect, but it wasn't perfect. . . . There's a lot of blame to go around."

Because all three—Castor, DeSimone and Tressler—were experienced in criminal law, they knew that sometimes it takes time for defendants to come around. They shared decades of criminal trial experience: DeSimone, 38 years; Tressler, 40 years; Castor, 22 years. They knew the evidence. They knew the difference between convicting someone of murder, first-degree with life in prison, and voluntary manslaughter, which carried a maximum of 10 to 20 years.

The trio knew the score well enough to realize that Robb's best option would be a guilty plea.

As they got closer to the trial date, Castor couldn't help but wonder—Is this going to be another Rabinowitz case? In that one, DeSimone had told him that his client would plead guilty just minutes before Castor was ready to address the jury. In that case, there was no plea deal.

The big difference here was that Castor was willing to allow Robb to plead guilty to a charge less than murder. That offer wouldn't be on the table indefinitely. He needed a signal that Robb was at least considering taking the plea, because once he began the intense preparation for trial, the process would take on a life of its own. Knowing all of that, Tressler, DeSimone and Castor had a talk in the judge's chambers after the November 9 hearing.

Tressler nudged the defense. If there was any interest, they needed to let him know.

CHAPTER 39

November 2007

For the family, the last thing they wanted was a trial. They especially worried about what it would do to Olivia. Even if she wasn't in the courtroom, it would be impossible to insulate her from the daily onslaught of television and newspaper coverage as the prosecution laid out its case.

Ellen's brothers Gary and Art were already on Castor's witness list in addition to other friends. They were prepared to tell the jury the tragic details of the Robbs' loveless marriage and the emotional abuse their sister had suffered over the previous ten years.

Everything was pointed at November 26—the Monday after Thanksgiving.

Sander kept the family informed of not only preparations for trial, but also prospects of Robb taking a plea. As a veteran prosecutor, Sander had most recently been captain of the narcotics enforcement team. He was also a captain in the Army Reserves Judge Advocate General's (JAG) Corps and in 2003 had served a six-month tour as trial counsel for V Corps in Darmstadt, Germany. It's no wonder that Castor felt he could count on Sander to keep everything moving forward. They wanted to be ready to go to trial just in case Robb demanded it.

Robb had remained steadfast that he wanted to go to trial until about two weeks before the trial date. That's when he started opening up to DeSimone and talking to him, asking more questions, analyzing where he stood. That's when DeSimone knew it would only be a matter of time.

DeSimone laid out for Robb what he could expect both from the defense and the prosecution.

Everyone was engaged in a delicate dance.

Tressler played a key role—by doing nothing.

He had yet to rule on the defense's request to conduct a hearing on whether Castor could use his forensic psychologists to describe the killing. The attorneys had asked him not to.

That was part of the strategy.

If Tressler had decided to order a hearing on the expert testimony, Castor would be forced to immediately file notice of his appeal. Once he did that, the case would leave Tressler's jurisdiction, making it impossible for him to accept any plea.

An important step in the unfolding dance was Tressler signaling that he was going to let Castor have the experts, but also give the defense the hearing they had asked for. For now, the judge's move was to do nothing and wait.

In his meetings with Robb, DeSimone carefully answered questions about the plea, the trial and how in this case, Robb had a chip in his pocket—a plea offer, which Patty Swinehart never had. She'd had no choice but to go ahead with the trial.

Robb had a choice—and a gamble. He could go to trial and win—walk away a free man. Or he could lose and spend the rest of his life in jail. Castor's plea offer gave him another option, but he'd have to admit publicly, and that included to his daughter, that he'd killed his wife.

DeSimone described what their case would sound like— how he would attack every piece of evidence Castor presented, and finally how he would make sure the jury knew what it had been like to live in that household. He'd tell them that Olivia had been embarrassed to bring home friends because of how the house looked. He'd emphasize that Ellen Robb's illnesses and shopping had overwhelmed them all. Epstein explained his chances of winning if Castor appealed their challenge on the expert testimony.

On the day before Thanksgiving, less than a week before trial, DeSimone and Epstein went to the jail to see Robb. They all knew it was time for a decision. DeSimone started, laying out the options. "I can't make this decision," he told Robb. "This is something you have to do. If you didn't do it, then you can't plead guilty, but if you did . . ."

Robb looked at both of his lawyers and told them, "I want to say something," as he tearfully began telling them what had happened on December 22, a story that the public would not hear for a few days. Just to make sure that he hadn't changed his mind, the attorneys returned to see Robb again on Sunday.

That day, the eve of the trial date, the only media outlet to nail what was really happening behind the scenes was the *Inquirer*. Emilie Lounsberry, a veteran court reporter, wrote that Robb was pondering a plea and the case might never make it to a jury. "Right now, he probably holds the key to the level of homicide for which the evidence will convict him," Castor told the *Inquirer*, adding, "this guy should plead guilty, but only he knows whether he did it, and only he knows whether he's willing to admit it."

The story said DeSimone had declined to comment on what might happen in court the next day.

Lounsberry reported that the prospect that Robb could sit in jail for as long as three years waiting for the courts to decide on whether the experts could testify against him made the prospect of a plea more likely. On the eve of trial, Temple University Law Professor JoAnne Epps said, "There's always an incentive to negotiate.

"There's uncertainties on both sides," she said, "and both sides might have an incentive to reach a certain result rather than to roll the dice."

Lounsberry also reported that the type of expert witness testimony Castor was proposing to use against Robb was untested in Pennsylvania and generally not accepted elsewhere.

The story quoted Colin Miller, a professor at The John Marshall Law School in Chicago: "The vast majority of courts that have been presented with it have found it to be inadmissible," said Miller, who has written about such challenges and the Robb case on his blog, EvidenceProf.

He added that courts had been reluctant because juries "do

put a lot of faith in expert testimony" and relying on opinions not rooted in science ultimately could be unfair to a defendant.

Reading the newspaper that Sunday, Castor felt satisfied that he was offering Robb what the case deserved—a voluntary manslaughter plea. He figured some may criticize him for it, but that had never stopped him before. He talked it over with Sander, a courtroom veteran and captain of the narcotics enforcement team. Castor believed the plea would be the right thing to do. He believed the murder had grown out of a fight between the parties, and Robb wasn't a killer in the sense that he could kill again.

On the other hand, Castor also knew he was giving up the chance to end his DA days with a big, showy trial—to go out with a public relations bang over a case that hinged on just how good he could be in the courtroom. And on how well he could match smarts with DeSimone. In many ways, the case offered what every prosecutor dreamed of—a high-profile case with a jigsaw-puzzle portrait of evidence. Castor had already told reporters he felt good about what he had. He was also satisfied that his strategy had closed off all avenues for the defense, including the fact that he could always come back to try the case no matter how long an appeal would take on the expert witness testimony. If Robb thought he could get away from Castor by pushing ahead for a trial, Castor had already arranged with Ferman that he be named a special prosecutor to come back and try the case.

The last step was bringing Tressler onboard. Castor had offered the plea. Would Tressler accept it? At a November meeting with all attorneys present, DeSimone asked whether Tressler would accept the plea if Robb agreed to it.

"Certainly, I'll take it," Tressler told them.

He had already read the probable cause statement, so he knew the facts in the case. He also had experience with the attorneys in the room. He knew Castor wouldn't sell out a case and DeSimone wouldn't sell out his client.

CHAPTER 40

November 2007

As the case moved forward, Marino drew the task of finding out about game theory and how it might be affecting Robb's handling of the case and the possible plea.

As a first step, the detective went to the Penn website and downloaded a copy of a final exam Robb had given to his graduate students in game theory. Other than convincing him that Robb was capable of playing games not only with the police but with the prosecutor, Marino couldn't make sense of it.

The test question was based on a classic problem in game theory known as "the prisoner's dilemma" in which the choices faced by two defendants are reduced to mathematical calculations.

If two people are accused of committing a crime together, and if neither offers evidence, they will both be freed. If neither accepts an offer, they gain too. But, if one betrays the other and gives up evidence, one wins, the other loses. The dilemma resides in the fact that each prisoner, following his/her own self-interest, will betray the other, making them both worse off.

Can Robb reduce his dilemma to a mathematical formula? Is there a plea bargain that fits the model? Could Robb have had an accomplice?

The day of the murder, Robb turned in grades for his

classes, which included Econ 682, a graduate seminar in game theory which, as Robb detailed in the course outline, is defined as "a player's payoff depends on other players' actions."

Here's a look at a take-home final that Robb gave his graduate students in 2004 for the course—the same one that Marino found as he researched Robb's specialty:

> There are two players, a plaintiff and a defendant. The plaintiff knows ahead of time whether he will win the case if it goes to trial, but the defendant does not. Instead, the defendant considers the probability of the plaintiff winning to be 1/3. (Formally, nature chooses whether the plaintiff wins or loses, and reveals this information to the plaintiffs only. The probability that nature chooses "win" is 1/3 and the defendant knows it is 1/3). All this is common knowledge. If the plaintiff wins his payoff is 3 and the defendant payoff is −4. If the plaintiff loses his payoff is −1 and the defendant's payoff is 0. These payoffs are also common knowledge.
>
> The plaintiff has two possible actions: demand a low settlement amount, m=1, or a high settlement amount m=2. If the defendant accepts a settlement demand of m, the plaintiff's payoff is m and the defendant's payoff is −m. If the defendant rejects the plaintiff's demand, the case goes to court.
>
> The problem: List all of the pure strategy perfect Bayesian equilibria. For each such equilibrium state which actions the two players choose and the posterior belief of the defendant as a function of m. Verify that each of these combinations of profiles and beliefs constitutes a PBE. Explain why other profiles of actions cannot be justified as PBE (i.e. show that there are no beliefs that satisfy requirements 1–4 that together with the profile of actions would constitute a PBE).

Here's another example of "the prisoner's dilemma" that applies more clearly to Robb's situation. This illustration in game theory is presented on the website of Dr. David Levine (*http://www.dklevine.com*), a leading game theorist who now teaches at Washington University in St. Louis. Dr. Levine offers it on his website as an instructive example:

> *In the case of a two-player game, the actions of the first player form the rows, and the actions of the second player the columns, of a matrix. The entries in the matrix are two numbers representing the utility or payoff to the first and second player respectively. A very famous game is the Prisoner's Dilemma game. In this game the two players are partners in a crime who have been captured by the police. Each suspect is placed in a separate cell, and offered the opportunity to confess to the crime. The game can be represented by the following matrix of payoffs*

	not confess	confess
not confess	5,5	–4,10
confess	10,–4	1,1

> *Note that higher numbers are better (more utility). If neither suspect confesses, they go free, and split the proceeds of their crime which we represent by 5 units of utility for each suspect. However, if one prisoner confesses and the other does not, the prisoner who confesses testifies against the other in exchange for going free and gets the entire 10 units of utility, while the prisoner who did not confess goes to prison and gets nothing. If both prisoners confess, then both are given a reduced term, but both are convicted, which we represent by giving each 1 unit of utility: better than having the other prisoner confess, but not so good as going free.*

> *This game has fascinated game theorists for a variety of reasons. First, it is a simple representation of a variety of important situations. For example, instead of confess/not confess we could label the strategies "contribute to the common good" or "behave selfishly." This*

captures a variety of situations economists describe as public goods problems. An example is the construction of a bridge. It is best for everyone if the bridge is built, but best for each individual if someone else builds the bridge. This is sometimes referred to in economics as an externality. Similarly this game could describe the alternative of two firms competing in the same market, and instead of confess/not confess we could label the strategies "set a high price" and "set a low price." Naturally it is best for both firms if they both set high prices, but best for each individual firm to set a low price while the opposition sets a high price.

A second feature of this game, is that it is self-evident how an intelligent individual should behave. No matter what a suspect believes his partner is going to do, it is always best to confess. If the partner in the other cell is not confessing, it is possible to get 10 instead of 5. If the partner in the other cell is confessing, it is possible to get 1 instead of -4. Yet the pursuit of individually sensible behavior results in each player getting only 1 unit of utility, much less than the 5 units each that they would get if neither confessed. This conflict between the pursuit of individual goals and the common good is at the heart of many game theoretic problems.

A third feature of this game is that it changes in a very significant way if the game is repeated, or if the players will interact with each other again in the future. Suppose for example that after this game is over, and the suspects either are freed or are released from jail they will commit another crime and the game will be played again. In this case in the first period the suspects may reason that they should not confess because if they do not their partner will not confess in the second game. Strictly speaking, this conclusion is not valid, since in the second game both suspects will confess no matter what happened in the first game. However, repetition opens up the possibility of being rewarded or punished in the future for current behavior, and game theorists

have provided a number of theories to explain the obvi-
ous intuition that if the game is repeated often enough,
the suspects ought to cooperate.

For the prosecution, the only thing unusual about charging someone like Robb was knowing that he would coldly analyze his moves and select what was best for him. Castor
already knew that that move was for Robb to confess.

CHAPTER 41

November 26, 2007

In the days before the start of the trial, Assistant District Attorney Sander was the point person to monitor whether Robb would take the plea. Castor wasn't really interested in talking to DeSimone. The week before the start of the trial, the best Sander could get from the attorneys was: "We think he's going to do it."

But even that was subject to change. Robb would have to decide, and he had right up to the last minute to change his mind.

Knowing that he was close to taking the deal was enough to signal to the detectives to hold off on rounding up the witnesses. They all had gotten notices about a month in advance, apprising them of the trial date. But that's a lot different from preparing them and reviewing with each of them exactly what they would testify to.

Castor and Sander arrived at the courthouse early on November 26. They hadn't gotten any final word from DeSimone, so they were preparing papers for three possibilities: Robb taking a plea in court; arguing against a hearing on the expert testimony; filing an appeal if Tressler announced that he was ordering a hearing on the expert testimony.

While Castor and Sander were prepared, they knew there was no scenario in which they would begin selecting a jury for a first-degree murder trial. In fact, even if the plea talks did collapse, DeSimone had signaled that he would need more time to be ready for the trial.

First, they had to get past the expert testimony issue, and Castor was adamant that his experts would not be cross-examined unless they were testifying at trial. He would never agree to give DeSimone a shot at questioning them in advance.

As Castor saw it, that would give DeSimone a tactical edge—knowing before trial began exactly how the prosecution's key witness would testify, and having that testimony to use when questioning him during the trial. Castor saw that as a prosecutor's nightmare that he planned to avoid.

Tressler had worked with Castor long enough to know he meant what he said. Likewise, Tressler knew that DeSimone and Epstein had done their homework on the issue. It was important and worth airing. All the public knew was that Tressler was still mulling it over. He issued no decision even as late as the first day of trial.

Before 9 a.m., Ellen Robb's family and friends filed into the first row of Courtroom #9, a large modern space with oak paneling behind the judge's chair. Gary and Kim Gregory took seats in the center of the row, Art Gregory, his ex-wife and daughter nearby. Ellen's friends filed in right behind them, all having a clear view of Robb and the witness stand.

Video and still photographers were lined up in the hallway waiting for Robb to make the "perp walk," the short trek from the elevator to the courtroom door when the photographers could actually get a clear shot of him.

Sander made an early appearance to get DeSimone's final word, and relayed it to Castor, who was in his office on the fourth floor. Both sides were present for the 9 a.m. start, even though proceedings wouldn't actually begin for about another hour.

At 9:10 a.m., Castor, dressed in a dark gray pinstriped suit, white shirt and yellow print tie, went over to the wooden rail separating the spectators from the inter sanctum of the courtroom. He greeted Gary and Art, and pulled up a chair to get closer to them. Ellen's friends were also straining to hear from the second row.

In hushed tones, he told them what they had been anxious to hear over the past eleven months. "Robb will admit that he killed Ellen after a confrontation in the kitchen," Castor told them. He explained what would be happening that morning, and warned them that it might be difficult for them to listen to it. Today would be the defense's day to present Robb's side. At the sentencing, the prosecution would get their chance.

Obviously relieved by the turn of events, one of them verbalized what they all must have been wondering: "Can he get out on time served?"

"He can, but that's not likely."

He shook hands with the brothers and returned to the prosecution table, where he conferred with Robb's attorneys.

Shortly after, four police officers pushed open the courtroom door and escorted Robb—looking more dressed-up than he had at his wife's funeral, in a light green patterned suit jacket, light shirt and dress pants—to the defense table, where DeSimone and Epstein gave him final instructions on what would be happening. Two minutes later, at 9:52 a.m., Tressler, dressed in his judicial robes, emerged from the judge's chambers and took his seat above them all.

Castor put on his reading glasses and rose to address the court. His first task was to actually charge Robb with voluntary manslaughter, since it was not one of the crimes that Robb had originally been charged with.

As Castor began to speak, Robb poured himself a glass of water from a pitcher at the defense table. He sat quietly as the district attorney declared in his charge that "Rafael Robb killed Ellen Robb without lawful justification, while acting under a sudden and intense passion, resulting from serious provocation from the person killed." Under Pennsylvania law, Robb was being charged with violating Section 2503 of state Consolidated Statute, Title 18.

Once the court and defense accepted his motion, Castor continued:

"In that instance, we have a proposed resolution for the court's consideration."

With that, Castor said Robb would plead guilty to voluntary manslaughter, a first-degree felony, and asked that sentencing be put off until after 90 days to allow for a pre-sentence investigation. Castor also promised that all of the other charges against Robb would be dismissed or, in court parlance, nol-prossed.

"That is the extent of the agreement we have reached in this case," Castor concluded.

From the front row, Ellen Robb's brothers glared at their brother-in-law as he put his right hand on the Bible and promised to tell the truth. Ellen's friends in the second row joined hands like a living chain trying to draw strength from each other as tension mounted.

With that, Robb sat in the witness chair and answered a series of questions from his attorney, described as a "colloquy." Addressing him as "Dr. Robb," DeSimone sought to show the court that Robb understood the charge and his plea, and his right to go to trial if he wanted to. It was time for Robb to finally tell his version of what had occurred in his home on December 22, 2006:

"So, that was a tragic morning of December twenty-second," he began, speaking softly.

"I took my daughter to school, like I did every morning.

"When I came back to the house, I got ready. And I was going to go to my office to turn in the—I had a few things to—go to the office, to turn in the grades.

"And before leaving for the office, I came down to the kitchen to talk to Ellen about two things: one was the preparation for the trip. She was supposed to leave for a trip, and Olivia, my daughter, to visit her uncle, who is here. So I offered to help them with the preparations.

"We were packing. And I said—I said, 'I'm going to the city anyway, so I can do shopping. Do you want me to pick something up?'

"And so we talked about that.

"And then I moved to the next topic, the one of greater

concern to me. This was—We talked about the return trip. I wanted to make sure that Olivia was coming back on time from the trip, because it happened before that she did not come back on time.

"They went on a trip. They didn't come back on time, and Olivia missed days of school. And I was very concerned about this possibility.

"I wanted to make sure that Olivia goes to school, and Olivia, herself, wanted to go to school.

"So we started the discussion about that. The discussion was tense. We both were anxious about it.

"And then—So there was a discussion—we both got angry.

"At one point, Ellen pushed me. I went—I fell on the counter.

"And then between the anxiety about my daughter and between this unexpected event, I just lost it.

"There was a bar in the living room, just a few steps from the kitchen. This bar I bought, I was going to install it. It was like an exercise bar.

"I grabbed the bar, and I started flailing it," he said, his right arm swinging through the air as if he had a bar in his hand. "I just kept flailing it until I collapsed.

"And this is what happened.

"And I'm very remorseful about it. And to say I'm sorry is to say nothing. It's not enough.

"I'm just remorseful, first, to the family. Second, for—to my family . . . in Israel, my parents. They didn't raise me like this. And third, to my daughter. I know she loved her mother, and I know her mother loved her, and now she doesn't have a mother," said Robb, letting out a sob, showing for the first time that he was touched by his own words.

"That's all I have to say."

With those words, Art turned to Gary and they shared a nod. Finally. After nearly a year of denials, Robb had finally come clean with his daughter, his wife's family and the public. He had finally stopped lying to police and to the court and to his attorneys.

He had finally admitted what Ellen's family and friends had known for so long. In the audience, they held hands and sobbed: Mary Beth Pedlow, Sharon Sellman, LuAnn Dubin, Patty Volpi, Karen Lander, Becky Rector, Becky Best.

Robb had spared them from testifying at a trial. He had spared his daughter, who had deliberately not been brought to court that day, for fear that he might not go through with the plea if he saw her there.

Later, DeSimone said that Robb had spoken to Olivia by phone from the county jail over the weekend and told her he planned to plead guilty. They had not seen each other since January when Robb was arrested.

As the court proceeding ended, just twenty-nine minutes after it had begun, Castor came back to the rail. He wanted to explain what they had just heard and to reassure the family that the plea was the right thing. Robb's claim that Ellen had pushed him was "bullshit," he said, but he had no choice but to take his story as he told it.

"This is the way the chess game of courtroom procedures are played," he told them, trying to explain that at least now Robb was in jail and would stay there for a while. This was the first step, and it was the defense's turn. He'd get his turn at the sentencing, which would be adversarial. Because Robb had used a weapon, it would add 1–2 years to his sentence. According to the guidelines he could get 54 to 72 months or 4 ½ to 6 years. "It can go higher," Castor told them. "At sentencing is when we get a chance to object. The sentencing considerations are for down the road."

Gary asked about the other three counts in addition to murder that Robb had been charged with. "We agreed to withdraw those," Castor told him. His pleading to a rage killing cleared all of the others.

Castor extended his hand to Gary and the other family members.

As Robb was led away, the lawyers hung back to let the family move out first. Gary and Art shook hands with Marino and Gershanick, the lead detectives, thanking them for their work on the case. The uniformed court deputies stepped into place just ahead of the family, ready to shield them from the cameras and reporters who were waiting outside the courtroom doors. The deputies would have surrounded them if they had wanted to leave quietly.

"No, it's OK," signaled Gary, in his executive navy blue suit and blue shirt; his wife Kim beside him in a simple black dress. The family had something to say.

Art, who was closer in age to Ellen, addressed reporters, reading from a written statement thanking the prosecutors and detectives, "all of those people who sought justice for my beloved sister Ellen.

"Everyone should continue to grieve for both Ellen and now for Olivia, who has lost both of her parents," continued Art, who is now raising Olivia in his home. Art, with Gary standing beside him and family members surrounding them, also gave a hint of the pain and regret that engulfed them:

> "In closing, I would like to offer advice to everyone, that was a lesson learned from an impossible-to-deal-with situation. It's never too early to get involved to help a neighbor, a friend, a family member who may be in peril.
>
> "The signs and symptoms may be more obvious than you may think. The effort required to help them is far less than you may think as well. Please remember it is never too early to get involved. It's far too painful to be a moment too late."

Gary said they wouldn't comment on physical abuse, but described the damage of the emotional abuse that Ellen had suffered.

> "There is no doubt that the relationship featured and was founded on a lack of love for many years. Violence takes place in many forms. I think verbal abuse is as damaging and detrimental as physical abuse. Whether or not there is physical abuse, we aren't commenting on, but clearly, there was longstanding verbal abuse, which eroded my sister's confidence, her joy and her passion and ability to contribute as she always had earlier in her life."

Added Art: "What kept them together was their undying love for their daughter, Olivia, and it was a situation where both of them put Olivia first, beyond anything else— unfortunately to their tragic end."

Asked if they believed that Robb was contrite in his statement to the court, Gary said the family was pleased to see that Robb had finally spoken "in a forthright manner."

And when a reporter asked him to tell them about his sister, Gary, the youngest of the three, choked up with emotion. "Clearly," said Gary as he fought to hold back the tears, "she was the most amazing individual, often described as an angel on earth, and I think that is accurate. I think that is obvious."

In his sister's memory, and in hopes of finding something positive in this tragedy, Gary announced that the family had formed a foundation, Every Great Reason (after Ellen's initials) "to carry forth her memory and lessons learned so that others can benefit from Ellen's life and all she represented to us."

They would talk more about it later that day during a press conference at Roberts Elementary School where Ellen's friends had placed the gazebo in her memory.

As traditionally occurs, Castor and DeSimone and Epstein took turns talking to the media.

With the cameras rolling, Castor did his best to silence any critics, whom he expected would object to his decision to allow Robb to plead guilty to the lower charge.

"At the very beginning I thought this was likely a heat-of-passion killing. The problem, from the defense perspective, he never admitted he did it," Castor said. "Once he changes his defense from an alibi defense to a heat-of-passion and sudden provocation, now all of a sudden our evidence tends to agree with his side of the story."

Responding to reporters' questions, Castor insisted that Ellen Robb's killing fit the definition of voluntary manslaughter. "I have never seen a burglar beat somebody to death and then not steal anything, which I thought was an interesting point in the case. Multiple blows far beyond what is necessary to bring about her death is indicative of a heat-of-passion killing, in fact, it is a classic heat-of-passion killing."

Even if the case had gone to a jury trial, Castor said, the facts supported voluntary manslaughter. "In my opinion, we arrived at where we would have gotten had we tried the case and he admitted he did do it, but in the heat of passion."

Castor also acknowledged that a trial could have resulted in an acquittal, or created issues that could have been appealed.

He described Robb as responding to the imminent threat of losing his daughter, for the vacation and possibly forever, since the divorce was certain. The lesser charge carried a standard range of four and a half to six years, although the judge could sentence him to anything—from probation to 10 to 20 years in prison to anything in between.

Asked about Robb's prison time, Castor would appeal to the judge, he said "We intend to argue a very, very substantial sentence be imposed. Obviously we think he's received whatever consideration for the heat-of-passion killing he's entitled to, and we added the voluntary manslaughter charge and came off the first-degree. Beyond that, he's gotten all he's going to get from us."

But one reporter wouldn't let Castor off so easily. Wasn't he sending the wrong message by allowing Robb to drop down to a manslaughter charge—that a man could beat his wife to death and get off with 4–5 years, cheaper than a divorce over a period of time?

While he was sympathetic to the victims of domestic violence, and urged the public to advise victims to get help, Castor didn't hesitate with his response: "I'm not in the message-sending business. I'm in the justice business, and this is an appropriate resolution based on these facts."

As Castor walked away, the cameras sought out DeSimone and Epstein, who had lingered outside the courtroom.

"I think this was the correct result. It's a very tragic situation," said DeSimone.

"Everything, as Mr. Castor said, dovetailed here. We had a

DA who was being reasonable. We have a judge who I really respect tremendously, and we had a terrible situation, as you heard, with the doctor, with the family and his daughter."

DeSimone went on to describe Robb as "very very remorseful, very sad. He didn't want this to happen. He's a PhD. He has no record. He's not a criminal. It is one of those things that he just loves his daughter so much, it happened."

"It was a very difficult case," he added. "We spent hours agonizing over it." Giving a glimpse of what he planned to argue at Robb's sentencing hearing, DeSimone underscored that Robb's hope was to do his time, which, under the court's guidelines, could be as little as three and a half to five years, and get back to his life and take care of his daughter.

In order to get the low end of the guidelines, DeSimone would have to argue that there were issues to mitigate the sentence Robb should receive. While he hinted to reporters that it would have to do with the couple's home life, DeSimone focused on Robb as father rather than Robb as killer. He urged reporters to recall what Robb had said when he'd pleaded guilty.

"He loves his daughter more than anything in the world. He took her mother away from her. He would never do that. It was a spur-of-the-moment situation. It was totally out of character."

Voluntary manslaughter is defined as a killing, but with no premeditation, such as a crime committed in the heat of passion.

"He took responsibility," Epstein told reporters. "The law defines this crime as exactly what happened, passioned manslaughter, not malice murder, which is bad people doing evil things, but recognizing the frailties of human emotion. That's what this case is."

Within hours, the University of Pennsylvania issued a statement saying it had demanded Robb's resignation from his tenured professor position. The resignation was submitted the next day and became effective immediately. Robb, who

was known at Penn by the last name Rob, was also immediately removed from the university's website. Their promise to
stand by Robb through the judicial process had officially
come to an end. His friends and colleagues at Penn were
equally shocked, including some who had believed in Robb's
innocence.

CHAPTER 42

November 26, 2007
Afternoon

The day Rafael Robb pled guilty to killing his wife was enveloped in dense, haunting fog with a light drizzle and gray skies. As much as Ellen's brothers had spoken about wanting something positive to come out of Ellen's death, the day captured the mood of friends and family gathering at the gazebo at Roberts Elementary in Wayne.

While they were relieved that Robb had pled guilty and spared them all a trial, there was no getting away from the pain and the deep loss they felt. It was like they were reliving the day when they'd learned that Ellen had been killed.

As one of Ellen's closest friends, Mary Beth set out to make sure the media heard about Ellen at her best. "Ellen had a great laugh," she told *Inquirer* reporter Tony Wood as the television cameras were setting up. "She wasn't above writing thank-you notes. If she felt she slighted you, she'd go out of her way to make it right."

As other friends arrived, Mary Beth shared hugs and tears with them. LuAnn, Patty, Sharon—The Friends of Ellen— while not organizing this event, were very much involved in creating a lasting memory to Ellen.

With umbrellas held aloft to protect them from the drizzle, family members made their way from the parking lot in front of the red-brick school. As soon as the cameras were in place, Gary was ready. With Robb's guilty plea behind them, the family was clearly looking to Ellen's legacy. How would her name be remembered in Wayne? Everywhere? Would she forever be the victim, the woman murdered—or could her name be connected to helping other women escape? As Gary put it, "I have to do this or it [Ellen's murder] would consume me."

Publicly, Gary tried to look strong, but he couldn't help the tears rolling down his face, and his voice cracking under the strain of the day. "This is a very tragic day for our family and the friends who loved Ellen so much. It's also a day of healing, a day that allows us to move forward and [continue] the healing process that has come about from my sister's passing."

He was surrounded by others who reached over to pat his back and give him support: his wife, Kim Wilson Gregory, his brother Art Gregory, Art's daughter Lauren and his ex-wife, Mary Ann Jones, other family and friends.

The Gregorys had summoned the media to the gazebo because it represented the best times for Ellen, or as her brother Art put it, it was "a place where Ellen was very innocent and able to be herself . . . When Olivia attended school here, she [Ellen] was very active. It was a bright period in her life."

They used the backdrop of the gazebo and the school to announce the formation of the nonprofit Every Great Reason Foundation, which would help women get out of abusive relationships.

"Our goal is to empower and enrich women with the opportunity to move forward in their lives," said Gary.

A website and materials distributed to reporters describe the nonprofit with the mission of providing "an avenue for women who are seemingly shackled to courageously move forward with their lives" (http://www.everygreatreason.org).

The family hopes that the foundation can give women in the same situation as Ellen the resources, the courage and the support to act. Ellen had taken steps to get out of her bad marriage, but did not move quickly enough. She had started by enlisting an attorney and finding an apartment for herself and Olivia, but she did not follow through. She didn't have the support around her to get her safely out of the house.

As Gary put it, "We allowed her to become trapped."

Gary also poignantly voiced his own regret at not helping his sister, and vowed that the same thing not happen to others in the same situation. "I have learned acutely, as we all have, as you think about all of the things you could have done differently. The little signs, the little observations, the things we should have known," he said, his voice cracking with emotion. "Instead, we didn't act with authority or decisiveness, and we didn't empower Ellen to the fullest of our capabilities. We'd like to have that mistake not happen again.

"Our mission is to make sure we are prepared to help others to recognize they have every great reason to move forward, to begin a new life, to get free of their bondage, to have the courage and resources and empowerment to march forward. We'd like to do so through a variety of resources brought in through the foundation. . . . Ultimately her demise will represent new life for others through the formation of our foundation."

As the foundation specifies on its website:

Our charter is to provide the road map, tools and access to counseling, support, shelter, food, child care, work and continuing education—so that these women and their families are empowered—with the resources and realization that they have Every Great Reason to begin a New Life.

In response to reporters' questions, Gary specified that, while he plans to start the effort regionally in the Philadelphia area, he sees a broader need. "The cause and the issue are national, and there is room for leadership on a national front for such an endeavor."

For the Friends of Ellen, the foundation offered a new challenge.

In a conference call with Gary right after Robb had pled guilty, the friends considered whether they could organize a fundraiser to coincide with the first anniversary of Ellen's murder.

"Let's do it," they said in unison, knowing full well that

they were setting themselves up for an almost impossible task of organizing a dinner and silent auction in less than a month, to take place five days before Christmas.

Even though she landed in the hospital needing a hernia operation, Patty Volpi kept working from her kitchen table, epitomizing the dedication of the women volunteers by dialing up everyone she could think of to get donated items: a hair salon and sports teams, including the Philadelphia Eagles and Phillies. Cheryl Friend lined up lots of other donations. They were all determined that Ellen's murder would help other women who needed the help to get themselves out of abusive relationships.

CHAPTER 43

November 26–27, 2007

Within hours of Robb's guilty plea, Castor was taking hits on television, in the *Philadelphia Daily News* and on the Internet for giving Robb the manslaughter option. Domestic violence advocates from Philadelphia lamented that prosecutors were hesitating too much on domestic violence cases after O. J. Simpson had walked away from charges that he'd killed his wife Nicole and her friend Ron Goldman. Not so, responded Castor. "I'm not afraid of anything."

While he had expected some criticism, Castor was confident he had made the right decision. The Simpson case had nothing to do with his offer to Robb. And he certainly wasn't afraid of taking a domestic violence killing to trial if he had the right case. His office got a flurry of calls and e-mails congratulating them for getting the guilty plea, while others wanted to know why he had let Robb off so easy. Assistant DA Sander answered some of those, explaining to the callers that the guilty plea was the best outcome for everyone.

In the *Philadelphia Daily News*, the *Inquirer*'s sister tabloid, which prides itself on reporting with "attytood," Will Bunch, in his column by the same name, wrote a piece titled, "PhD justice?" With this opening line, "OK, is it just me, or does anyone else think this guy is getting off way too easy here?" Bunch zeroed in on the numbers: The standard sentence for voluntary manslaughter is 54 to 72 months (4 ½ to 6 years) but DeSimone said he would be seeking a lot less—more like the minimum range of 42 to 60 months (3 ½ to 5 years).

Bunch took the controversy home:

Apparently, there was an issue over whether some of the evidence that prosecutors felt they needed for a murder conviction was circumstantial. Maybe, but it seems like we've seen a lot of these cases where the well-educated and the wealthy aren't prosecuted so aggressively or not prosecuted at all—like the case of another Penn professor, Tracy McIntosh, for example.

Bunch wrote that he'd heard DeSimone

arguing on KYW [radio] that Robb should get a light sentence in part because, "He's a Ph.D."
   Is that an aggravating or mitigating circumstance? You don't even need to be a rocket scientist to know that attacking your wife with an exercise bar is wrong.

By invoking McIntosh's name, Bunch reminded his readers about the internationally known brain trauma researcher who had gotten probation for sexually assaulting a student, the niece of a friend who had asked him to give her a tour of campus. After a public outcry over the sentence, the Philadelphia DA appealed its leniency and won the right to return the case to the court for a re-sentencing. McIntosh was sentenced to a 3 ½-to-7-years' sentence.

While they were relieved that Robb had admitted killing Ellen, her friends were worried that he would get a light sentence and literally get away with murder. They organized a letter-writing campaign to Judge Tressler requesting that he give Robb the maximum prison stay.

As one of the letter writers, Mary Beth Pedlow urged him not to believe Robb that the killing had happened the way he said it did.

Rafi has finally confessed to what most of us knew from the beginning, though as I stood in that courtroom I wanted to scream, "Liar!" Rafi said that he and Ellen argued and that in the "heat of the moment" he lost his temper and grabbed an exercise bar and started hitting. I don't believe him!

Pedlow told Tressler that she had questions to raise, because Ellen wasn't there to defend herself. She asked how it could be that the dog, who had the run of the house, had no blood on him

". . . and for that to have NO blood on him meant that Rafi had to put him in the upstairs bedroom BEFORE he started hitting Ellen, which also gave Rafi time to calm down and walk away or premeditate his crime."

Pedlow wrote that she believed that Rafi had struck Ellen from behind while she was wrapping presents

and she turned and fought for her life, because Ellen would have fled the house rather than fight Rafi if she could have, but he never gave her a chance to leave.

Only Rafi knows what truly happened that morning and one day he may tell the truth, but I see no remorse in this man, only a sad ex-professor trying to calculate the fastest way to get out of jail.

Pedlow said she missed her friend, their phone calls and shopping trips.

This woman has been a part of my life longer than my kids and husband, and I feel sad that many will never get to know this wonderful person.

In arguing for a maximum sentence, Pedlow pleaded with Tressler to "show Ellen the compassion that Rafi never did by locking him up for a long time."

Other friends were also writing the letters around the same theme—Robb should pay for killing Ellen Robb with a lot more than a minimum sentence. Becky Rector wrote the testimony she never got to deliver in court, hoping to convince the judge that Robb had been abusive to her friend and urging that he be "greatly punished for his crime . . . The thought of him getting off with just a few years is wrong and unjust."

In their long telephone talk, she and Ellen "were completely honest with each other about our lives," Becky wrote to the judge. "Maybe that is why she decided to confide in me and tell me of the extensive abuse perpetrated by Rafi. Maybe it was the fact that I live in New Jersey and wouldn't confront Rafi. Whatever the reason, I feel like I let her down in not doing something more. I will have to live with this guilt. I can't stop thinking about her. I can't sleep at night and have been very sad. I am still not through the pain and I don't know if I will ever be."

Actually, the sentence is where the big legal fight was headed. Castor, armed with victim impact statements from Ellen's family and friends, would argue that Robb had gotten his break with the lesser charge. On time, he deserved the maximum that Tressler could give him.

As Castor had told reporters right after the plea, he would ask for a "very, very substantial sentence."

Still, Castor would argue not only that Robb had already gotten a break with the reduced sentence, but that Robb had tried to cover up his crime by creating a story that Ellen had been killed by a burglar.

The real preparation for the sentencing hearing would occur on Robb's behalf, starting with Robb himself writing to Tressler to explain how his sixteen-year marriage had ended on December 22 in a bloody rage-induced killing.

DeSimone planned to emphasize Robb's contributions as a teacher and researcher, and his unique role as Olivia's sole surviving parent. If the court believed that Robb had killed his wife in a fit of passion and not because he was a malice killer, then it could accept that Robb deserved a chance to make it right to his daughter. A minimum sentence in the range of three and a half to five years would allow Robb to get out and be young enough to still care for her in her teenage years. Whatever Tressler would give him would be minus the nearly two years he had already served in the county jail.

By putting off sentencing for several months, DeSimone gave himself sufficient time to prepare for the hearing. In addition to Robb's letter, he enlisted a psychologist to interview both Robb and gathered letters from colleagues and friends who saw another side of Robb.

He also planned to show Tressler that Ellen Robb's excessive shopping was a glimpse into the chaotic life that the Robbs had lived. While he was in jail awaiting sentencing, Robb made regular phone calls to Olivia, who by now was legally in the custody of her Uncle Art and living with him in Haddonfield, where she attended middle school.

Her father was still very much in Olivia's life, having agreed that Olivia could live with her uncle as long as Robb was consulted on all major issues, including health care, education and religion. Art also agreed to make reasonable efforts to have Olivia visit her father in jail and to return her to him in the event he was acquitted. But her dog Copper didn't make the trip across the river. He needed a new home. The trauma of the last year had left him shaken.

While his attorney worked to present Robb in the most sympathetic light to the judge, Robb remained in the Montgomery County jail but made numerous sheriff-escorted trips to Philadelphia area hospitals at his own expense for thyroid surgery and treatments and evaluation of his injured shoulder.

CHAPTER 44

Danger

Ellen had probably had no idea the danger she was in when she'd taken the first steps toward divorcing Rafael. As anyone trained to help domestic violence victims could have told her, the time when a relationship is ending is when women are most at risk for something lethal to occur. That's why counselors suggest that women have a safety plan before they initiate a divorce, one that includes where she might go if she needs to, having access to a telephone at all times as well as money and a car, and giving her children a code word for when they would call other family members for help.

During 2006, there were ninety-two persons murdered by a partner in Pennsylvania, including four in Montgomery County. Ellen was one of them.

There is no record of Ellen seeking help from police, from the domestic abuse hotline operating in the county or from Laurel House, the county's domestic violence program, which operates a shelter and even connects victims with legal help. In the same year Ellen was murdered, about 200 women and their children sought shelter through Laurel House and 700 called the hotline. Organizers say those numbers reflect the tip of the iceberg. Most domestic violence victims—like Ellen—suffer in silence. About a quarter of all women in the United States are abused by "an intimate partner" sometime during their lifetime, according to a 2005 survey of 70,000 people in the United States and its territories by the Centers for Disease Control and Prevention. The survey also found that 11 ½ percent of men reported being victimized, which was defined as threatened, attempted or completed physical or sexual violence or emotional abuse by a current or former spouse or partner.

While there has been a drop in murder by partners, women are more likely than men to be killed, according to a study by the U.S. Department of Justice.

In 2005, 1,181 women were killed by a partner, a third of all women murdered. That's up from 26.1 percent in 1995 when 1,311 women were killed by a partner. For the same period, the share of men killed by their partners dropped from 3.1 to 2.5 percent.

Ellen Robb's death was counted in Pennsylvania as just such a case.

While there was no evidence that she had been physically abused, her friends and family told authorities about emotional and verbal abuse that affected her physical and emotional health.

She'd withdrawn from friends as she sank deeper into depression. While she told a few close friends that she was having trouble with her husband, her friends say she was too ashamed to tell them what had become of her life. She had lost her self-esteem and feared that her husband would soon succeed in convincing their daughter that Ellen was too ill to care for her.

The problem, says Beth Sturman, executive director of Laurel House, is that women often can't believe that the person they loved, and may still love, would kill them. And the people around them, including the professionals who are helping them, often can't believe that the situation is so dire that they need to escort the woman out of the house for her safety. Ellen had been under the care of doctors and therapists at the time of her murder. She had also seen an attorney.

Sturman said Ellen's murder has highlighted the need to educate victims, family members and especially attorneys that the most dangerous times for victims of domestic violence are during a breakup and for the next two years. What happened to Ellen has also spurred the expansion of a special counseling program at Laurel House where women can come in and talk to a counselor even if they aren't ready to leave. The emphasis on getting women to leave the home may discourage some of them from seeking any help, Sturman noted.

She plans to introduce a pamphlet for attorneys to put in their waiting rooms. The program already works with doctors and therapists—adding lawyers would help get the word out about the need for women to get help when they are seeking to end a relationship. The same kind of message has gone out to hair salons, a place where woman may feel free to talk to other women.

The pamphlet will tell them that separation and divorce is a heightened time for physical violence and how they need to have a plan for their exit.

Oftentimes, just starting the legal process can trigger a fight and lead to other violence. It's especially a problem when both husband and wife continue to share the same home.

"Ellen's murder helped to underscore that we had tremendous work to do," said Sturman. It's an issue highlighted in the research into domestic violence. Nearly a third of women homicide victims reported in police records were killed by their partner, according to a federal study. Men who killed their wives said that threats of separation or actual separation were the triggers that had led to the murder, according to studies quoted in a 2000 research report titled "Extent, Nature, and Consequences of Intimate Partner Violence" published by the U.S. Department of Justice.

In Maryland, police departments are increasingly using a program in which police called to a scene ask a series of questions aimed at identifying those most at risk of being killed, and get them immediate aid or counseling. "If it saves only one life, then it has done what it was supposed to do," Captain Daniel Hall of the Prince George's County Office of the Sheriff, which started the program in January 2007, told *The Washington Post*. A federal grant is allowing the model to expand nationwide.

On the day Ellen was murdered, there were eleven women

and eleven children staying in the Laurel House shelter. Two other women had called the hotline. The newest hope for abuse victims is the Family Justice Center, which was first developed in San Diego and now operates in thirty-one American cities (none in the Philadelphia area) and five locations in Canada, Mexico and England. The idea is to offer abuse victims a one-stop center where they can get all of the services that they need, such as legal, counseling and police. The model has been adopted by the U.S. Department of Justice and is credited with playing a major role in the ninety-percent drop in domestic violence homicides in San Diego since 1985.

CHAPTER 45

December 20, 2007

The gathering at The Radnor Hotel on West Lancaster Avenue on the Main Line had all of the looks of a holiday gathering for one of the many companies with offices in the King of Prussia area.

Five days before Christmas, when many were home wrapping gifts, Ellen's friends and family gathered for the first annual fundraising event of the Every Great Reason Foundation.

Calling itself Philadelphia's Main Line Hotel, the Radnor has the classy understated elegance of a building that is used to catering to its clientele. For the 100 guests who turned up for Ellen Robb's event, there was a sense of relief. With Robb's guilty plea, they could now talk openly of Ellen's struggle and how much they regretted not helping her.

As they walked into the dining room, guests were greeted by a continually running photo show of Ellen from childhood to motherhood. Conspicuously absent was any photo of her marriage or any photos of her with Robb. A bouquet of Ellen's favorite yellow roses graced every table.

As if reading their minds, the evening's speakers—Wallis W. Brooks, an assistant district attorney in Montgomery County, who runs the domestic violence unit, and Dr. Sandra Levenson, a suburban chiropractor who describes herself as a survivor of domestic violence—both urged the listeners not to blame themselves for Ellen's death.

"People may regret that they didn't do more," Brooks told them from the podium. "Despite our best efforts, tragedy occurs. Give yourselves credit for what you did do. You loved her. You were her friend, and you grieved for her, and now, you are here."

The goal, she said, is for every little girl to grow up without the pain and fear of abuse. "May Ellen's daughter, Olivia, see that day."

The words were soothing, especially coming from her. A former state representative, and assistant U.S. attorney, Brooks decided to give up politics to prosecute criminals. She's most at home in the domestic violence unit, where in four years she's prosecuted over 1,000 cases. "This just seems so right," she told them about her mission.

The women around the tables nodded in agreement. They each had their story of how they knew Ellen and when they had last spoken to her. From Brooks, they learned that what had happened to Ellen over the previous three years was typical for women who were being victimized. Their friend had pulled away from nearly all of them—failing to return phone calls or even to answer the door.

Brooks described a systematic pattern in which the abuser often gains control through physical and verbal abuse, controlling the finances, even destroying work clothes. The abuser may have isolated her from friends or family. She may be physically ill and feeling embarrassed that this was happening to her.

"It occurs at all levels of society," she added. "Unfortunately, a woman is at the highest risk to be killed when the abuser feels he has lost control and can't get it back . . . when she's leaving."

Leaving wasn't easy, but she finally found the strength to do it, Sandra Levenson told them.

"I made it. I walked out the front door."

A petite woman dressed in a stylish suit, Sandra looked every bit the professional chiropractor. But there was another time, she told them, when she was also a victim who endured abuse to the point where she routinely made excuses to her children for the black-and-blue marks on her body. "I had run out of excuses."

She said people often ask why a woman stays. It's a question from people who don't understand. The reality is, you become paralyzed over what to do next.

Ellen's friends had seen the paralysis. They had also seen that she had wanted out. She had taken the first steps.

At the center table sat a little girl with long brown hair, dressed in a black-and-white spaghetti-strap dress, who couldn't hide her tears. Perhaps for the first time, Olivia Robb was hearing about her mother from a different perspective. As much as she loved her father, he had admitted that he'd killed her mother. It was quite a burden for a little girl to carry.

When he stood up to address the crowd, Ellen's brother Gary shared Olivia's tears. "We don't carry the guilt. The criminal carries the guilt," he said through sobs.

Gary told how he had elected not to stay with Ellen on the night of December 21. He had stayed at a nearby hotel so he could do some work the morning of December 22. When he arrived, he was shocked to see the yellow police tape being set up around the perimeter of the Robb home, and an ambulance parked out front.

Gary had quickly jumped out of his car, he recounted, and was immediately taken to the Upper Merion police station "and descended into the world of domestic violence."

It's a world where four women die every day.

Three million suffer from physical abuse every day.

One in three Americans know someone who has suffered in the past year alone.

"Here we are on the Main Line in Philadelphia," he told them. Women could become victims regardless of their race or their income status.

Gary, the successful executive, had taken on his sister's cause, much in the way he must take on new business challenges. Gary vowed that the foundation in his sister's name would save others from her fate. "We'll do it one woman at a time, until we have successfully eradicated this issue."

The foundation's objectives stemmed from Ellen's experiences: There's a need for awareness, the need to recognize that abuse is happening and not that it's "just a bad marriage." Every woman needs a road map. Ellen had emerged from the quicksand of her life, the slow emotional torture that had "eradicated her spirit" to having a plan to move out. "There were no economic constraints. She was good to go." But women leaving abusive situations also need help to get out when they are ready to go.

In the language of business, Gary said he would look for the "best practices" in use to help women and share them across the country. "We want to raise the game on domestic violence so we can move forward," he said. "We're very excited about the mission we're on."

CHAPTER 46

January, 2008

Castor had made it clear to Robb in public and to his attorney in private that he would stick with this case through a trial and sentencing, regardless of what happened in his political life. As the top vote-getter on November 6, 2007, Castor was preparing for a new chapter in his career as the chairman of the three-member board of commissioners that now included a Democrat, former congressman and the number-two vote-getter in the race, Joseph M. Hoeffel. Castor took for granted that James R. Matthews would support him for chairman and Hoeffel would have no choice but to go along, since a 2–1 vote rules.

In a glowing December 16, 2007, story on Castor by *Inquirer* reporter Larry King, the outgoing DA said he was ready to take on his new job, and his rivals Hoeffel and Matthews, with whom he'd clashed on the campaign trail, said they too were ready to work with him. They both said they had moved past the campaign, when Hoeffel had called Castor "Bruce the Almighty" and Matthews, although they were fellow Republicans, had jabbed Castor for having an ego that was so big "it could float the Titanic."

Matthews told the *Inquirer*: "He has cautioned us that he is an autocrat, but he's not used to working together with people, so bear with him. He's aware. But he will learn quickly."

Two days later, Matthews and Hoeffel held a stunning joint press conference in the county courthouse in Norristown and announced that they had made a deal for the Republicans and Democrats to share power. Or, in other words, they would rule in Montgomery County and leave Castor out in the cold. While the voters had elected two Republicans and one Democrat to the county commissioner jobs, they had also elected Democrats to five of the nine other county-wide offices: controller, clerk of courts, prothonotary, register of wills and coroner. "We see a government of shared authority, responsibility and, moreover, accountability," Matthews said as he stood next to Hoeffel. "We're going to have a government of inclusion."

Castor held his own news conference later in the day, chiding Matthews for throwing away what voters had given them. He left the door open to a reconciliation, even offering to support Matthews for chairman as long as they didn't empower Hoeffel. "I think it's impossible to minimize me," Castor said.

A rapprochement would never come. Matthews and Hoeffel made good on their promises on January 7 by voting for Matthews as chairman and Hoeffel as vice-chairman. Castor sat alone on the sidelines. As he told *Inquirer* reporter Tom Infield, "It's apparent the two of them intend to run the show and leave me in the dark. I don't think that's what the voters had in mind when they elected me."

It certainly wasn't what Bruce Castor had had in mind when he decided to step away from the all-powerful DA's office.

To underscore his disdain for his situation, he told the *Inquirer* that he had put his county commissioner certificate where it belonged, above the toilet near his office.

Castor could end up having the last laugh. Ken Davis, the GOP chairman who retired, was replaced with Robert Kerns, an attorney and Castor ally. And once the dust settled on the election and its aftermath, Castor had the satisfaction of hearing from many party committee members who told him he had been right about Matthews all along. The outcome gave Castor the confidence that he'd have the support he needed for any race in the future. In the meantime, he was the third vote on all decisions affecting the county. Within months, the party committee had voted to censure Matthews.

With Robb's sentencing delayed until May 5, 2008, five months into his new situation, Castor would get a chance to step back into his old world, into the courtroom, where he commanded respect. Getting as much prison time for Robb as he could would be his last official act as district attorney.

CHAPTER 47

May 5, 2008

Ellen's friends' biggest fear was that Robb would, in essence, be getting away with murder. To them, he had become the Ivy League killer who now had one of the Philadelphia area's top criminal lawyers to argue on his behalf.

But who would argue for Ellen? Who would tell Judge Tressler that someone had to pay for killing her?

In letter after letter, Tressler heard from Ellen's supporters. Her friends, her family, everyone had their own stories of the vivacious personality that had been snuffed out by her abusive marriage. In heartbreaking candor, they appealed for justice. Allowing Robb to leave jail after serving the 4 ½ to 6 years' standard sentence for voluntary manslaughter was simply not enough, they wrote, urging him to sentence Robb to the maximum 10 to 20 years.

Rather than just let the sentencing happen, DeSimone had taken the initiative to do everything he could to convince Tressler that Robb deserved the lighter end of what the guidelines called for. Tressler already had a 15-page pre-sentencing report from the county probation department that detailed the Robbs' life, together with letters from Ellen's friends and family urging maximum jail time. At the sentencing hearing, DeSimone would give the judge additional letters from Robb's professional colleagues and others reminding Tressler of his professional brilliance and his devotion to his daughter.

But before Tressler could turn his attention to how much jail time Robb should get, the defense had one last card to play. Days before the sentencing, DeSimone, with Robb's blessing, filed a motion asking the judge to order the prosecution to turn over to him Ellen's psychiatric records. The prosecution had gotten them through a grand jury subpoena early in the investigation when they were thrashing about searching for her killer.

DeSimone's motion raised the prospect that the summer of 2008 would become a battle of the psychiatrists.

On a bright and warm spring day, Ellen's friends and family filed into the first row of Tressler's courtroom. They had hoped for a final chapter in her murder, but had learned days earlier of DeSimone's change in strategy.

Castor and Sander took their places at the prosecution table and DeSimone waited for Robb to be led to him by two county sheriffs.

Castor, who was continuing with the case as an unpaid special prosecutor, walked to the wooden rail that separates the spectators from the inner courtroom and pulled up a chair so he could talk privately to Ellen's family and friends in the first row. Ellen's brother Art and his family represented the Gregorys, Mary Beth Pedlow and Becky Best, Ellen's friends.

"You know there is not going to be a sentencing today?" Castor asked as he leaned toward them. As they nodded, Castor explained that Tressler would have to decide how much time Robb was to spend in jail. By law, he was required to set a minimum and a maximum sentence, and the minimum could not be more than one-half the maximum. The judge already had a report from the parole office on Robb, and the prosecution would have a chance to object to anything presented by the defense aimed at convincing the judge to go easy on the sentence.

The good part, he added, was that Robb was already behind bars, and the delay didn't change that.

The judge's clerk summoned the attorneys into his chambers for a short conference, during which DeSimone told the judge what he hoped to get from the psychiatric records while Castor strenuously objected.

The hearing was supposed to start at 1:30 p.m. It was

2:05 p.m. and Robb was finally being led into the courtroom wearing the same black outdoor jacket that he had worn the day of his arrest. Looking lean and alert, Robb glanced toward the first row just as Art turned himself away.

Once the sheriffs removed his handcuffs, Robb, who was dressed in his own light green pants, pale green shirt and patterned suit jacket, settled in to listen as his attorney outlined their latest move.

Addressing Tressler in open court, DeSimone explained that he planned to have Ellen's records analyzed by a psychiatrist who would prepare a report for the court. The information would allow the judge to sentence Robb in the "mitigated range." In other words, DeSimone was trying to convince Tressler that what the psychiatrist would have to say would convince him to lighten Robb's sentence to something less than the standard 4½ to 6 years.

DeSimone insisted that the new information would help Tressler understand what Robb had had to live with. Once the judge learned about Ellen's psychiatric problems, he would understand why Robb had snapped, or, in his own words, why he'd "just lost it" and grabbed an exercise bar and beaten her beyond recognition. As DeSimone told Tressler, the psychiatrist's report of life in the Robb household would help the judge "understand the bigger picture to the whole situation."

Ellen's psychiatric records were "not relevant" to the sentencing, Castor responded. All of the issues DeSimone hoped to raise had already been taken into account when Robb was allowed to plead guilty to the lesser charge of voluntary manslaughter. What DeSimone was doing now would only hurt Ellen's memory. Her character "will be further smeared by these proceedings."

The lasting message would be "that somehow the victim is responsible for her own demise," Castor told the court.

For his part, Tressler concluded that he first had to look at the records himself before deciding whether to hand them over to the defense.

"Our purpose is not to argue anything that would be disrespectful to the victim," DeSimone said.

Outside the courtroom, DeSimone carefully insisted that "I want the judge to get a full picture of why this happened." He wasn't out to trash the victim. Rather, he was trying to present a more complete view of his client, who had no prior record and who had a daughter he loved dearly. "This is a tragic situation," DeSimone said, repeating his earlier description of the case. "Ellen Robb was a nice lady. This is a tragic, tragic situation."

When the cameras turned to him, Castor didn't mince words. "All of the sentencing breaks that he's entitled to, he already got at the plea," he insisted. "It's only when it appeared that we were going to crush him in court did he come clean."

If DeSimone were to put up a psychiatrist to testify about Ellen's mental condition, he could expect a tough cross-examination, Castor added. And the prosecution might just have to call its own expert to review the records. The promise suggested a sentencing featuring dueling psychiatrists. While DeSimone's skilled examination would attempt to show that Ellen's illness had left her incapable of caring for her daughter, Castor would zero in on what Ellen had told her therapists about the years of emotional abuse she'd endured.

As May turned into June and then July with no order from Tressler, DeSimone pursued his strategy by obtaining, through his client, records of joint psychiatric sessions for Robb and Ellen. Even if Tressler ruled against him, DeSimone would be able to have an expert testify about the couple's problems.

But first, he would come under fire from *Philadelphia Daily News* columnist Ronnie Polaneczky, who condemned DeSimone for trying to unearth Ellen's personal psychiatric woes:

That Rafael's attorneys had the temerity to ask for the review is repugnant. What a violation, to drag words uttered by Ellen in confidence to her counselor into the sentencing of her killer.

And what an irony, too:

The state of mind of Ellen's unknown killer wasn't deemed by Rafael's attorneys to be pertinent to the case when Rafael was pretending to be innocent; but his dead wife's mental health is deemed pertinent now that Rafael has admitted he's not.

If Rafael really wanted to show remorse to his daughter, he'd not attempt to defame her mother's memory by exposing Ellen's personal struggles in a courtroom.

Isn't it enough that he took her life? Must he use her own words to take her good name, too?

The column stung DeSimone, especially, because he just wanted the judge to understand why Robb had snapped. If Tressler could see the situation the way DeSimone did, perhaps he would shave a year or more from the sentence.

On a sweltering day in mid-July, Tressler released an order directing that Ellen Robb's psychiatric records be turned over to the defense and Rafael Robb's psychiatric records be given to the prosecution. Each side could now get their own psychiatric expert to delve even deeper into the failed union of Ellen and Rafael. Was there a smoking gun that could actually explain why Robb had killed his wife? It would take a hearing in the fall to find out.

Ultimately Tressler would have the last move. Even once the experts had spoken, it would be up to the veteran jurist to decide whether to side with DeSimone, who was arguing for a light sentence in the 3-to-4-year range, or Castor, who would seek the maximum 10 to 20. Tressler was also free to sentence Robb to some combination of prison and probation.

In arguing for the lighter sentence, DeSimone would focus the judge's attention on Olivia. In a written report to Tressler, and in courtroom testimony from a psychologist he had hired to interview Robb, DeSimone planned to remind Tressler that Robb was Olivia's sole surviving parent, and they shared a deep parent–child love. Sentencing Robb to a long prison term would only further hurt the child.

But perhaps the only words that mattered were those that came from Robb himself. Working for months from his county jail cell, writing in longhand, Robb crafted what he hoped would be an emotional appeal to Tressler to give him a break. If only the judge could understand how horrible his life had become. As Tressler moved to take up Robb's sentencing, the professor had been in jail for nearly two years. So far, he had escaped the harsher existence of the state prison. At least here, he could telephone Olivia every day if he wanted to pay for the calls. With a light sentence he could be a free man in less than two years.

CHAPTER 48

Olivia

Regardless of the outcome, Olivia Robb bore the brunt of the tragedy. Raised as an only child in a dysfunctional family, Olivia had learned how to love her parents—separately. Now, she had to learn to reconcile their irreconcilable differences.

Although she lived with her mother's family, she remained devoted to her father who remained a force in her life, not only because he paid for her living expenses, but because father and daughter had shared a special bond.

At the December 20 fundraiser for the foundation in her mother's name, Olivia displayed remarkable maturity by engaging with the guests and even drawing the winners for a spa raffle. But, she also sat quietly, tears rolling down her face when the speakers talked about domestic violence and the damage it causes to its victims and their children.

The reality was that Olivia would keep her relationship with her father. Her uncles knew that and actually encouraged it. Gary answered quickly when he was asked about Olivia on the day Robb had pled guilty. He said he thought it "would be wonderful" if she could resume a relationship with him. "He's her father and the only surviving parent . . . it's important that we all move forward." There was a recognition that, despite the tragedy of Ellen's death, Olivia would be able to continue loving her father dearly. When asked by the television reporters about Olivia, Art sounded protective, cautioning them to realize that the little girl had lost both of her parents. "That's something we have to keep in mind when speaking of her." On a practical level, her world had been shattered and upended. She was going to a new school, lived in her uncle's home and had little that was familiar to her. Even her dog, Copper, was gone.

Back on Forest Road, a vase of yellow silk roses remained in the front window of the now-deserted Robb home. Some of the neighbors had complained to Mary Beth that the window needed curtains to keep out onlookers. Mary Beth shrugged. Ellen had liked the open picture window and the way it showed off the yellow roses. As long as they remained there, they would remind anyone driving or walking by that Ellen had lived.

CHAPTER 49

Nov. 19, 2008

Nearly a year after Rafael Robb admitted to bludgeoning his wife to death, he returned to face Judge Tressler to hear his sentence.

DeSimone and Epstein had laid the groundwork for Robb's leniency bid with letters from Robb, his sister, Ruth Dvorak in Israel, six academic colleagues, several of whom had done research with him, and a report from a forensic psychologist. Arthur Fishman, a longtime collaborator from Bar-Ilan University in Israel, described his old friend as having an international reputation in game theory and industrial organization with a focus on the strategic behavior of companies. Yet he was "easy going and unassuming with a wonderful sense of humor and a calm, philosophical view of life."

For Robb to have brutally killed his wife was shocking to them all—so out of character for the mild-mannered son of Nazi concentration camp survivors.

The more than thirty friends and family of Ellen who crammed into Judge Tressler's courtroom that day were ready to hear all of that.

What they weren't ready for is what came next during a more than two-hour hearing.

Under questioning from DeSimone, Dr. William Russell, a forensic psychologist, described what he had learned from

Robb and the couple's psychiatric records. He described Ellen as suffering from severe emotional and mental health problems that left her unable to care for herself and her daughter, Olivia, who slept with her and took a bottle until age six.

She had been treated for obsessive-compulsive disorder, depression and attention deficit disorder, for which she was prescribed twenty-seven different medications since 2000. Referring to photos that DeSimone presented to the judge, Russell said the home illustrated characteristics of hoarding, with boxes stacked floor to ceiling, many containing the newly delivered items Ellen had purchased on the Internet. She would pull out her hair and excessively wash her hands. Her preferred pattern was to stay up late and sleep during the day, disrupting Olivia, who was often late for school.

Ellen's problems, which began shortly after Olivia's birth, forced Robb to get Olivia to school and prepare her dinner—even if it was a frozen one. As the years passed, Robb, increasingly worried about Olivia, was "storing up, storing up, storing up anger," Russell said. On the day Ellen was planning to leave and take Olivia with her, all of Robb's anger finally erupted, leading to the hot-blooded killing of his wife. While Ellen complained in therapy sessions about problems in their marriage, the records "reflect how much of their relationship problems were rooted in her behavior," Russell wrote. In court, he said Robb had "understated" their problems.

As Russell spoke, Ellen's friends and family hung on every word as they watched their worst nightmare unfold. Robb had admitted to killing Ellen, and now he was being painted as a victim. How could that be?

In cross-examination, Castor tried to turn the tide by asking Russell if he knew about Becky Rector's claims that Ellen told her Robb had given her a black eye. Tressler shut him down, saying the record showed no evidence of physical abuse. Since the rules of evidence would not allow others to testify about what Ellen had told them, it fell to Ellen's brothers, Gary and Art, to speak for her. They described how much they loved and missed her and how her marriage to Robb had changed her from a bright personality to a recluse.

As Olivia's guardian, Art pleaded with Tressler to protect her. How could Robb have taken her back to their home days after the bloody killing and have her "sit in chairs still blood-spattered today . . . while he lied to the world about what he did with his own hands?" He said he has had to argue with Robb over paying for counseling for the fourteen-year-old, who was not present.

In hopes of giving the judge a window into Robb's relationship with his daughter, Art took out a letter from Robb received by Olivia just the day before:

Hi Honey:

Just to make it easier for you I am enclosing a self-stamped self-addressed envelope. All you have to do is print out picture(s) of you, make a copy of your report card, enclose them in the envelope, and drop it in a mailbox. In return you will have your holiday gift coming to you in no time.

I'd hate to delay sending you the gift, but I won't do so unless I get these items. Remember also that I will be shipped out of the area soon. So, if you don't send the items within a day or two, I won't get them for few months, if at all. Won't the love of money propel you into action?

Luv & Kisses
Dad
XOXOXO

With that, Art turned over to a court deputy Olivia's report card and a photo and urged Tressler to at least keep Robb in prison until Olivia turns eighteen, and preferably until she finishes college.

"There's not a single day that I go through without thinking about my sister and Olivia," Art told the hushed courtroom as Robb sobbed quietly, reaching for a tissue in front of him at the defense table, the very tears that Castor would later mock as "crocodile tears" and urge Tressler to ignore.

Ellen had become a recluse and suffered from depression,

but that was because of her "horrific marriage" and the "mental abuse" she suffered, Gary said.

But if she had become so depressed, why didn't someone admit her to a state hospital? Tressler asked him.

Gary explained that Ellen had been in "mental quicksand," paralyzed by fear about Olivia, losing her home and how she'd support herself. He said he knows now that Ellen's behavior was a pattern of "someone in an abusive relationship."

On Dec. 22, 2006, she had made plans for a "brand-new life," plans that "were already in motion." But to his horror, when he arrived to pick her up to return to Boston with him, he saw only an ambulance driving away from her home, leaving him with "a lifetime of inconsolable despair."

As Castor explained later, he agreed with the defense that Ellen suffered from obsessive-compulsive disorder. Just looking at the house told you that, but "I just think that Robb drove her to it," Castor said.

In his final plea to Tressler, DeSimone rebutted any message from the brothers that Robb was responsible for their sister's illness. "This woman was a victim of severe mental illness," he declared. ". . . This isn't domestic violence."

Saying he felt sorry for Ellen, DeSimone asked aloud why no one had helped her. His question stung many in the room. "We had reached out to Ellen many times," Gary said later. "As consistent with women in particular in domestic violence—verbal, mental or physical—they often recede from the world. They often are shameful of their situation." Ellen often diminished her problems, he said, telling her brother, "I'm fine."

But DeSimone kept the focus on what Robb's life was like, describing living conditions as untenable and telling the court he couldn't have lived in that house, "not for five minutes, not for ten minutes." It was no wonder, he said, "this man snapped . . . it took a lot for him to go over the edge. It was mental illness that did it."

Castor rose to mock the idea of Robb as the victim, telling Tressler "the victim is Ellen Robb," and that she needed to be heard.

To underscore what Robb had done, Castor read a lengthy

passage from Ellen's autopsy, describing her crushed head and hands as she tried to fight off her killer. "That's the final moment our victim here gave to his wife," he said. And rather than bemoan what he had done, that was when "the game theorist kicks in," and he tries to manipulate investigators by staging a break-in, lying to police and creating a phony alibi, Castor added.

Finally, it was Robb's turn to speak. He stood at the defense table and read a statement, apologizing to Ellen's family and his daughter, calling his actions on Dec. 22, 2006, "a horrific misdeed" that occurred as a "moment of madness" that couldn't be stopped.

"I and I alone am responsible for Ellen's tragic death and all of the pain I have inflicted on others. More than anyone I have scarred our daughter, Olivia, for life. I can't imagine what goes through her mind when she is asked about her parents."

All eyes focused on Tressler. Robb was no victim, he declared, but he believed that Robb, who suffered from stomach and thyroid cancer, was remorseful, and would not kill again. He had committed a "horrendous crime—the worse physical bludgeoning I've ever seen in my entire life," Tressler said.

There was no doubt for him that it was a rage killing, Tressler said, mimicking how Robb, when he pleaded guilty, had waved his arm to show how he had pummeled Ellen with an exercise bar. Castor was right to offer him voluntary manslaughter: "He was in an absolute rage that day . . . he did lose it."

He singled out Olivia, saying he hopes "she overcomes the disadvantage she's just been given." And Ellen, who was "severely, severely ill. . . . There are a lot of people who failed this woman."

With that, Tressler asked Robb to stand up, and told him that he had considered giving him a mitigated sentence—in the lowest range—but had changed his mind after reading Robb's letter to his daughter. Other than the killing itself, "nothing offends me more than that letter," Tressler told him.

"You are *not* going to manipulate your daughter. That's not going to happen."

Robb showed no reaction as Tressler handed down his

sentence: five years minimum to ten years maximum in state prison plus ten years probation. He was required to pay for the cost of the prosecution and to create a trust fund for Olivia so that "she will be protected."

In the back of the courtroom, Ellen's friends and family hugged and cried. They were stunned. Not only had Robb not gotten a maximum sentence, but Ellen's mental health had become the focus of the hearing. Her medical record was "mischaracterized in the most egregious manner," said Gary. The judge never heard that Ellen was sickest the last two years before her death and had been the volunteer of the year at Olivia's school in 2004, or that she suffered from colitis, which led to frequent changes in medication.

Castor said he wasn't surprised that the defense focused on Ellen's psychiatric problems and the condition of the house to explain why Robb blew up. He didn't like it, but it was legal. For his part, DeSimone said he "didn't victimize the lady"— he just put Robb's crime "in context."

In a closed-door meeting in the courtroom, Castor heard the wrath of Ellen's supporters from her friend, Sharon Sellman. "My friend was not portrayed properly in there, and I don't think justice was done for her at all," said Sharon as she tearfully left the courtroom. Castor failed to "defend her in any way whatsoever. There were plenty of things that should have come out in there that did not. She was victimized twice. For someone who belongs in a mental institution, it's amazing how she found her own apartment and went to a divorce lawyer," she said.

Castor told them he was proud of how they had prosecuted the case and had gotten Robb to admit to the killing. While the sentence was less than what he had asked for, it was in the standard range and more than what the defense wanted. He understood their frustration, but the rules of evidence don't allow anyone to testify about what Ellen had told them. Robb could come up for parole in three years—he gets two years' credit for time served—and Castor told them they should plan to testify against him. (By then, he just may be in Harrisburg himself. He's thinking about making a run in 2010 for lieutenant governor.)

The family's last chance to stand up for Ellen will come in a civil suit that will seek a financial settlement for Olivia. Having the money will free her from the kind of control her mother endured, Gary said. She can then decide for herself whether to have a relationship with her father.

Robb's sentence left Gary resolute to work on behalf of domestic violence victims "to create awareness, so at the end of the day we don't have someone getting five years for the most brutal murder that a judge has ever seen."